PRAISE FOR *SURFING AQUARIUS*

"A hip, entertaining, and stunningly informative account of how to thrive and prosper through embracing the spirit of community in the coming Age of Aquarius. A must read for all those interested in 2012 and what lies beyond!"

—JIM DREAVER, author of *End Your Story, Begin Your Life*

"*Surfing Aquarius* is brilliant! It's really so much more than an astrology book. Dan Furst is a fun and informative tour guide on a journey into these forthcoming times of transformation and change. Running the gamut from astrology to quantum physics to economics to medicine to relationships, this book explores the consciousness necessary for us to successfully embrace the years ahead."

—JONATHAN GOLDMAN, author of *The Seven Secrets of Sound Healing* and *The Divine Name*

"*Surfing Aquarius* is a great guidebook to understanding and experiencing new levels of awareness. You don't need to be into astrology to appreciate the information and techniques that Dan Furst offers in this powerful resource for the coming times."

—ANDI GOLDMAN, coauthor of *Chakra Frequencies*

"Among the archetypal figures, the most important one that our era desperately needs is the Trickster. The witty, jokey Trickster shows up (usually as a male figure) when a community becomes overconfident. He challenges self-righteous, greedy, pompous demeanors, deflates ego-inflation, and reestablishes a tipped balance. In Surfing Aquarius, Dan Furst is positively performing the role of the Trickster. He is smart, funny, and constantly challenges the narrow-minded."

—EDE FRECSKA, coauthor of *Inner Paths to Outer Space*

SURFING
AQUARIUS

HOW TO ACE
THE WAVE OF CHANGE

DAN FURST

WEISERBOOKS
San Francisco, CA / Newburyport, MA

First published in 2011 by Weiser Books, an imprint of
Red Wheel/Weiser, LLC
With offices at:
665 Third Street, Suite 400
San Francisco, CA 94107
www.redwheelweiser.com

ISBN: 978-1-57863-501-6

Library of Congress Cataloging-in-Publication Data is available upon request.

The author is grateful to those who have kindly given permission to reproduce or adapt their
graphic images in this book:

Precession of the Vernal Equinox on page 20 adapted from Andrew Raymond's *Secrets of the
Sphinx*. Chart available at *www.revealer.com/review.htm*.
Aquarius from the Dendera Zodiac on page 40 by Mark Wilcox.

Cover design by Jim Warner
Interior by Maureen Forys, Happenstance Type-O-Rama
Typeset in Adobe Janson Text Pro with Futura and Clarendon display highlights

Printed in Canada
TCP

10 9 8 7 6 5 4 3 2 1

CONTENTS

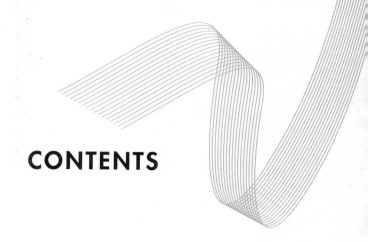

ACKNOWLEDGMENTS

The author is grateful to all the generous souls who helped in the intending and birth of this book:

The gifted, industrious people at Weiser Books with whom I've been honored to work with on *Surfing Aquarius*: Jan Johnson, who saw the book's promise; Amber Guetebier, Rachel Leach, and Susie Pitzen, who shepherded it through editing and production; Lisa Trudeau, Pat Rose, and Martha Knauf, who've blessed me with invaluable guidance on publicity and help with my Living Aquarian tour; and Jim Warner and Maureen Forys for giving the book a beautiful cover and interior design.

Pat Paquette and Jane Randolph for reading and commenting on drafts of the book.

James Marcus for invaluable help in facilitating communications, and for dancing, not just walking, the talk of celebration.

Kevin Hughes, the finest webmaster imaginable.

Kara Steele, for preparing the final manuscript. Michael Costuros, whose patient coaching has helped me get up to speed with 21st-century Aquarian networking media.

And all whose hospitality and kindness have helped me in my research and travels, most of all in my Living by the Moon tour of 2009–2010: Gretchen Grace Lindsay, Alex and Eliza Howard, Dillon Naber and Melissa Hunt, Chuck Priest, Michael Weber, C. L. Hickerson and Andrew Trump, Bev Bockover of Dancing Moon Books, Jim Weigl, Fred Wolfson, Daveed Korup, Clifford and Betsy Alexander, Lawren Leo and Domenic Leo of Creative Medicine,

Kelly Furst, Diana Huntress, Marcia Keegan and Harmon Houghton, Shems and Basira Nickle, Tracy Shaw, Chuck Page, Joe Anderson, Katie Starr, David Weber, Adam Lebow, Ruth Trimble, Chris Cohen, Barbara Bonelli Pryor, Sheldan Collins and Valerie Shepherd, Mark Wilcox and Rebecca Sweet, Shazna Jai, Kathleen, Van and Joya Fleming, John and Athena Kliegl, Rick and Joan Furst, Judith Raymond, Jacqui Lown, Laura Lamettery, Kimba Arem, Jonathan and Andi Goldman, Steve and Janine Larrick, Thraicie Hawkner and Jane Hansen of The Eye of Horus, Elysia Gallo of Llewellyn Worldwide, Paula Cartwright, Aaron Freeman and Sharon Rosenzweig, Dave and Diane Lametterey, Scott and Layli Magers, Peggy Phillips, Greta and Bruce Bollinger, Dan and Gail Schiffer, Rachel Lindsay, Bob and Penny Howard, Maureen St. Germain, Frediano Pichiotti, Pavel Maximov, and Nina and Randy Cochran.

INTRODUCTION

AQUARIAN AIRLINES!

DISCLAIMER

Before you get your boarding pass, Aquarian Airlines presents a disclaimer that may affect your wallet, your ego, and your comfort. This flight has no first class, business class or any other class that allows anyone to board first or enjoy any other privileges, though passengers with small children or physical disabilities will of course get the special consideration they deserve. Everybody gets the same meals, music, movies, and reading materials.

All movies are rated "A" for Aquarius because they preserve your intelligence, or actually stoke it.

Champagne is mandatory on this flight. By coming aboard, you agree that if you don't want to drink your champagne, you have to give it to someone else who does.

If the luggage you get back at baggage claim seems lighter than what you checked before you got on today's flight—Wonderful! Your bag may contain opinions, which have no value anyway, and they may shift their positions during the flight, and even disappear. Aquarian Airlines provides no compensation for the loss of any opinions. We do offer our heartiest congratulations.

We're about to board, ladies and gentlemen, and we ask you now to read the next few pages and acquaint yourselves with both the risk factors and the safety features of our aircraft. We direct your attention to the front of the cabin for some footage of an amazing but true story.

ASTROLOGY ALERT!

In the next two chapters we'll explore some mythic material about constellations and planets as they were understood by ancient priestesses and mythmakers. We'll even look at some astrological material about planet positions and relationships: for example, what we may expect when Neptune enters Pisces, the sign of his "rulership," for the first time since the revolutionary decade of the 1840s.

When such things appear during the first half of our flight, you may get an *Astrology Alert!* If you're at least willing to tolerate the mention of astrology, just sit back and relax. But if you find astrology really infuriating—we'll soon look at a famous story about a person who felt exactly the way you do—you can skip the next few paragraphs or pages and ask for some more champagne. If a person near you is so astrophobic that he or she begins to froth and perspire, you can help them reach for the star sickness bag in the seat pocket in front of them.

If we're going to understand Aquarius, astrology is unavoidable. Some basic star lore, at least the main symbols delivered without abstruse calculations or technical language, is essential to our journey. It is important to get clear about what astrology does and does not mean here. Three main points apply:

The Evidence Is There. Astrology is the oldest continuously practiced science on our planet, relying as all true sciences do on collections of data gathered through the practical experience of observing the evidence, and organizing it in mathematical formulae that can help predict what will happen when similar conditions occur again. Astrology was comfortable with the premise that similar events be *predictable* and *repeatable* long before the 17th century, when "natural philosophy" began to evolve into "science."

Before astronomy and astrology became separate sciences, and astronomy felt compelled to denigrate his intuitive side, the rulers of ancient Mesopotamian city-states built their ziggurats high off the ground to elevate their star priests far above the lights and noise of the city, on a platform from which they could watch the planets moving through the signs of the zodiac, and calculate their relationships with each other. Their data were correlated with reports from couriers riding in from every sector of the realm with information on what had happened, and exactly when, in an attempt to match what was going on in the sky with what was happening on Earth. From the very beginning, astrologers relied on hard data, painstakingly compiled and evaluated. These early scientific studies, conducted in order to understand and predict what may happen under specific planetary conditions to the country as a whole—individual horoscopes were still far in the future—are the basis of astrology interpretations still in use today. From the beginning, the numbers were there.

Each Soul Is Free and Responsible. True and legitimate astrology is never fatalistic or fear-fixated in predicting that because certain planetary conditions are in effect, certain events—the scarier the better, for fear-tripping fake astrologers—will inevitably happen in the lives of individual people and nations. An alleged star-reader who tries to manipulate a client through fear is not an astrologer, but a doom pimp.

What a genuine astrologer does, when "reading" for another person, is estimate how given planetary conditions may affect the client's actions and objectives in his or her areas of interest and concern, and recommend which windows of time are most or least favorable for the new job or the promotion, for forming the team or starting the family, for launching the new enterprise or waiting a while and spending more time on the drawing board. Like his admired colleague Rob Breszny, the author emphasizes that *Free Will Astrology* is the only honest game in this town. The free individual is never fated or determined to do or not do anything, and we are completely responsible for our choices. The stars do not make us do anything, any more than the Devil does.

Astrology Is a Spiritual Art. It is a tool for soul work and patient spiritual practice, not some mere lucky charm for predicting when one will meet a new lover or find a hundred-dollar bill in the street, though a skilled astrologer can tell when these events are more or less likely to happen. One of the implied agreements that an astrologer accepts is the commitment to devoted study performed over a span of many years. As in any spiritual vocation, this decision and practice are not taken lightly.

The other implied agreement, by far the deeper one, is that the astrologer accepts that he or she will now invest a lifetime in the inner work of refining body, mind, heart, and soul so that in time they outgrow all fear and grasping, greed and envy, and all need for fame and recognition, until what is left is the insightful mind, the compassionate heart and the generous soul, ready to lead the client as subtly and lovingly as possible toward the discoveries that will be most wholesome and medicinal. Thus, like the true spiritual art of alchemy, astrology is a process of burning away all the weaker and meaner impulses of the body and the ego until all that is left in the crucible of the heart is the gold of love.

One astrologer who accepted this mission and practiced it faithfully, from his student years at Cambridge University until his eyesight began to fail in his old age, was the famous mathematician and physicist Sir Isaac Newton. He concealed with the greatest care, until late in his life, the notebooks that he filled with his data and meditations on astrology, alchemy, numerology, and other gnostic sciences. This secret writing grew over the years into a body of notes more voluminous than the published pages of the *Principia Mathematica* and Newton's other works in the field of conventional, "respectable" science. Newton was convinced that physical science and esoteric study are two different but complementary paths, one intellectual and mathematical, the other intuitive and symbolic, toward the same goal: of understanding the secrets of the universe.

Newton also knew for certain what an uproar would ensue if word ever leaked out that the most eminent scientist of his age was also a believer in "occult practices" that the scientific establishment of the time hotly denounced as idle superstition at best, perilous folly at worst. All was placid until the astronomer Edmund Halley, for whom the comet is named, learned Newton's shocking secret and became determined to confront his august colleague and demand an explanation. An intricate game of hide and seek followed, in which it seemed that the more fiercely and indignantly Halley pursued, the more cleverly and elegantly Newton slipped away. Newton seems at least to have understood the higher mathematics of how much to tip a footman or doorkeeper to get him to feign ignorance or point a false trail leading a pursuer away from his quarry.

In the end, of course, Halley tracked Newton to one of the clubs the great man favored, got past the sentry, and boomed on Newton's door. Newton opened it to find Halley in such a self-righteous boil that he could barely speak, then calmly said, "I have studied it, sir, and you have not," and closed the door. What else, really, can one do? When a man chooses to close the door of his mind and behave as a bigot—that is, one who vigorously hates and opposes an idea, or a creed or a skin color, without having experienced it—then like will attract like, and doors will be closed on him. At least this was how it went until Piscean "poetic justice" began to transmute into Aquarian comic justice.

We are engaged now in opening doors, removing all obstacles to understanding whatever you want to attempt, and moving wherever you want to go. Look around you now, and you'll notice that the top half of our Aquaricraft is as clear as glass, so you can see the sky above you, and everything around to the sides. Soon enough, not long after we get to cruising altitude, the whole craft, the fuselage, the floor and the carpet, everything, will go completely transparent, so that you'll feel that you're in a chair in the air.

This may be disorienting at first, but you'll get used to it. You're perfectly safe, because this is an Aquarian journey, in which each one is taken care of by all the others, and each one looks out for everybody else. There is no separation, and that's why, as you know, we have no assigned seats. So if you start out sitting next to a separation case or a loud skeptic, especially if you're in a window seat, please be patient. You'll be free to move about the cabin soon enough, but we hope you'll lend us your love, work with us, and help the one next to you break through his fear of being united with the rest of us.

That's right. The scenario has shifted 180 degrees. You probably remember how before this moment, when we were all still flying the TransPiscean routes, we had to invest so much energy in helping people cope with the *separation anxiety* of having to lose or be parted from the people, the places, the things each one loved most. That was back when almost all of us built our lives around a few loved ones and other things that were most precious to us, and we had little or no feeling about anything else. Now the opposite situation, the last thing we would have expected, is what draws our time and ingenuity. We are having to devote ourselves as we never could have imagined before to helping people cope with *union anxiety*.

So let's be as gentle and compassionate as we can, and understand that the ones who fight hardest against accepting equality with everybody else are sometimes precisely the ones who have worked hardest and made the sincerest efforts to contribute something to their fellow human beings. Imagine what it must be like to be a person who's had a lifetime of achievements, who has proudly carried his ideology and opinions like an honored old warrior, has even won a Nobel Prize or married a movie star or appeared as himself in an episode of a popular situation comedy, and now has to accept that everybody is right and nobody is wrong, and nobody is more important than anybody else.

You'd be terrified too, and like the "pure" scientist next to you, you might be shivering, sweating, and gasping, caught in so much union anxiety that you haven't even loosened your tie, unbuttoned your collar, and remembered to breathe. Let us be kind, accept that we are here to help each other get through the fear, and see that even if the one we soothe is so stuck in the material paradigm that he "knows" with all his passion that God is only a phantom and a scam, still, much more than we may know, imperatives of kindness are at work here, in this moment. You may get to be an agent of liberation. This person's panic is a precious opportunity, and we are honored to help him break into love.

So let us not bicker about opinions and priorities, and questions about how it is that people who won't object to war and racism, to oppression and cruelty and greed and all the other horrors that human beings can pour against each other, are able to feel such fury at the idea that our lives on Earth somehow move in synchrony with the planets in the sky. In the end, what is most intolerable to those who are afflicted with acute astrophobia is the humbling possibility that when we're stuck the hardest in ego postures of being certain that we're "right," our senses are about as accurate as gossip, our intellects are only calculators of very limited range, and the Universal Soul might know, and be trying to show us in its gorgeous star show, truths more profound and ultimately more useful than anything that the rigid methods and beliefs of materialist dogma will ever reveal.

Why has astrology kept going for 6,000 years, through all the persecution and ridicule, even the embarrassment of being featured in the tabloid newspapers that we pretend not to look at when we're going through the supermarket checkout line? Because the night sky is the Book of the Soul, and has always shown those who want to see the roads that lead to the Source.

Now, in the time window of 1999 to 2012, we have been shown already, and we will keep being presented, a sequence of spectacular sky pictures. Each one is designed to focus our attention on the themes and images of our awakening, especially as they apply to the Aquarian agenda of uniting human beings in the common intention of loving and lifting all people, and honoring our sacred home in the heart of mother Earth. For now, it's time to look at the basics about Aquarius, and see how the Great Ages of the last 8,000 years have led us to where we are now, at the doorway of the Aquarian Age.

Our journey is about to begin. Only one more important announcement needs to be made as we leave the boarding gate.

IT'S TIME TO TAKE THE JOYSTICK!

Yes. This is the last thing we need to tell you, as we taxi toward the runway and position ourselves for takeoff. The time is coming, sooner than you know or we're allowed to tell you, when you are going to take the controls and pilot our vehicle. Not you as the only individual who's reading your copy of this book, of course, but you as one of many who are joined with everybody else aboard our flight in a common intention to go to the same place, in the same loving adventure, so that everybody gets there safely and happily.

This may seem very risky at first, especially when you see that the people who were our pilot and copilot at the beginning of our flight are happily taking their turn to knock back the champagne, and seem not to have a care about anything. They know they can rely on you, all of you, acting with the nearly unlimited clarity and love that you share with all the human beings and other species who are joined in the Aquarian Hive Mind, to bring us home confidently and easily.

Thank you for choosing Aquarian Airlines, and have a pleasant flight. Sit back, relax, and Keep Holding That Frequency.

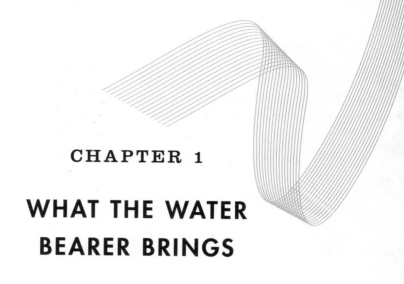

CHAPTER 1

WHAT THE WATER BEARER BRINGS

As billions of people on our planet know by now, we are about to enter, or we may already be in, something called the Age of Aquarius. Almost everybody who lived through the 1960s, and liked at least some of what we did then, can sing from memory what "everybody knows" about the Age of Aquarius:

> *When the Moon is in the seventh house,*
> *And Jupiter aligns with Mars,*
> *Then peace will guide the planets*
> *And love will steer the stars.*
> *This is the dawning of the Age of Aquarius.*
> *Harmony and understanding,*
> *Sympathy and love abounding . . .*[1]

The opening lines about the planets, from the "tribal love rock musical" *Hair*, are better as poetry than they are as star lore. The Moon is in the seventh house every day, and Jupiter and Mars align with each other every few years. Nothing unusual in any of this. But the point of the song, the prophecy and the expectation, is that we look forward to the Age of Aquarius as a time when we no longer clash and struggle with each other, but live together *harmoniously* in a peaceful order that will naturally express itself in music. It will flow spontaneously from the hearts of people who have chosen to relate to each other and their planet in loving and healthy ways.

We will live in a home key of understanding one another. We will learn and practice the sympathy and true compassion of caring not just for a few loved ones who matter to us, but for all people and all things. Sympathy and love will not be the only things that are "abounding." One of the essential Aquarian ideas that already shapes our new ways of thinking is the belief in *abundance*, and in our ability to create it in our lives, our communities, and all through our amazingly fertile Earth.

The Age of Aquarius, like all the other Great Ages before it, brings its new social organizations, new political systems, new scientific discoveries and technologies, new religions and art forms and images and symbols. Many relics of the earlier Great Ages show this. Surviving works of art from the ancient Age of Taurus (4500–2300 BC) are filled with images of bulls and cows from Mesopotamia, Egypt, Crete, and India. Ram and sheep icons in the Age of Aries (2300–100 BC) are even more abundant, in everything from Rama in India, to Jason's Golden Fleece, to the rams sacrificed by Abraham and other Israelites, to the ram's horn helmet of Alexander the Great, to the pivotal figure of Jesus, symbolized as the Lamb of God.

Now the Age of Pisces, which has spanned the last 2,000 years and more under the Christian symbol of the fish, is coming to an end. We will either welcome happily or enter unwillingly the next Great Age, of Aquarius the Water Bearer. But like it or not, love it or fear it, Aquarius comes. The next Great Age always does.

For many of us, the Age of Aquarius is closely connected with the year 2012, which some interpreters of the Mayan calendars have described as the "End of Time," and which other prophets see with the usual range of everything from doom to delight as a moment when Earth and her people will suffer unimaginable catastrophe—or will cross through a door of liberation and transformation for human consciousness and all life on Earth. For the most optimistic among us, 2012 may even be the curtain-raiser for the Age of Aquarius, the overture to the grandest and most spectacular opera that human beings will ever stage or dream.

While we undergo now and in the years to come changes in our planet and ourselves that are literally tremendous—causing people to tremble and things to shake—2012 is not the moment of doom. That's not where Spaceship Earth is going. What will happen is that *our perceptions of time will change completely* as we enter a whole new field of consciousness. That is what the "end of time" means. The coming change is not in the destruction of our planet. Rather, the coming Shift of the Ages is a dramatic clearing and speeding up of our way of perceiving things. To explore this Aquarian theme, that we have the power to change our world and our lives by changing the way we see and think about them, we start with a simple story.

THE HUNDREDTH MONKEY

If you think this sounds like the title of a Zen Buddhist teaching story, you're close. The original story does come from Japan, and it does have something to say about how a *satori*, or flash of insight, can light up not just one mind, or a small group of minds that share the same discovery, but the collective mind of an entire species.

The story has been discredited, but lives on as a transformational paradigm that continues to inspire many. Here's what the Hundred Monkeys allegedly did: In 1952, scientists introduced a new food item to the macaca fuscata monkeys living on Koshima Island, near Tokyo Bay, to see how the monkeys might hoard, compete for, or share their new bounty. The scientists dumped a fresh supply of sweet potatoes on a beach at the edge of the island each day. As Ken Keyes, Jr., reported, the monkeys shared the new food about as kindly as monkeys will.[2] The scientists' gift was a hit, except for one thing: the unpleasant grit of dirt and sand that clung to the sweet potatoes. An 18-month-old female whom the scientists named Imo ("potato" in Japanese) started to wash her sweet potato in a stream before eating it. Soon her mother and her young playmates were doing it too. Over the next six years, the scientists watched as all of the young monkeys, and some of the adults too—99 monkeys altogether—began washing their sweet potatoes.

Then, in 1958, the unexpected happened. The scientists were startled to see that one morning, when the hundredth monkey washed his sweet potato, suddenly *almost all the monkeys*, except for a few old adult hold-outs, started doing it. A new idea that had been tried over the last six years by only one or two monkeys a month had exploded overnight, and now, all at once, all the monkeys were catching on. Soon there was even more stunning news: Monkeys on other small islands nearby, and on Japan's main island of Honshu, were now washing their sweet potatoes too. All of a sudden, a new way of doing an essential task had flown across ocean and rice fields, and was now *a common instinct* shared by *all* the monkeys.

Amazing!, thought many excited people once the word got out. There must be a collective monkey mind, a telepathic field that holds all the monkeys together in a single web of consciousness. And if monkeys can do it with potatoes, human beings, who are much more intelligent and evolved, should be able to do the same thing for ending war and hunger, beating cancer, losing weight, helping our children be happier, putting the zip back in our marriages, and getting love to unpack and stick around for good. And it shouldn't take us any six years, right?

But . . . after all this excitement, the original story turned out to be a fabrication. The research team had cooked their data by moving monkeys from one site to another. Nonetheless, the story's implications for freeing the human mind, for reversing old habits and healing our planet, are enormous. If the Hundredth Monkey paradigm worked with human beings, we could in fact be infinitely more powerful and creative than we ever imagined. We could even find that we won't just be lucky to be here when the Age of Aquarius arrives. We will be the ones who create and bring it.

MORPHIC RESONANCE AND COUNTING EGGS

Even though the Hundredth Monkey story proved to be a fake, other stories show how quickly new habits can spread through an animal species. In 1921, Rupert Sheldrake reports, blue tits in England learned to anticipate when the milkman would deliver the milk in the morning, and used their beaks to open the paper tops of the bottles. By 1947, blue tits in Holland, Sweden, and Denmark were doing the same thing. More than word of beak was going on. These English milk tricksters—tiny non-migratory birds who normally never venture more than a few miles from their breeding place—could only have started this new habit independently in various places, as new knowledge spread through an entire field of shared consciousness.[3]

The ability of these birds and other species to learn and adapt at once, as one, is the core of Sheldrake's elegant idea of *morphic resonance*—the premise that the behavior of an entire species may "morph" in some way, when enough individuals begin to *resonate* with a new image, trick, or perception so strongly that their discovery moves outward, like waves of sound, until the new pulse is felt and understood by every single animal in the "morphogenetic field."

The implications, as they say, are staggering. If it's possible for human beings to do by intention what birds can do by instinct, then it's possible that our whole impact on the field of collective human consciousness doesn't have to be unconscious or a matter of waiting, for either Godot or Aquarius. We can create it. The challenge that we are offered in the window of opportunity in and after 2012 is to make a conscious, concerted effort to hit the critical mass that helps us understand who we are, and what we can do *now* to help and cherish one another, and save our home on Earth.

Will we do it? Can we join in communities of loving intention and send each other and our planet the energies of love and courage, compassion and joy that bring a new era of peace and planetary healing? Not only can we do it, we have a technology that lets us check our progress. Since the late 1990s, Princeton's Global Consciousness Project (GCP) has been using a network of Random Number Generators (RNGs) called "eggs"—because they work like electroencephalogram (EEG) sensors—to gather evidence of a global consciousness that may be affected by events of global import, and may respond to events by holding specific emotional frequencies.

"The underlying motivation for this work," the GCP explains, "is to discover whether there is evidence for an anomalous interaction driving the eggs to non-random behavior. In a metaphoric sense, we are looking for evidence of a developing global consciousness that might perceive and react to events with deep meaning."[4] Put more simply, the GCP created a way of monitoring the emotional pulse of the whole global field of human consciousness. We can see how a single event can register instantly throughout the grid as it impacts the hearts of people everywhere. You get one guess as to which shocking, violent event of a decade ago made all the needles jump. In December 2001, a GCP report recounted how, on September 11, 2001, "[t]he whole world reeled in disbelief and horror as the news of the terrorist attack and the unspeakable tragedy unfolded. The egg network registered an unmistakable and profound response."[5]

If we can all react at once in grief and fear to a terrifying event, is it also possible that we can work actively with each other to create the opposite effect? Can we intentionally produce a harmonic surge of love and joy that can be felt everywhere, even by those who didn't know others were working together to help them feel better? This, too, has already happened. The template for synchronizing millions of people in the intention and frequency of love has already been tested successfully.

On November 8, 2003, the day of the "Harmonic Concordance," an international team led by sound therapy master Jonathan Goldman did a global sound meditation in which people all over the world simultaneously chanted the sacred syllable *Om* while holding the intention of lifting and transforming the planet through the practice of love. The GCP reported weeks later that it had heard the worldwide Om. "Analysis of the data around the time of the lunar eclipse on November 8, 2003," Goldman wrote, "shows a major harmonically related increase in the energetic measurements. The results are quite impressive—you can definitely see the peak at the time of our most coherent sonic resonance! We can make a difference!"[6] A similar result was achieved on May 20, 2007, when over a million people in 65 countries aligned on Global Peace Meditation and Prayer Day—and, as we'll see at the end of this book in Aquarian Planet, such experiments multiplied, and continue to yield encouraging results.[7]

DO WE REALLY HAVE THE POWER TO CHANGE EVERYTHING? INSTANTLY?

One premise of this book is that we can. We will, and we'll have to, if we're going to find each other bearable and our planet livable. The first experiments toward lifting the human morphogenetic field started years ago, and are still going on today. Intentional communities have formed and are proliferating. They will gain momentum as more and more people wake up, recognize the opportunity, pick up the tune, and join the global meditations and ceremonies in sounds that lift and transform.

Why don't more people know about this already? The easiest answer is another question: Is it likely that mainstream media outlets, which have now deteriorated almost everywhere into advertising agencies for dominator elites who control their people by keeping them in ignorance and fear, will spread word about anything that offers us a way to take back our lives and communities, free ourselves from fear, helplessness and boredom, and lift us all through the practice of love? Not likely. The talking class is hard-wired for debate, not concord; stuck in conflict stories and unlikely to see a clear path for themselves out of the old battles and bruises, much less mark the trail for anyone else. Even "reporters" who are honest and courageous tend to squint hard at anything that claims it's going to enlighten all of humanity at once, especially if the recipe for change lists "spirituality" as the main protein. They "know" that until now, it's been inconceivable that most people, much less everybody, everywhere, will ever agree on anything. No matter how a new thing might help solve our misery and confusion, we simply can't expect that *everyone* would want to give it a try.

THE BIG SHOWDOWN? NO. ONLY IN THE MOVIES.

Not only that, but some people think there'll be a showdown fight to decide our future. They're already checking to see how they look in black leather and metal spikes, and they're getting ready for their *Armageddon*, even though they don't know for sure who they're going to fight. All they know so far is that they're going to fight somebody, they'll be disappointed if they don't, and when it all comes down, a lot of the good guys and all of the bad guys will die. The problem with this whole Dustup of Doom is that it will, as people in Hawaii say, nevah happen. The change that transforms humankind and our planet won't come through a Last Battle. It will come instead when all the lights go on.

Does this mean we will miraculously get through the years ahead without turmoil and conflict? Of course not. There will be violence, especially among fanatics for faith and those who want a bigger slice, even any slice, of what they see as a shrinking pie. And the living body of Mother Earth is cleansing itself in a fight for life, just as the human body purges itself of toxins by vomiting and sweating, by coughing up phlegm from the lungs and discharging fluids through eruptions in the skin.

The Earth changes that will continue and may well get more severe in the years to come are by no means mere payback for what human beings have done to their planet. The Earth is but one player within a scenario of transformation that now manifests throughout the solar system in solar flares of unprecedented sweep and number, in huge storms on the supposedly dead planet Mars and a surge of X-rays from the equator of Saturn, increased global cloud activity on Uranus and weather anomalies on all the planets. Some of these changes—such as a 300 percent increase in atmospheric pressure on Pluto even as the planet moves *away from* the Sun—are theoretically impossible.[8] But they *are* happening.

The question is not whether there will be cataclysms on Earth. There will be. The key question is whether we'll respond to them every time with fear and rage, or whether we can respond sometimes, then more often, with courage and resourceful love that help us stay afloat together rather than drown one by one. The Aquarian gamble, in essence, is that we're betting on human beings to learn the language of compassion and service, and transcend old conflict paradigms that have so often been our first response to trouble.

One new perception that's about to drive up and honk is that by 2012, we will begin to see conflict itself for what it is: not some "reality" or rule of "human nature," but only a habit and illusion that human beings have bought into for several thousand years simply because we didn't know we could choose and create something better.

Is it possible that we can actually change "reality" itself? To answer this, we have to define some terms—new ones, and old ones that are now picking up new meanings. We'll look at some of them now, all grouped in pairs, or in one trio. You'll see that the sets of ideas in the next few pages are all ways of looking at the transition from Pisces to Aquarius through two lenses: some old assumptions that most of us have carried unexamined through our lives, and some new ideas that are about to enter the stream of our awareness, or are already here.

"Reality is an illusion, albeit a persistent one."—Albert Einstein

What does "reality" mean? Most of us think it means the same thing as "truth." We accept the word, without ever having picked it up and looked under it, as a kind of standard for deciding what exists and what doesn't, what happened and what didn't, who's sane and who's crazy. Our opinions about whether we believe each other—whether that thing that I just saw go by was a UFO or only a backlit bird, whether I should be allowed to go out in public or kept in a padded room and not allowed near any spicy food—pretty much come down to the way each person or thing measures up against "reality," whatever that is. But the word does have a specific meaning.

Reality comes from the Latin *res*, for "thing." It's based on the premise that the test of truth is in the supposedly solid world of things that "must be true" because we can see them and touch them. The premise of reality is that if we can grasp something with our senses, we "know" it is there. "Realists" are the people who say "get real" to the other one who disagrees with them, even though the other sees something that seems equally real to him. Two people may even agree that they have "different realities," when what they have, in fact, is just different opinions. But at least they agree that the thing they disagree about is really there, and they're not making it up. Each of them, he thinks, knows this much: if we both see it, it's real.

At least, the two friends believe, we both know this. The world does not change. Yes, things grow old and die, and then new things sprout or are born from the dead things that nature recycles. But the new things are always like the things that were there before. Except for freaks here and there, Nature doesn't just invent new things, not even the new bird flu or the new cockroach that's resistant to Baygon and uses it for flavoring. The new things are still just another flu and another cockroach. The world stays the way God made it, or the way it just is. It's not going to change. That, for those whose world is made of things, is just reality.

Now let's look at another word that, unlike reality, is loaded with change. In contrast to reality, *actuality* is the world of *action*, of *energy* rather than things. Actuality is the idea that things that look solid are in fact in motion, both in themselves and in relation to each other. An *actualist*—we may as well coin the word now until we get a better one—sees the world not as solid things, but as energy fields that are balanced and held together by electrical charges. The root ideas that underlie this one have been on the table for a century now, ever since Max Planck won the Nobel Prize for *quantum theory*, the idea that the substances of nature and their physical states differ from each other not by their properties as things, but by the *quanta* (that is, amounts) of energy that they emit as they move. And they are *always* in motion. The only question is whether these "bodies" that are not really solid matter are moving faster or slower, going in the same direction or changing direction, or becoming something else.

The actualist doesn't see people or things as bodies. He sees their states of action and motion. What appears to a realist to be a world of solid things appears to an actualist to be a *flow* and *transformation* of energy. Unlike the realist's world, which does not change, the actualist's "world"—or what appears to be one—is constantly changing, and not just haphazardly. For many who see energies rather than things, and perceive the "world" as a huge and mutable assortment of energy arrangements, All That Is is changing purposefully, as the whole world is in conscious evolution toward a goal.

Whatever we may call the end point, whether Ascension or the Omega Point or Oneness with a "God" or Universal Soul, we are all heading there. For all of us, the final union is the point that drives the swirl of change that only looks chaotic because we have not yet seen the pattern. But once we all get there together, we'll understand the design. This moment of shared truth is our holy destiny.

As actualists see it, the old reality is changing into Aquarian actuality all the time, as we understand that resonating with quanta of Energy drives change, while reality slows it. This retarding function of reality is useful for now, as the power of an engine must be restrained by a brake. Reality has had, as the saying goes, a hell of a run. But as human beings continue to evolve into spirit, "reality" will become obsolete.

DEAD BOLTS AND LIVE WIRES

We have in front of us now a choice between life and death, and between the cultures that grew up around these two ideas and organized their values into action and meaning. We have a *life culture* that believes our abundant Earth can keep living forever if we take care of our planet and each other. And we have a *death culture* that sees us clashing more and more violently as we compete for resources that are getting scarcer and scarcer, so that "developed" nations live in annual cycles of consuming as much as we can until it all runs out and we die.

As we've just seen with realists and actualists, the life and death cultures have their distinct vocabularies too. The language of the death culture is dead simple: I'm dead certain that you're dead wrong. Over my dead body. To die for. And the ultimate death culture statement: "Whoever dies with the most toys wins." Not whoever gets the most toys and lives to enjoy them for a long time. Whoever *dies* with them.

The life culture has its vocabulary too—much of it, predictably, in verbs that actualists use to communicate that they are stoked, juiced, jazzed, buzzed, or otherwise excited; or who talk about getting a *charge* from some high-voltage person or high-powered experience; or being *wired*, either from electronic stimulation or from one's own state of high nervous energy. We'll look more at these metaphors of electricity in chapter 3, "The Eleven Principles of Aquarius."

These contrasts between death and life correspond to the two broad cultural groups that now live on our planet, as Thom Hartmann and others have described them.[9]

OLD CULTURES AND YOUNG CULTURES

The "young cultures" of the last 7,000 years have dominated their slaves and enemies, controlled resources and expanded to seize more, and have validated themselves as "haves" who own and consume as much as they can. Only the ones at the top, and other criminals at all levels, are actually predatory. The tiny minority of dominators and "winners" who drive the young cultures can maintain their perch at the peak only with the support, willing or unwilling, of a vast, seething structure of competitors, wage slaves, and "losers," all paying their money and labor out of fear of poverty and punishment. They're kept in their places not so much by the physical barrier of prison walls—though the youngest cultures build more of them than anyone else ever has—as by their beliefs about what they can't do, can't have, and can't be. Like the boy in Gurdjieff's story, they are trapped inside an invisible circle made only of their dread of what will happen if they try to step out.[10]

"Old cultures" lived on Earth for 10,000 generations before the young cultures appeared. The principles of the old cultures are, as we shall soon see, the same as Aquarian core values: friendship and equality within the tribe and in relations with other tribes, the life-long security of a community that is one's true wealth, a conscious and modest use of only as many resources as are really needed, a reverence for all life, and a core belief that all things are interconnected in a design that human beings celebrate in ceremonies of thanksgiving and inclusion, communion and blessing. And whether one believes that the circle is cast again and again, or that we are about to transform and ascend into a whole new dimension of perception and experience, it is understood in the old cultures that the Earth will continue. Life will go on.

Now, as we come closer to 2012, the contrast between the two cultures has become extreme, even grotesque, and has urgency unlike anything we've ever seen. Our planet has two populations: one that seeks to spiritualize consciousness and move beyond the illusions of matter and limitation into the highest frequencies of serenity and bliss; and another that remains stuck in physical pleasures and addictions, toys and opinions, the adrenaline rush of hate, and anything else that helps to block the realization that something's got to give here, and it may be me.

Now the issues of life and death come down simply to a practical question of whether we do or do not have the ability to change ourselves, individually and collectively, and thereby change the conditions of our lives. Are we helpless ever to lift ourselves up out of ignorance and greed, violence and hate? Are we condemned never to outgrow war, poverty, and ignorance, never to escape from life as a relentless, slashing struggle to climb up higher, or just to stay alive? Or—do we have the power to pull off the unthinkable achievement of a life that is happy, beautiful, and loving for us all? And can we even do this instantly, without working long and hard to bring it about?

The answers are predictable by now. We'll look at them more closely in chapter 2 as we see how the preceding Great Ages have molded our beliefs about ourselves, our world, and God, and how the features of the Age of Aquarius are already starting to change the ways we live and work, care for our bodies and our relationships, and reconceive our core beliefs about who we are and where we're going.

The Aquarian transition will be tough for those who anticipate bloodshed and misery so vividly that they seem avidly to desire it, and may bring it about for themselves and others standing close enough to get hit by the ricochet. But the good news is that more and more people who play the coming years positively and proactively will show how each one of us, and the intentional groups we're forming, can *manifest* the outcomes we want. We'll do this when we understand the terrain we're about to cross, and the scenario of union that punishes none, and welcomes all. The new practice and science of *manifestation*—of bringing about what we want through a focused, committed process of bringing our aims from intention to practical outcome—is in fact one of the new Aquarian art forms. Like any art, it requires discipline. How do we get from here to liberation and liftoff? Practice, practice, practice. A few years from now, not even the sky will be the limit. But we shall have to work at it.

If, as Branch Rickey claimed, luck is "the residue of design," then this is the time to prepare. To understand what we really need to live. To decide what kinds of families and communities will best serve our aims, and how we can best live in service to our planet. To learn to live like scouts who move on the ground soundlessly, observing everything, taking nothing away, leaving nothing behind, and reporting what we've seen accurately enough that others can find and follow the trail we've marked to the place of safety where we embrace one another in generosity and joy.

As we get more skilled in learning the feel of the land, we will notice that the time gets shorter and shorter between the moment when we first form the intention of what we want, and the moment when we realize it. As we manage to achieve our desired outcomes more quickly, it will appear to others, and we may even think to ourselves, that we're getting luckier. But what is truly happening is that we're only manifesting our desires faster than we could before. In fact, this book will now start to move faster, and the pieces of this introduction will get shorter, as we glance at a few things that will and will not pop up in the landscape as we go along.

GOOD, E-WORD, AND LOVE

The word "evil" will be used exactly once in this book, and there it went. It will be called the *E-word* from now on, whenever it must be quoted from another source. The plain truth is that the E-word is toxic. The more a person thinks it, writes it, and says it, the more he or she will perpetrate the kind of behavior that the E-word describes.

The actuality is that there is no Good, and there is no E-word. There is only love, and the absence of love. That is all. The actions of a person who treats others with love and kindness will have results that others are inclined to call "good," and those who treat others with hate, violence, and indifference will produce different outcomes that others are inclined to call "E-word." But the root actuality is that there is only love, and the absence of love. This is why there are now two kinds of people in the world.

ONES AND TWOS

The Twos are those who believe in Good and E-word, and see the world as a conflict between light and dark, us and them, take it or leave it, pro and con, with us or against us, and every other dream of duality that doesn't exist in nature, but only in the minds of those who feel naked if they have nothing to hate. Twos believe that human beings are corrupt and sinful, and therefore need to be corrected and controlled, ideally by a savior, but by the police and the penal system if nothing else is available. Twos are afflicted in these times by a terrible epidemic of Insight and Sudden Awareness that reduces their numbers daily as more of them awaken, and unexpectedly become:

The Ones, those who believe only in love, and in creating love when it is absent or in limited supply. Ones believe that human beings are good and loving, and share a common dream of creating beauty in freedom for Mother Earth and all her people, who are always One. The number of Ones increases daily on the planet, and once a Two becomes a One, he or she doesn't go back. The awakening is decisive. It changes the person into one more closely aligned with soul. Some Ones even know that they already outnumber the Twos, and will help lift them into insight and freedom.

One thing that will really happen sooner or later, and that those of us now on the planet could live long enough to see if human beings expend effort, is that all people will give up their illusions of Good and E-word altogether, and will realize that if their choice is between love and the absence of love, there is really only one choice, and it may as well be made now.

A KIND FAREWELL TO THE PISCEAN AGE

One pitfall in writing about the beauty and promise of the new Age of Aquarius is a bias in favor of all things Aquarian, and against all features of the Piscean Age that is now coming to an end. It is all too easy to demonize the Age of Pisces, to set it up as a kind of straw era to which the Aquarian Age will be superior in every way.

Let us be clear. Every Great Age, like every individual soul, lives within a wide array of possibilities, ranging from the most fearful, hateful, and cruel to the most loving, wise, and compassionate. For the record: Pisces is the most spiritual and mystical of all signs. It feels the universal human heart more immediately and intuitively than any other, and has the honor to be the creator of sublime beauty in theatre, music, and dance. It is the first of the Great Ages to open the possibility of individual salvation and union with the divine not just to kings and sages, but to every sincere heart.

Yet the end of the Piscean Age, as we see it play out, shows us one of the recurring rhythms of the Great Year as it passes very slowly from one sign to the next. Each new Great Age unleashes the most energetic and creative qualities of the new sign, moves through climactic centuries in its middle and late phases, and finally reverses its initial themes as it begins to fade. This doesn't mean that each Age is "positive" at the top, "negative" at the coda. Rather, it means that the sign's basic polarity shifts.

The Mars-ruled Age of Aries, for example, began with predictable violence and fire, and with such assertive individuals as Abraham and Rama. In the middle phase the Arian Age climaxed with such events as the destruction of Knossos, Troy and Nineveh, Jericho, and other hapless cities of the Promised Land, as the world witnessed for the first time the obliteration of whole cities and their peoples. Yet in its final centuries, the Age of Aries produced Zoroaster, the Buddha, Confucius, Lao Tzu, Pythagoras, Socrates, and Jesus, the Lamb of God. However we explain this transformation from physical to mental and spiritual warriorship, something clearly changed in the center of gravity and the compass of meaning.

The same is true with the Piscean Age, which began with such events as the ferment of liberty in the late Roman republic, the spread of Taoist and Buddhist ideas about the sanctity and interdependence of all life, and the Sermon on the Mount—and has degenerated into a grim, hierarchic struggle to control human societies and natural resources. The mystical Piscean ideal of life in complementary balance has decayed into a merely intellectual duality based on opposition, judgment, and endless, pointless conflict. It is not that the Piscean Age has been inferior in any way. Every Great Age has its beauty and purpose. But the energies of the waning era are largely played out now. It is time to open the old windows that have been shut against change, and to bring in the new. It is time to fly with the Angel of Aquarius.

CHAPTER 2

THE GREAT YEAR

The Age of Aquarius is due to begin sometime soon, or is perhaps already underway. Some people say it started in the year 2000, or even a little before, and others think we're still in transition and that the Aquarian Age will begin in 2050 or later. It may have started last year, or this year.[11] This book will show how our resonance with the Age of Aquarius, whether we see it and get it or not, gets stronger every year.

How long will Aquarius run? The numbers say until sometime around the year 4,150, since each of the Great Ages spans some 2,150 to 2,160 years. But the numbers may soon cease to matter, as it's quite possible that before this century is out we'll fly through the barriers of third-dimensional consciousness and experience both space and time in ways that we can only vaguely imagine now. If Mayan prophecies are correct in saying that 2012 will liberate us from the limits of time as we've perceived it up until now, then the Age of Pisces that has just ended, or soon will, could be the last Great Age that we track from start to finish with the traditional time measurements we use now. Once 2012 comes, and the Age of Aquarius along with it, we may kiss the Great Ages goodbye, pitch the clock, and retire the measuring stick to a folk art exhibit.

How did the Great Ages of the past bring us to where we are now, bringing precise and vivid symbols that help us understand our history better? It's time to look at the grand mythic package of the astronomical cycle called the Great Year.

THE PRECESSION OF THE EQUINOXES

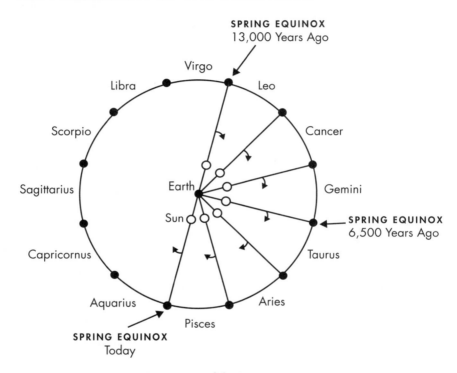

Precession of the Equinoxes

This picture shows what happens, though we don't perceive it, every March 21 on the Spring Equinox. The plane of the ecliptic—the orbital path that the Sun seems to travel through the zodiac—crosses the plane of the celestial equator at a point on the zodiac wheel that creeps very slightly to the west every year. This "backward" movement is called *precession* because, unlike the *procession*, or "forward" movement in which the Sun, Moon, and planets seem to travel west to east through Pisces, Aries, and then Taurus, precession shifts the Spring Equinox point very slowly in the opposite direction, from Taurus to Aries to Pisces and now to Aquarius.

By an ancient system of reckoning that the Greeks received from Egypt, the equinox point shifts to the west by $^1/_{72}$nd of a degree each year, and thus it takes 72 years for the equinox point to move one full degree on the zodiac wheel. This is why 72 has long been a major mythic power number that occurs in many ancient legends. Multiply 72 years by 30 degrees in each sign, and it takes 2,160 years for the equinox point to move slowly west through an entire sign of the zodiac. Multiply this by 12 signs on the wheel, and it will take the equinox point 25,920 years to travel all the way through the zodiac and return to the same point again. Plato called this immense cycle the Great Year, and some still call it the Platonic Year in his honor. For him and others living near the end of what they knew as the Age of Aries, the 25,920-year cycle was a year of God's time, far longer and grander than a mere 365-day year of human solar time.

Modern astronomers now reckon the precessional cycle at a length of about 25,800 years, so that by their numbers the equinox point takes 2,150 years to move through one sign of the zodiac, and about 71.6 years to move through a single degree. One way or the other, whether we use very old or recent reckoning, it remains true that for those interested in tracing the great epochs of human history, "The zodiac is the master calendar or the face of a clock for the Platonic year."[12]

How to know when each Great Age begins? Imagine that you're looking at the eastern horizon at the moment of sunrise on the Spring Equinox. If you could look right through the Sun, the point you'd see on the zodiac wheel behind the Sun's center is the equinox point for this year. So if you'd been looking at the Spring Equinox sunrise 12,900 years ago, the point behind the Sun on the zodiac wheel would have been very early in the sign of Virgo, about to move "back" into Leo. Fast forward to some 6,500 years ago, and the equinox point would have been in early Gemini, about to go "back" into Taurus. Fast forward again to now, and we will soon see Aquarius the Water Bearer. In fact, in many ways, he has already arrived—but it's hard to predict his coming precisely. Why?

FADE OUT, FADE IN

If we think for a moment in motion picture terms, the transition from one Great Age to the next is not a cut, but a fade. The symbols and patterns of meaning that dominate one Great Age may retain their potency well into the next, and far beyond. The Cow, ruling symbol along with the Bull of the Age of Taurus, is still sacred in India, still universal in meaning. Christianity and Islam, the two great religions that were born in the Age of Pisces and have spread throughout the world, are not going to disappear abruptly when the Age of Aquarius begins, though both may change into something more Aquarian, at least at the grass roots where the faithful live and worship.

The fade into the next Great Age can begin centuries ahead. One obvious forerunner of the Aquarian Age is the century of Enlightenment culminating in the French Revolution, not only in the technical innovations of the Industrial Revolution and Ben Franklin's experiments with electricity, but in new political and social currents: the impetus to free people from corrupt and oppressive authorities, the affirmation that legitimate power resides in the broad base of the citizenry, and the embrace of Aquarian values of liberty, equality, and fraternity.

And the world is not waiting until 2012 or later to get fascinated with the main symbol of Aquarius, the androgynous Angel who is the happy integration and balance of male and female qualities. In recent decades, angel images have been proliferating in art, movies, and television, and popular books suggest how anyone can form a relationship with angels and ask for their help. Yes, much of this is showbiz. But it is worthwhile to glance for a moment at an Aquarian angel who shuffled into our view almost a lifetime ago, and is still around. The angel candidate Clarence, from Frank Capra's *It's a Wonderful Life*, is noteworthy here not just because he's a kindly old guy who helps others. He's also at work on his own soul evolution. When he nails his assignment by saving George Bailey, Clarence gets his wings, and transmutes instantly into a higher and finer being. *He evolves spiritually*. And so, by implication, can we—for Aquarius aims not just at revolution in the street, but at evolution in the soul.

SIX GREAT AGES

It is time now to look more closely now at four of the Great Ages that are long past, at the one that is passing now, and at the new one that is about to arrive. The time span listed for each is based on the premises that a Great Age is 2,160 years long, and that 2012 is the beginning of the Age of Aquarius. Is this an instance of "wishful timekeeping?" Maybe. No one knows for certain where the exact transition years are from one Great Age to the next. But for our purposes here, 2012 is at least one of the better choices, and could prove to be right. We're about to look at a half-cycle of the Great Year.

Table 1 shows the zodiac sign and time span of six Great Ages, each one's technologies, myths, and symbols, and three other items that are the rest of the template that we'll use for looking at the Great Ages.

Table 1: Great Ages from Cancer to Aquarius

SIGN	HOUSE	ELEMENT	RULER	ERA	TECHNOLOGIES
♋ Cancer the Crab	4	Water	Moon	8788–6628 BC	Agriculture, Lunar Calendars, Herbal Medicines
MYTHS AND SYMBOLS: Triple Goddess, lunar deities, and myths of fertility and renewal. Mother Earth.					
♊ Gemini the Twins	3	Air	Mercury	6628–4468 BC	Writing, Language, Communication to Extended Families, Clans
MYTHS AND SYMBOLS: Gods of knowledge and literature, The Trickster, rivalries between brothers. Goddess of Truth.					
♉ Taurus the Bull or Cow	2	Earth	Venus	4468–2308 BC	Cities of brick and stone. Wealth. Standards of Weight and Measure. Art
MYTHS AND SYMBOLS: The Minoan Bull dancers, Apis Bull of Egypt, winged bulls in Mesopotamia, Isis, Hathor, cow deities in India.					

SIGN	HOUSE	ELEMENT	RULER	ERA	TECHNOLOGIES
♈ Aries the Ram or Lamb	1	Fire	Mars	2308–148 BC	Metallurgy and Iron Age. Glass. Coinage. Solar calendars and calculators. Armies
MYTHS AND SYMBOLS: Zoroastrianism and other fire religions, Jason and the Golden Fleece, Khnum, The Judaic ram symbol, Buddha and Alexander. The Lamb of God.					
♓ Pisces the Fishes	12	Water	Neptune	148 BC–2012 CE	Navigation. Religion and other hierarchies. Binary math and other dualities
MYTHS AND SYMBOLS: The Fish as symbol of Christianity, and myths of duality: black vs. white, light vs. dark, God vs. Satan, higher self vs. lower self. Whales and dolphins.					
♒ Aquarius the Water Bearer	11	Air	Uranus	2012–?	Modern electronic media. Computers, the Internet and cybertechnologies. Air and space travel
MYTHS AND SYMBOLS: Angels and other androgynous/asexual beings, light warriors and cyber-tricksters, return of the Goddess. Myths of evolution and metamorphosis.					

THE BASIC TEMPLATE: HOW TO READ THE ESSENTIAL FEATURES OF THE GREAT AGES

Astrological House (First through Twelfth): An astrological chart is divided into 12 equal sections called *houses*. While the houses and the 12 constellations or *signs* of the zodiac are not the same thing, they naturally correspond to each other. The eighth house of death and regeneration, for example, is linked with the transformative sign of Scorpio, just as the third house of communications is related to the communicative sign of Gemini.

Element (Earth and Water, Air and Fire): These four elements appear as common symbols from ancient times in almost all cultures.

Ruling Planet: the seven classical planets (Sun, Moon, Mercury, Venus, Mars, Jupiter, and Saturn) and the recently discovered planets, Uranus, Neptune and Pluto. Each zodiac sign is said to have a ruling planet that symbolizes its activities and energies. The ninth house of government, law, philosophy, and long journeys is ruled, for example, by the majestic king of the Olympian gods, Zeus/Jupiter.

SIX GREAT AGES: A CLOSER LOOK

♋ The Age of Cancer: 8788–6628 BC

The Age of Cancer came and went thousands of years before the first writing of actual history. But we do have evidence from ancient villages showing that from about 8000 BC, an agricultural revolution begins, and we acquire farming skills so effective that the field that could feed only a family before can now support an entire community.[13] One result of this is a population spike that comes when we can grow a lot more food. Our lives become less nomadic, as we no longer have to move as hunters following a migrating herd, or as gatherers going along a food route from one plant supply to the next. We can now farm and live in the same place that we call *home*.

Astrological House: Fourth

So it's appropriate that the home is the focus of the fourth house, and along with it the mother, who has traditionally borne and raised the children, and handled the rest of the *economy* (from a Greek word that means "home measurement"). This is why the mother truly has power during the matriarchal Age of Cancer. It is obvious to everyone that as mothers are the bearers of life—and not just the human mothers, but those in the animal herds as well—the mothers must be protected, honored, and empowered.

Element: Water

One likely connection between water and the Age of Cancer in this clearly matriarchal era is that water is especially honored as the sacred feminine element, and religious rituals must have included water ceremonies of purification and blessing. On the practical plane, farmers develop early methods of irrigation.

Ruling Planet: the Moon

While the majesty and danger of the Sun are evident enough to everyone, the planet that has the greater practical value for planning and organizing life is the Moon, who not only has an obvious link with the menstrual cycle of women, but is also seen to be born anew, waxing and waning in a predictable cycle. A 13-moon annual calendar of nearly the same length as later solar calendars (13 × 28 days = 364 days) could have been invented, with intercalary days or moons added when the lunar calendar got out of synch with the seasons of the Earth's life cycle. Beyond the Moon's practical importance, she is the main religious symbol of the Age of Cancer as well, and the world's most beautifully visible image of the possibility of life beyond death. Someone first framed this question in the Age of Cancer: If we grow toward fullness as the Moon does, and we wane as she does too . . . are we also then reborn after we die, to live again, just as she does?

Zodiac Sign: Cancer, the Crab

The crab's water environment fits the Age of Cancer. So does the way it moves. Who works by moving every day like crabs, going side to side over the ground? The farmers, who have worked the rows of their fields in the same pattern since the Age of Cancer. The month from late June until late July, when the Sun is in Cancer, is the time to work patiently and methodically, the way farmers do, as the crops grow toward fullness.

♊ The Age of Gemini: 6628–4468 BC

The population growth spurred by more expert agriculture in the Age of Cancer brings larger family and social structures than humans have seen before. This leads to more complicated patterns of speech and the forerunners to our first languages. Early written pictographs, meant to stand as actual symbols of other things, appear. This huge step forward develops mightily in the Age of Taurus into Egyptian hieroglyphs, Mesopotamian cuneiform, and early Chinese writing. Language, and its most civilized expression in *written letters*, does not develop fully in the Gemini Age. But that's when writing begins.

Astrological House: Third

The constellation Gemini has always been easy to find because of its two first-magnitude stars that the West calls the Twins, Castor and Pollux. Other peoples have thought these stars were brother and sister. So it fits that the third house rules sibling relationships, and the activities of transportation, communications, and commerce, all associated with the deity who would be known to the Egyptians as Djehuti, or Thoth, and to the Greeks and Romans as Hermes/Mercury. By the Age of Gemini, families are getting bigger, with more siblings. Given the greater potential for rivalry and conflict that comes with larger families, more sophisticated thought and speech are now needed to help articulate the religious laws and communal rules, and the things that sisters and brothers must or must not do to or with each other. More abundant food supplies also lead to the earliest barter economies, to more active travel to trade with other communities, and to the earliest ways of marking with symbols who is exchanging what for what. All of the third house relationships and activities fit the Age of Gemini like an ancient deerskin glove.

Element: Air

Air is the medium of all sound and speech, so its link with the communicative Age of Gemini is clear enough. As clans grow to live in clusters of villages, they learn how to project their voices in speech and singing, and to use drums to send sound signals to kin and neighbors living and working hundreds of yards away. Gemini dwellers don't know yet how sound waves move through air, but they are using it for their communications.

Ruling Planet: Mercury

The earliest well-known version of this mythic hero is the beloved ibis-headed Egyptian *neter* Djehuti, or Thoth, revered as the inventor of letters and the patron of all intellectual arts.[14] As the month of late May to late June, when the Sun is in Gemini, has been the end of the academic year in many countries for thousands of years now, the young scribes of Memphis and Thebes likely prayed to Djehuti in the spring as devoutly as today's college students beg the Lord to save them from this morning's hangover, and help them survive the final faceoff with Calculus 105.

As Djehuti becomes better known west of Egypt, he splits into two mythic types: Hermes Trismegistos ("thrice-great"), the robed and bearded master of learning and occult sciences; and Hermes/Mercury, the slender boy with the winged helmet, heels, and staff who flies with unimaginable swiftness to deliver messages from Zeus/Jupiter to humans who cannot begin to keep up with Mercury's velocity or wit. So it's fitting that he has always been the patron of speakers, writers, merchants, and thieves. The first tricksters, so good at fooling others that they seem to have a heroic genius for it, may have appeared in the age of Gemini. Beyond all the tricks, the superb new gift of Thoth/Mercury is the concept of *thought* itself, the notion that human beings have some faculty that enables us to plan, invent, and discover—and it moves with a speed that nothing else can match.

Zodiac Sign: Gemini the Twins

Above all, the Twins embody *relationship*. All three air signs of the zodiac are "dual" signs symbolizing the relationships of siblings (Gemini), spouses (Libra), and friends (Aquarius). But the only one of these that is joined by blood, and has been sanctified since ancient times by peoples who see in the link of brothers and sisters a bond of trust that no other bond can equal or break, is better understood in the Age of Gemini. The treasures of brotherhood and sisterhood enter our consciousness now.

♉ The Age of Taurus: 4468–2308 BC

The Age of Taurus develops *wealth* as something to be created and accumulated as the basis for prestige and power in larger political, social, and economic communities. The earliest city-states of the Taurean Age are usually deemed the first *civilizations* because they are established in permanent settlements of buildings made of durable materials, and kept in order through laws, administrative rules, trade practices, and religious rites.

Astrological House: Second
The second house is the house of money, understood in the Age of Taurus as wealth in its most tangible forms of precious metals and stones, crops and livestock, land, buildings, and works of art. These things become the basis of royal power and social position during the Age of Taurus, when rich people—and their inevitable relations, poor people—first appear. It is no accident that the first Young Cultures that are well-known from historical writings and artifacts appear now, with their qualities of aggressive expansion through wider spheres of territory to seize crops, food animals, and land; and the concentration and resulting maldistribution of wealth between powerful haves and hapless have-nots. In the Taurean Age, great rulers are not yet known mainly for their armies. But they are known for how many talents of gold, heads of oxen, chests of frankincense, and thousands of slaves they've acquired from lands beyond their own. They create systems of currency and taxation to keep it all flowing. When Babylon sprouts and grows rich and gorgeous, wealth is heady, and no one seems to be thinking yet what agony the lack of wealth, or even the having of it, can bring. The idea that "the love of money is the root of all E-word"—an example of how an idea as unstoppable as wealth consciousness must engender its reverse image of poverty consciousness—is many centuries from now, in the Age of Aries.

No matter what seeds of wretched excess get planted now in the Age of Taurus, one of the inestimable new gifts it brings is an awareness of *the importance of beauty, and the value of art.* It seems now, as it never has before, that some things have great value by virtue of their beauty alone, and that some people may be rewarded and honored for their skill in creating works of beauty, and nothing else. In other words, we have *professional artists.* While no one claims that the first true artists arrived in the Age of Taurus, it's clear that the Taurean Age was the first to recognize that beauty is essential to civilized life, and to design a system of training and support for those who create beauty.

Element: Earth

This one is obvious. The Age of Taurus begins to use Earth herself as a resource and material for the first enduring buildings, which range in size and ambition from one-room mud huts to huge temples and city walls made of dressed stone. Human beings shape Earth for buildings and monuments, for clay tablets used in commerce, diplomacy and learning, and the first refined earthenware vessels and sculptures.

Ruling Planet: Venus

Just as the Age of Taurus invents the business of art and beauty, it also coins a new mythic type not seen before: the goddess of love and beauty whose devotees believe that sexuality and beauty, in and of themselves, have a holiness that exalts and ennobles the one who meets and knows them . . . and endangers the one who turns his back on love.

The role of Venus is not to bear children, though she does, nor to turn a woman into an exquisite work of art. Nor is she here to embody the lust and languor of women who really love sex. Her true purpose is much worthier and weightier, and has been almost invariably missed by those who are insecure about their own sexuality and suspicious of everyone else's. This is why false terms such as "temple prostitute" have been misapplied to the Age of Taurus women who were revered as priestesses of love.

We get a clear hint of this true Venus role from the most famous surviving book of the Taurean Age, *The Epic of Gilgamesh*. When the forest wild man Enkidu returns from his encounter with the temple "harlot," the animals who had always loved and played with him flee. His scent has changed, and so has his nature. No longer a rough, violent animal, he is now a *man* of finer sensibilities. His experience of the sacred feminine has begun to lift him into new spiritual awareness, and a realization that sex is holy. Thus the true mission of the love goddess is not to inflame and delight men, but to awaken in them an awareness that spiritual love and erotic love, when done consciously in a sacred manner, are one and the same.

Zodiac Signs: Taurus the Bull and Taura the Cow
The earliest ancestors of the planet and goddess whom the Romans called Venus were the Mesopotamian deities variously known as Ishtar, Astarte and other related names, and the Egyptian Het-Hor (Hathor), a form of the beautiful mother *netert* Aset (Isis). These two Egyptian forms of the Mother Goddess are almost always depicted with Cow's horns that embrace the disk of the Sun, define its place in the universe, and affirm that no matter how mighty the Sun may grow, the sacred feminine is primary, as the bearer of life.

As the Age of Taurus enters its middle centuries, the sexual polarity of the ruling symbol shifts, and the Bull now represents the Taurean forces of power, stamina, and above all male potency, which was the virtue for which the Egyptians adored each incarnation of the Apis Bull. As long as the Apis Bull was strong, it was believed, the males of the kingdom would keep engendering healthy children. It's noteworthy that the Apis Bull is a gentle, stately beast who has no urge to charge and crash into anything. All this Bull has to do is love the Cows, so it is no mystery that he appears content.

Later still in the Age of Taurus, though, the main symbols change from the placid Cow and the serene Apis Bull to the huge bulls who roam wild in the eastern Mediterranean and are the ultimate test of a warrior's courage and craft. This is why the bull's head and deadly curving horns are symbols of gods and kings alike. For the people of Crete—home of the half-human, half bull Minotaur—the most exciting and perilous of all sports is the fearsome challenge of vaulting over a charging bull and living to tell the tale.

By the end of the Age of Taurus, the pitiless kings of Assyria are on the move, and aspire to the muscularity of winged bulls that embody sexual potency and *military might*. The Age of Aries, with all of its aggression, is about to arrive. Here in the Age of Taurus, we see clearly for the first time how the grand creative forces of each Great Age— and with them, the ruling symbols—mutate as the Age nears its end into something different from, even opposite to, what the Age stood for in its growth and its prime. By the end of the Age of Taurus, the dominant image is no longer the gentle Cow, but the massive, terrifying Bull. We'll see ruling images change in the same way in the next two Ages.

♈ The Age of Aries: 2308–148 BC

The Age of Aries is well known to us from chronicles, the first actual books of history, and the great works of faith and literature that are our first treasure house of myth: the Torah and the rest of the Jewish Bible, the poems of Homer and the Greek tragedies, the Rig Veda and other great works of devotion from the Hindu and the early Buddhist and Taoist traditions.

Astrological House: First

The first house, bordered by the "Ascendant"—that is, the zodiac point that is on the eastern horizon at the time for which the chart is cast—is the expression of *personality*: that is, the individual moving outward to interact with his environment, to place his own stamp of will and desire upon it, and announce what he wants from the world. Thus in the Age of Aries the most ambitious ones make their heroic journeys of conquest and trade, adventure and soul insight on a scale never seen before. Odysseus sails through ten years of amazing dangers to get home to Penelope and Ithaka. Jason and his Argonauts journey in search of the Golden Fleece, one of the Age's great symbols—like the Holy Grail in the Age to come—of the prize of inestimable value that clearly represents something more than material wealth. In a parallel myth from India, the hero Rama, whose name means "Ram," journeys into the forest with his consort Sita to hunt the Golden Deer.

The young man who will be the patriarch Abraham, in a classic first house act of aggressive emergence, destroys the idols in his father's shop and moves south to seek a new relationship with God. His people make a similar move centuries later when the Israelites leave Egypt for the Promised Land. Like the Jews, the Pandava brothers wander in long exile until they return for the great battle that gave its name to *The Mahabharata*. And perhaps the most furious idealist and relentless glory seeker of his age, Alexander the Great, rides into battle wearing a ram's horn helmet and leads his army over unheard-of distances to immortalize his name—the ultimate first house achievement.

Element: Fire

The applications, from the sublime to the tragic, are evident enough here. The new faith founded by Zoroaster of Persia is only one of many that worship fire itself as the sacred element that illuminates and purifies. Parallels abound in India, China—which use fire as a means of divination, heating tortoise shells until they cracked to reveal patterns of meaning—and other Age of Aries cultures. Fire also brings miracles of metallurgy at this time. While the Bronze Age apparently began before 2300 BC during the Age of Taurus, the key breakthroughs in working bronze clearly come during the Age of Aries, when bronze weapons, tools, and vessels help the aggressive Greek culture to expand into empire, and Shang Dynasty China perfects bronze casting. Later in the Arian Age, iron gives the Romans the advantage that is for them what bronze is for the Greeks.

The Age of Aries also plays the tragedies of fire. Earlier aggressors were content to take what they could carry, wait for their target to recover and grow rich again, then come back to plunder it again. But the Young Cultures of the Arian Age do not merely turn their rivals into cash cows, but feels a need to destroy them completely. Now we hear for the first time of great cities—Troy, Carthage, probably Knossos—put to the torch by conquerors who fear a mighty rival's recovery and revenge.

Ruling Planet: Mars

The war god called Mars by the Romans first appears among the Greeks during the Age of Aries, and is called, not surprisingly, Ares. He embodies masculine force, energy, and drive, charging outward in a spirit of aggression, which literally means "going toward." The ultimate new organizational product of this Mars-ruled era is, of course, the Roman army, which perfects, before the next Great Age arrives, the Piscean principle that *hierarchy* of position in a chain of command outranks natural relationships of birth, faith, or blood.

Zodiac Sign: Aries the Ram—then the Sacrificial Lamb

The mythic animal of the Age of Aries is the Ram, who is both creative and intrepid. One notable new deity who appears in this era is the ram-headed Egyptian *neter* Khnum, the creator who fashions individual human beings on his potter's wheel. Two other major figures do not normally strike us—there's an Aries expression—as ram figures, but actually are. Young Siddhartha was trained for war by a father, who was determined that his son would lead the Gautama clan against the other kingdoms of Nepal. The rest is well known. Siddhartha's spiritual hunger moves him to slip out of the palace and see for the first time, at 29, how the teeming, suffering world tries to live. From then on, like a first-house hero who would rather move than sit, the one who will be the Buddha practices austerities and meditation until he finds his awakening, then spent 40 years and thousands of miles as an itinerant teacher. His method is often brief and direct, as one expects an Aries to be. The Buddha's Aries identity is hard to miss in Buddhist art, since the Aries symbol is prominent in the line of the Buddha's nose and eyebrows. Here is the Ram of God, moving actively in the world to increase happiness and relieve pain.

Several centuries later the Lamb of God appears in the pivotal figure of Jesus. While he is of course the defining figure of the Age of Pisces, the one who was symbolized by a fish and taught others to be fishers of men, he is also the one who transmutes the main Aries symbol by changing from the firebrand who whips the moneychangers out of the temple and allegedly says, "I come to bring not peace, but a sword," into the Lamb who yields himself to the sacrifice, so that his blood may purify all of humankind.

♓ The Age of Pisces: 148 BC–2012

The Age of Pisces needs no prelude as we know it well, and we will see here many examples of the institutions, thoughtforms, and symbols that have defined it.

Astrological House: Twelfth

In ancient astrology, the twelfth house was often regarded as the house of enemies, just as the eleventh is the house of friends. Modern astrologers tend to emphasize instead that the twelfth house rules spirituality, secrets that are about to emerge, and all things that must remain cloaked until it is their time to be seen. Thus the twelfth is the house of the mystic who perceives the subtle interconnectedness of things.

Element: Water

The Age of Pisces has learned to redirect water in projects such as the Suez and Panama canals, and ambitious dams in the United States, at Aswan in Egypt, and the Three Gorges in China, and has also developed technologies of water that are so familiar we no longer notice them. Steam engines and boilers. Hydraulic lifts, water gauges, liquid crystal displays, and other devices that exploit water's properties of being non-compressible, and seeking its own level.

At the end of the Piscean Age, we also see the Return of the Goddess and a new vision of the medicinal and purifying power of water as the element of the sacred feminine. It's been well over a century since Helena Blavatsky published *Isis Unveiled*, and with it opened a new surge of interest in the river goddess who knew the properties of herbs, and used her mastery of healing to bring her husband Ausar (Osiris) back to life—not once, but twice. It is no wonder that Isis rises again at the end of the Piscean Age, and points to the empowerment of women in the Age of Aquarius.

Ruling Planet: Neptune

The planet Neptune was first predicted and observed in 1846, and soon afterward astrologers designated him as the ruling planet of Pisces. As Neptune has an orbital period of 164.8 years, it will happen, interestingly enough, that Neptune will soon complete one full orbit since his discovery in 1846. In fact, Neptune's entry in 2011 into Pisces, the sign he "rules," is one of the key milestones on our way to 2012 and Aquarius.

Neptune, known to the Greeks as Poseidon, rules the sea in all its darkness, depth, and mystery. While the journey by sea is an ancient archetype in stories from the Ages of Taurus and Aries, it is in the Age of Pisces that explorers sail across the ocean, even all the way around the world, for the first time. The mastery of modern shipbuilding, of the navigational compass and maps showing safe sea routes, all become indispensable in Europe's competition for overseas empire.

Now, as the age of Pisces comes to an end, this all shifts radically. Great warships now carry warplanes and missiles designed to strike from the Aquarian element, the air. The competition for water resources gets grimmer and deadlier as big agribusiness seeks to control food production, the last rainforests are cut down to make grazing land for future hamburgers, and the once-abundant tuna stocks of Sicily have been almost fished out to provide the finest sushi for Japan. Neptune is likely to feel much disrespected by all this, and one wonders in what ways besides the Aceh Tsunami, Hurricane Katrina, and the Deep Water Horizon disaster he will express his displeasure before the Age of Pisces is out. No dire *Day After Tomorrow* predictions here. But this Piscean conflict story, with a ruthless Young Culture exploiter of land and sea versus a hero scientist working bravely to alert Earth's people to the danger, is also an Aquarian document in its implied message that our only hope is in growing numbers of awakened ones united in our determination to save and restore our planet.

Zodiac Sign: Pisces the Two Fishes

The link between the Fish and Christianity comes from the early centuries of the Christian movement, when believers identify themselves to one another by drawing two curves to make a fish, or *ichthys*, an anagram for "Jesus Christ, God and Savior." As everyone knows, some of the original disciples of Jesus are fishermen whom he empowers to be "fishers of men," and one of the Latin titles still used by the pope of Rome is *Piscator*, "the Fisherman."

The Agony of Duality

Earlier eras certainly believed that some souls may survive the death of the physical body if one has led a virtuous life. But Christianity and

Islam are the first world religions to teach that every soul can achieve immortality and the bliss of paradise. Both these faiths also imagine the body and the soul as adversaries locked in a struggle that must end in Heaven or Hell, with each human being torn between the body's desires to pig out on food, pass out from wine, get laid and get rich, and the soul's desire to rise and seek the rarefied, airy delights of the spirit. The wealth-loving Taurean Age would have been amazed to hear that lucre is "filthy," and Age of Aries warriors would have rubbed their bronze beards in puzzlement at the idea that the main battle is not between princes or peoples, but between God and the Devil for each human soul. The great religions of the Piscean Age are the first ones to imagine that the soul is pure and the body is dirty, and that human bodies and souls are not just split in duality, but are *at war with each other.*

This Piscean theme of conflict has shown up everywhere for the last 2,000 years in everything from the war within the soul to dog-eat-dog business, the battle of the sexes, sibling rivalries and family feuds, thesis and antithesis, class struggle, split personalities, and seemingly so many million other ways for human beings to align against each other, and struggle within themselves too. To many people in the Christian West and the Muslim East, it may seem that conflict is not only the lifeblood of the drama, but the law of life itself, the essential truth of the way it is here in the three-dimensional world.

This is why the two fish in the Pisces symbol so often point in different directions that express *opposition.* It is this desire to move apart that defines the essential loneliness of the Piscean paradigm, as each one is faced, especially in the middle-class cultures of the last three centuries, with the choice of conforming or rebelling, breaking out or fitting in, living as an other-directed person who serves others and meets their expectations, or as a self-directed one who does not necessarily defy society, but refuses to let it limit him.

The result, as we reach the end of the Age of Pisces, is that conflicts are everywhere, and life has never been so fractious. It is no wonder, then, that national governments look for ways to unite their people without having to incarcerate them, and even horrors like the events of Sept. 11, 2001 may seem "a blessing in disguise," as Donald Rumsfeld actually called them—a means to pull a polarized and centrifugal country into cohesion. The Aquarian Age is already showing us much more pleasant ways to do this, for our communities and our whole global village, but for now, we will witness a continued pulling apart in all of the areas ruled by the sign of Pisces.

As Pisces rules secrets of all kinds, we can expect that human beings will continue to divide into seekers of mysticism and esoterica on one side, and on the other obsessive "security" experts determined to hide everything from high crimes and state secrets to trade formulas and the silliest skeletons in the closet. It can't all be hidden, of course, and this is why we now see a parade of lurid, shocking, elegant dirty laundry that not even Fellini could have imagined. This great director, incidentally, had a quintessentially Piscean world view. "I must have opposition," he said in his last filmed interview. "Someone to annoy me, someone to oppose me. I need an enemy to do anything good."[15]

≈≈ The Age of Aquarius: 2012–?

Like all of the five Great Ages that have preceded it, Aquarius fits the astrology template in its new organizational structures and technologies, key ideas and ruling symbols.

Astrological House: Eleventh

The eleventh house is the house of friends, and as the Age of Aquarius begins, we can now outgrow the dualism of having friends *and enemies*. Aquarius brings the radical idea, unimaginable to many in the Age of Pisces, that everyone is a friend. Will Rogers was a herald of Aquarius some 80 years ago when he said, "I never met a man I didn't like." In the Aquarian Age we'll finally, really, understand what he meant.

Element: Air

This one is easy to predict, from what we've seen about the first air period we've covered, the Age of Gemini. The technologies of travel by air that were pioneered at the end of the Age of Pisces, and have even sent explorers to the Moon and unmanned probes out beyond Pluto, will continue. We've already begun to find, and will soon perfect, ways to travel by air using individual air cars and strap-on power packs, so we need no longer fly prescribed routes in buses with wings, but can go where we want.

The Age of Gemini villagers who used drums and voices to send alarms and other signals through the air would be amazed to see what we send through the air now: TV and radio waves, cell phone and Wi-Fi signals, and so many other unseen rays of information that we can imagine an atmosphere in which words and numbers, pictures and sounds are zipping around and through us all the time. Someone, before long, will figure out how to get rich from this. If we know that wireless money transactions are whizzing through the air all the time, and billions of dollars are moving back and forth and every which way through our bodies in every hour of the day and night, it's only a matter of time before somebody figures out—like the Black Sea peoples in the Age of Aries who fastened fleeces in their streams to catch flakes and bits of gold—how to read the money signals in the air and skim them. When this happens, who needs an ATM when you can be an AMT, an Aquarian Money Trickster who intercepts the money signal in mid-air?

Ruling Planet: Uranus

The ruler of Aquarius is Uranus, the planet discovered in 1781 by the British astronomer William Herschel. Uranus is one of the more gruesomely unhappy figures in Greek myth. When considered only in terms of his mythic story, he is, in fact, the one element in the six templates we've looked at so far who seems not to fit the qualities that astrologers assign to Uranus as a showman of magic and trickery, a protean master of electricity and other dazzling effects who endlessly shifts his own shape and reinvents himself, and brings about change, usually unexpected and dramatic, in everything around him.

Uranus was the primordial god of the sky, son of the Earth goddess Gaia, who produced him unassisted, then mated with him to bear a dozen titans who first ruled the universe. Uranus was knocked off his throne by his son Kronos, better known as Saturn, who castrated his father with a sickle and threw the genitalia into the sea, where they engendered several new beings, most notably the goddess Aphrodite/Venus, who was born from the sea foam. Once she appears, nothing more is known of her father. Not the most cheerful choice for a new planet. What was the point of choosing Uranus, a tragic ruler who is deposed and cruelly mutilated? Did the scientists who named Uranus want him to represent a time when the old order was about to crack and give way? Why not choose instead someone daring and heroic, who leads the revolt and topples the tyrant? Why not Prometheus, bringer of fire?

Whatever the answers, Uranus in myth and Uranus in astrology are two very different figures. Uranus, as astrologers see him, embodies the desire for freedom. And as freedom is never gained easily, Uranus is the planet of changes to be brought rapidly and easily when possible—but when necessary by revolutionary means. Uranus has an exciting effect on whatever he touches. This is why he is associated with individual inventiveness rather than conformity, with experimentation rather than comfortable acceptance, with the positive altruism of one who knows that something better can be created if we will make the effort, and with quick flashes of intuition rather than more deliberate reasoning. This quickness of Uranus shows as well in the sudden attractions that can bring new lovers and friends together and that can feel like electrical charges that flow from one person to another. So it makes sense that Uranus is also the ruling planet of electricity, and of technologies that use it, including the electronic media, especially motion pictures.

Zodiac Sign: Aquarius the Water Bearer

The ancient image of the Water Bearer, as we see especially in Egyptian zodiac images like this one from the temple of Hathor at Dendera, most likely evolved in Middle Eastern cultures that saw the waters of the Nile, the Tigris, and the Euphrates, and the *wadi* rain freshets of Petra, as crucial to their very survival. These peoples invoked water deities in ceremonies throughout the year, and underscored the crucial role of water in all of life by placing a Water Carrier between Capricorn the Sea Goat and Pisces the Fishes, as though to say that yes, the year may begin in fire and move through earth and air, but it ends, then renews itself in the sacred birth element of water.

The link between Aquarius and water is inescapable now at this time of planetary water crisis, as great stretches of Earth's surface become desert and corporatists who call water "blue gold" aim to buy it up—yet, at the same time, we begin to understand "Messages in Water," as Masaru Emoto calls them, and we understand as never before that as water goes, so goes everything. The challenge of Aquarius and the question of water are the same thing. They both invite us to decide whether water is an *It*—a colorless, odorless, tasteless thing to be controlled and traded—or a *She*: a single, conscious being who is sacred and the same in every cup of water we share, every drop of rain that falls on us, every lake and river we cross, every ocean that is the eternal source of birth and wisdom. It is clear which of these ideas about water is based in outworn beliefs about hierarchy, competition and scarcity, and which expresses the truest Aquarian values of community, cooperation, and abundance. It's time now to look at these and the other Principles of Aquarius.

CHAPTER 3

THE ELEVEN PRINCIPLES
OF AQUARIUS

Why *Eleven* Principles? For one, the eleventh zodiac sign of Aquarius corresponds to the eleventh house of the astrology chart. This house rules friendship, one of the Aquarian Principles, and eleven is the number of renewal, representing a new cycle that begins after a unit of ten is completed. The point of eleven, like everything else, is all in how we see it. For people obsessed with doom, everything is a threat, and it's the eleventh hour, the fear sweat before midnight. For those who see the future as a breakthrough into love and joy, everything is a blessing about to come our way. It's time to welcome the elegant eleven, striding gorgeously like models gracing the sparkliest runway in Milan.

REVOLUTION!

The only one that gets an exclamation point, as there is nothing modest or uncommitted about it. The energy of Aquarius is revolutionary. This is why, ever since Uranus was discovered in 1781, he has always been prominently placed or "stressed" in or just before impulses to revolution get strong enough to crack the dam, even break it. In the 1780s, the revolutionary decade of the 1840s, the First World War, the Russian Revolution, the collapse of the Berlin Wall and the Soviet Union between 1988 and 1993, Uranus was approaching, or already in, his home sign of Aquarius.

As revolution is a highly charged word that stirs fear in many quarters, it's useful to get clear here about what it does and does not mean in the Age of Aquarius. It simply means a "turning back," and implies that power has somehow been cluelessly surrendered by, or arrogantly taken away from, the broad base of the citizens who are its true owners—and that this power is abused for a time by a small segment of the society who exploit it to elevate and enrich their families, cronies, and backers.

When revolution comes, it redistributes power from the few back to the many, or at least claims to. It need not be bloody, and need not be seen in gallons of blood per day or brick dust from falling forts and prisons. The Czech Republic's "Velvet Revolution"—led by, of all people, a playwright—is a good example of what can happen when the desire of the people to reclaim what belongs to them aligns with the insight by those who have been the landlords that it's time to pack the dishes, turn over the keys, and vacate the building. Normally, of course, the landlord doesn't want to surrender even the umbrella stand, much less the deed to the property, so it's no wonder that people think of revolution as Paris mobs watching heads tumble from the guillotine. Or Bolsheviks and their bayonets storming the Smolny and trashing the Tsar's Winter Palace, or hordes of Chinese peasants wiping out the entire landlord class in and just after the Red Revolution of 1949.

The actuality about revolution is not in a power structure that will give way only under violent pressure. But, understandably, many people still hold fearful *expectations* of how it must go. Typical is the German controversy in 2004 over the Schroeder government's decision to make deep cuts in national unemployment benefits. *Die Zeit* called it "A German revolution," and *Newsweek*, with the knee-jerk dread typical of American fear culture, opined that "As with any revolution there promises to be blood."[16] There wasn't.

So—what if change doesn't have to be violent? As we move now from the lobby into the opera house where the *Aquarius Overture* is playing, we get a program note from Gandhi's *Non-Violence in Peace and War* (1948): "A non-violent revolution is not a program of seizure of power. It is a program of transformation of relationships, ending in a peaceful transfer of power."[17] This transformation in our perceptions is everything. It is the essence of the Aquarian opportunity. The thing that will give way in the revolution is not the building itself. It is our assumption that we need to storm it.

EVOLUTION

Take the R from Revolution and we get Evolution. The Age of Aquarius seeks the evolution of the *soul*, and embraces the premise common to many traditions in both East and West that each person is capable of *soul growth*. Each of us, in today's metaphysical language, is responsible for achieving our *soul desires* and *soul objectives*, and realizing the goal of spiritual perfection to which every soul aspires. This new way of thinking is very different from the usual Piscean Age ideas about the soul, especially as seen by "realists" (see chapter 1), for whom, if the soul exists at all, then it's like that thing in *The Da Vinci Code* that everybody is trying to get at all costs, or guard with their lives.

For the great Piscean religions, the soul is that precious insubstantial mystery that we do everything to "save," or run the risk that it will be "lost." The foolish may be tempted to sell it to the Devil for a chance to get rich or be the king of somewhere, though the wise safeguard the soul for "God," usually believing He (masculine pronouns appear here only for brevity's sake) is someone other than themselves. But very few think of the soul as getting bigger or smaller, healthy or sick, coarsened into something as opaque as mud, or refined and lightened into something finer. For guilt-carriers, the idea that a soul can evolve to unite with the Source, to *become* it, is not on the game wheel at all.

Aquarian people, however, can live with the notion that we can get closer to "God" and even come to resemble Him. To do this, we undertake the *soul work* that we do by *working on ourselves*. Works such as

Thomas Moore's *The Care of the Soul* are not merely about how we keep the soul in a cool, dry place, but what we do with it. This task involves each one's decision to accept the divine assignment of our own creative risk and adventure, and stop fearing things like Hell. It isn't there. It never was. In the Age of Aquarius, Hell will be seen as a vicious scam invented by dominators bent on controlling others through fear. The only other use of Hell in the years ahead—apart from idioms such as "run like hell" or "lie like hell"—is in the axiom that if you're a religious person, you're afraid of going to Hell, but if you're a spiritual person, you've already been there.

The true risk that the soul takes is not Hell, but the pain of spiritual growth. It is as unavoidable as the growing pains of children, or the pain of wisdom teeth. That agony, that dark night of the soul, must come, when I see that I have been so much less loving and forgiving and kind than I had thought. I must face and get through the guilt that is an essential rite of passage, and the horrible illusion that I am pinned under a mountain of karmic debt. The spiritual person always goes through this kind of inner breakage and reconstruction. The person who stays religious occasionally does. Yet there is no helping it. There is a thing in the soul that we are meant to find, and polish until it shines. Yes, there can be pain in finding the soul's darker recesses. But the greater danger is in leaving the soul unexplored. In the Aquarian Age, evolution is each soul's duty to itself and others, as the outer environment can't change unless the inner soul work is done. As the Dalai Lama put it, "Unless there is inner peace, there can be no world peace."[318]

UNITY

Unity does not imply uniformity. Rather, it involves finding a way to bring our unique soul gifts into a harmonious design that honors each one, and brings all into the healthy loving *community* that is the collective expression of the unity within each one. In the Age of Aquarius, we'll outgrow the old Piscean conflicts and postures of opposition. Transforming these old habits will not be a piece of cake, or even two—Devil's Food and Angel Food in honor of all that ingrained duality. We'll have to act as a team, to find harmonies that work for all while still respecting the joy that each voice finds in its own tune. We will play in healthy competition—it means "strive together"—that helps us bring out the best in each other, and gets us closer to our goal.

Our unity, like our evolution, will come from within. We will realize what the Book of Proverbs meant in saying, "A wholesome tongue is a tree of life, but perverseness therein is a breach in the spirit." When we see we gain nothing in speaking or even thinking against others and ourselves, then the tree of life will take root in each of us, and grow. We will flourish in unity to create the New Earth, where in time there will still be a diversity of cultures, but fewer of the painful divisions that come when duality exists not for balance, but for blood. There will be fewer artificial walls—and in time, no countries, borders or checkpoints, separatist religions, passports, or trade barriers. There will be much less to impede us any more in our wish to live in freedom and move where we will.

FRIENDSHIP

Friendship, as we know, belongs to the eleventh house in the astrology chart, and is naturally linked with Aquarius. What are the qualities of friendship as Aquarian people practice it? It is based on mutual *generosity*, and the desire to give and receive love and praise, and perhaps also to exchange the endearing and beautiful things that friends have always loved to give and get as symbols of the deep bond that links them. But there is no *need* to do this. The posture of two friends, all friends, is one of shared confidence that is no longer based on a need for outer validation through tokens of affection or assurances of love. One thing we'll know how to do for ourselves is to find the inner validation that comes always from the giving of love, never from the fear of being unloved.

Our empowerment from within, and through friendship, will change our understanding of what power is. In the simplest terms, power just means the ability to do something, or the force that propels it. The electric juice that drives power tools. The muscle to hit the ball over the fence. Yet for many, power has come to mean a poisoned treasure that corrupts its possessor, as in Lord Acton's phrase, or in Gibbon's belief that "Of all our passions and appetites, the love of power is of the most imperious and unsociable nature, since the pride of one man requires the submission of the multitude."[19] Something will have to give here, as the Aquarian Age requires *the empowerment of everybody*, not just major players. A whole new understanding of power is on the way, as we discard what the Young Cultures have long assumed: that power is the way to make others do what we want, so the more one gets other people to work his will, the more powerful he is.

We'll look more at this perverse ego cocktail in chapter 5. For now, we affirm the core values of Aquarian friendship. It is based on *equality*, and this is why innovative organizations now emphasize *teamwork* over competition, and the superior potential of "win-win" relationships. In Aquarius, everybody's equal, and everybody wins. Just as one-up, one-down relationships of winners and losers are a classic expression of Piscean conflict and duality, the win-win relationships that have already entered our vocabulary are as Aquarian as it gets. The last main ingredient of Aquarian friendship is *trust*, which requires the next Aquarian value.

TRANSPARENCY

Dishonesty is usually the product of fear, though yes, exceptions apply. Jacob, one of the Taurean Age patriarchs, tricked his blind, dying father Isaac and stole his brother Esau's patrimony. Some conmen in all ages screw the other guy just for the sheer high of getting away with it. But the dishonesty our societies have now—brazen, habitual lies that the mighty throw in the faces of their people, knowing that none will object—are different in quality from the lies of Odysseus, the signature trickster from the Age of Aries, who lied in self-defense when he found himself in an unfamiliar place and had to figure out, before revealing himself, whether the local people like to greet strangers, or eat them.

But Odysseus did not lie all the time, or *dissemble*, as villains in Shakespeare and other Renaissance courtiers do, heeding Machiavelli's advice that one who intends to succeed, even survive, in the world of the court had best learn to keep his heart under his sleeve, and speak only as much of his mind as the prince wants to hear. It was late in the Piscean Age that *dissimulation* became an art form, a way of life that obliged the artist of subtlety to keep two personalities, like two wardrobes: one for outer public business, the other for inner, private life, if any. The risk is obvious. The Japanese, whose *honne* ("root truth") is always kept hidden behind one's *tatemae* ("stand front"), have been known to wonder whether, at the end of a long career, one actually has anything under his kimono.

Now, as we near the end of the Piscean Age, the line from the old pop song, "It's a sin to tell a lie," does not begin to convey the trouble that all this lying and concealment have created. If Alexander Pope was correct in writing that the man who tells one lie must then invent ten others to support it, it's not surprising that the famous profiteer Dick Cheney had at least four heart attacks and can no longer keep all the falsehoods straight, while the president he operated became as jumpy as Macbeth. The point of these cautionary tales is not just that if the habitual liar's heart does not give out, his sanity will, so human beings will have to get truthful in order to survive. The main idea is that if love does indeed cast out fear, then in our practice of love we must grow more transparent to each other.

As we master intuition and telepathy, then go beyond them and are linked in a global hive mind, we'll give up the keeping of secrets as a dishonest habit that divides and diminishes human beings—and is even a navigational hazard on our journey. Can thousands of birds fly and turn as one if they are keeping secrets and telling lies? Surely not. They are as one mind because they're transparent to each other. And so shall we be.

MAGIC

So far, the Principles of Aquarius are not new words at all. They are new ways of looking at ideas that have been with us for a very long time—or whose meanings we forgot, but are beginning to understand anew. *Magic* is one of these. It hardly means anything now. The lovers who have just given each other an unusually good time purr that they have made magic. A new food-slicing appliance is called a kitchen magician, and Ozzie Smith is called a magician at shortstop. Fans argue whether Magic Johnson was as great as Michael Jordan, who was later actually an executive with the Washington *Wizards*.

"Black Magicians," though, can allegedly do perverse things to us. If they get really scary, we go see a movie with special effects by George Lucas and his team at Industrial Light and Magic. This, certainly, is as Aquarian as a company name can be, as it conveys high skill at creating and blending brilliant light images, and Arthur C. Clarke's idea that "Any sufficiently advanced technology is indistinguishable from magic."[20] This is the true sense of the word *magus*, from which *magic* derives: special technical knowledge that is mysterious and wonderful to those who do not know the secret of its effects. Can we all be Magi in the Age of Aquarius? Yes. Will we all have to memorize every scroll in the library of Alexandria to do it? No. How is this possible? If there was no royal road to geometry, as Euclid said to Ptolemy I, can there be some chute under a magic welcome mat that will drop us right into the arcane learning of the magus through gravity alone?

Yes. As Aquarian friends who are transparent to each other, we know that teamwork with friends is essential. We pool what each of us knows so that all of us will know it, and we create the magic of the *mastermind*. Here is another term whose meaning changes now. It used to mean the brains of the outfit, the superintelligent and usually solitary figure whose strategic vision comprehended far more than anyone else's. Often the mastermind was a dark or suspicious figure, like Ming the Merciless or James Jesus Angleton.

Not anymore. Now we have masterminds of a very different sort. When Aquarian people use this word, it means a group of likeminded friends who communicate their objectives and plans to each other, hold strongly the intention of each one's success, and meet to report accomplishments, refine the language of their goals and plans, and refocus their intentions. Thus each one commits his or her time and vision to supporting the others, and in turn draws help and strength from everyone else. Does a mastermind produce "magical" results? Yes. Is it really magic? We're not telling. Those who have not yet started to work with a mastermind will have to find out—soon, we pray—for themselves.

COMEDY

Is comedy really something new in the Age of Aquarius? No. Ever hear of Nick Bottom, Figaro, or *Don Quixote?* The word itself—and its fearful twin, tragedy—came from the Greeks in the Age of Aries. We know from *The Epic of Gilgamesh* that kings had jesters back in the Age of Taurus. Who was the first human being to feel that sudden bouncing in the belly that we call laughter? Did this first happen in the Age of Gemini, the mental sign under which people were likely to enjoy the odd mismatches of ideas that trigger laughter? Maybe the first pie was thrown in the Age of Taurus, when it could have been a sign of wealth to waste food just to get dumb laughs. Maybe in the Age of Aries, one patriarch said to another, "Two Sumerians walked into a bar." Who knows?

What we can suppose, though, is that in some ways tragedy is to Pisces as comedy is to Aquarius. Unlike classic Greek tragedies, in which the hero is caught in an *inner* conflict between the nobility of his nature and the arrogance of his pride, tragedy of the Age of Pisces adds layers of *outer* conflict, in which the hero is up against the villain, and the kingdom is at stake. In the end, good people may survive, as they do in *Macbeth* and *King Lear.* Or the catastrophe may be as dark as *Hamlet,* with the hero and his enemies all dead, the Queen poisoned, and the prince of Norway striding in to take over Denmark. The main idea is that opposition and duality, so implacable that conflict can lead to only one horrific outcome, is the essence of tragedy in the Age of Pisces.

In recent centuries, the fierce combative force of tragedy has entered the gentler domain of comedy too, and satire has gone feral from the

18th century. But true comedy, as those who play it most luminously know, is not a vehicle for murderous colors. The essence of comedy is not conflict, but *dumb mistakes*. Friends and lovers fall out through mistaken identities, get-rich-quick schemes, harebrained adventures, and illusions born in a goofy gulch between expectation and desire. But no matter how words wound and passions fly, nothing in comedy cuts mortally deep, and in the end the truth clears it all up, everyone is forgiven, and there is feasting and marriage to affirm that we're all in union again.

Now which of these models, the blood on the dais or the cakes on the table, is likely to serve better our goals of survival and happiness? And since tragedy and comedy both claim to convey the truth, which is it? It can't be both. Can it?

The best answer is to say that tragedy conveyed beautifully the dark and conflict-ridden Young Culture view of a vale of tears in which life is nasty, brutish, and short, and the only hope of real happiness is in salvation and Heaven. And comedy conveys the Old Culture and Aquarian view of human beings and their world as a festival in a garden filled with beauty and wonder. Both tragedy and comedy are right for their time. This is why comedy will be one of the great art forms of the time that now begins—and one of the noblest challenges of the Aquarian Age is the rediscovery of compassionate comedy that affirms the folly of the mind when it splits off into separation, and the wisdom of the heart when it comes back into union. Fortunately we have a blueprint in Joseph Meeker's *The Comedy of Survival*, which shows that the values we must embrace to care for each other and our planet are those of the most life-affirming comedy, which sees under all the jokes and tears the core principles that all life is sacred, all roles are included, and in the end all are welcomed in the celebration of joy and abundance, mercy and love.[21]

ABUNDANCE

It's integral to the spirit of comedy, which affirms that human life is precious, and ought to be continued through the usual means of making new babies and feasting our bodies with good nourishment and cheer. But right now, as the natural world of our Earth is in such turmoil, is the very idea of all-embracing abundance more a cheeky daydream than a responsible idea of what's going on? Our population surges as energy resources dwindle, fish stocks disappear, plants and animals go extinct, rain forests shrink, thousands of people die daily of starvation and illness in Gaza and the Sudan while thug militias block relief and diplomats explain politely that the word "genocide" doesn't really describe what is going on. Where is the abundance in any of this?

It is actually everywhere, if one can give up looking through the tragic lens of *scarcity*, in which Young Cultures see all of life as a snarling competition for resources that we'd better be armed to the teeth and hard in the heart to grab before they disappear. Is there any Aquarian generosity in this worldview? About as much as Lyndon Johnson once expressed when he was asked why so many people of other countries resent Americans, and he replied, "They want what we've got, and we're not gonna give it to 'em."

This is how people think when they are in scarcity mind. It gets more unsustainable by the year, as Americans stake their claim to Iraq's oil by keeping military bases on top of it, and agribusiness giants try to corner the market on life itself. Is the problem really one of scarcity, or one of inept misuse of our resources or glaringly greedy attempts to seize and control for the use of only a few of the things that belong to all humans and other living beings? Buckminster Fuller knew the answer. He once remarked, "There is no shortage of anything. There is only an abundance of ignorance." But how could even Buckminster Fuller not know that our planet really is running out of some things, like fossil fuels?

Fuller actually saw the glass as more full than empty—and he was also too gracious to say, "Please look in the sky and let us know if you see anything very bright and yellow up there." Yes, we're about to run out of oil. Kurt Vonnegut wrote brilliantly about the cold turkey surprise that he expected to show up soon.[22] But in our cutthroat race to tap what little sunlight is left in petroleum, most of us have ignored the source of unlimited sunlight that's been there all along, and the unlimited power of the energy *field* in which we live, and which we'll explore at the end of our journey in Aquarian Planet.

The former American president Jimmy Carter, for all his depth and sadness, will grow in stature in the years to come as a true Aquarian figure who started and assisted projects of personal empowerment, community building, and sustainable development. He created the U.S. Department of Energy in order to solve the problem of addiction to fossil fuels. He installed solar energy panels on the roof of the White House. The man who ousted him, Ronald Reagan, an Aquarius (Feb. 6) famous for his sunny disposition, bought the Armageddon doom scenario and alluded to it during public appearances. His first action upon moving into the White House was to have the solar panels removed, thus recommitting his country to dependence on oil. The price of his folly continues to rise.

Fortunately, those who lack the military power to take the oil are using their wits to find the philosopher's stone of clean energy. When they do, the Age of Aquarius will earn the honor of unlocking the secret of solar energy. The Japanese, who long ago mastered the team-working skills of the Aquarian Age, now produce half of the world's solar power, thanks in part to government support, which helped Japan's solar power industry grow by 90 percent from 1997 to 2003. Today firms like Sharp, Mitsubishi Electric, and Sanyo Electric are poised to do for solar power what they've done for decades with cars and electronics.

If the Japanese don't break through, someone else will. Once we tap the indescribably abundant energy of the Sun and the field, energy will be abundant. We will no longer need to foul our air and water by burning coal or oil. Energy pirates, like those who rigged electricity prices in California and then laughed about cheating "Grandma Millie," won't exist. Another who won't exist will be the man I met in India in 1979. He was so upset when I entered his shop that any ear would do to hear his venting, even a foreigner. It was bad enough, he yelled, that 17 of his 22 children were girls, who'd leave home when they got married and be useless for taking care of him in his old age, if he didn't drop dead first from raising a dowry for each one. Even worse, one of the sons he'd been counting on had decided to become a monk!

In Aquarius, we will begin to kiss this insanity goodbye. Understanding energy and other arts of abundance will transform our lives. We will no longer have to live in fear of scarcity. And because we will know how to live in community, we will no longer fear that no one will take care of us when we're sick or old. It is not a matter of producing more. It is a matter of using better what is already there, waiting for us to find and share it. Yet true abundance consciousness is much more than trusting others enough to feel safe. It has the "positive" emphasis of living in gratitude and appreciation, honoring our true wealth of friendship and community.

ELECTRICITY

And riches like electricity. Mercifully, this section will not be a rant about the "Con" in Con Edison, or the dubious ethics of anyone else who sells electric power. It will not even be about how electricity is a key principle of Aquarius because this sign rules all kinds of electrical equipment and machines.

One intriguing Aquarian invention is the semiconductor, which turns on its head our assumption that all electrical systems, like every other duality in Pisces, must have positive and negative poles. We could even be at the brink of understanding that we no longer need the plus-minus paradigm, or the resistors or transformers that stop or slow the flow of power. The negative pole, for all we know, may be in our state of mind, not in anything about the electricity itself. Why does direct contact with lightning kill some people, while leaving some unaffected and bringing others into sudden awareness of psychic or clairvoyant gifts? If lightning is only a physical force, then the lightning bolt should have the same effect on each one it hits, either frying them all or turning them all into Edgar Cayce. What accounts for the difference? Is there something in the souls or the emotional bodies of the ones who survive that saves them, even consciously taps the lightning for better illumination?

In the Age of Aquarius, electricity is the spiritual force that shakes the foil in Gerard Manley Hopkins' "God's Grandeur," and the magnetic force in Whitman's "body electric" that sends us spinning away from each other just far enough that our attraction can bring us together again, more lovingly than before. Attraction runs on the confidence that what I need—abundance of all kinds—wants to come to me, and all I need to do is send out the love that will magnetize it. Electricity is the energy of attraction, most obviously in magnetic forces. And in us, too. Life will get so much easier when we turn from thinking what we have to do and have to get, to allowing ourselves simply to attract and choose, love and receive. We will be electrical bodies, our vitality recharged by our communities, attracting through conscious effort—not "effortlessly"—what we need.

BRILLIANCE

Aquarius is light and fast rather than ponderous, and this applies to the Aquarian arch-symbol of lightning, which moves from sky to Earth in an instant, transmitting a huge bolt of energy in a flash that lasts only a second or two. Energy transmissions in Aquarius have that kind of brightness. And are that short in duration, as it is the nature of brilliance to be brief and evanescent. It's not much of an exaggeration to say that Aquarius is to Pisces as a rock concert or a rave is to one of the great cathedrals built in Europe in the Middle Ages. The darkness at the ground level of a cathedral, even when its candles and lamps are lit for high mass, has the effect of drawing one's focus up, into the mysterious light realm where God dwells, and in, to the quiet contemplation of one's soul. It may even lead one into the mystical dream realm where angelic messages and other sacred visions come, like the hypnagogic states that the Noh plays of Japan induce in those who are willing to surrender control by the intellect and senses for a while, and watch the play through a lyrical imagination.

Darkness isolates; brilliant light unites. This is why the lighting at rock concerts and raves is a trick show of quick lighting flashes on the stage and spotlights that move through the audience, never staying in one place long enough to create discomfort, but *uniting the crowd* with colorful light fields that change every few seconds, like a fireworks display. At a rave, rapid changes of light are matched by quick changes in sound, as DJs match tempos and changes of music to the emotional beat of the crowd itself, blending each song into the next when excitement is at its peak. Do the dancers at the rave feel their heady, sweaty dance as the kind of sacred ecstasy that the rites of Dionysus induced in ancient times, and that tribes today re-create in fire circles with chants and drums? Maybe not, though many ravers take a drug called Ecstasy as a kind of endorphin insurance to guarantee the high that they'll get from dancing anyway, if they trust their body's own chemicals. But some of the ravers—and at the beginning, only some may stoke the consciousness of all—do see that the rave gives them a chance, however fleeting, to give in to the beat and the heat and join hundreds, even thousands of others in a moment that is holy because all are united in an experience of joy and love.

Yes, the quick sound and light pulses of the Aquarian transition reflect how busy we've become in the "developed" world, and how our lives have become much faster. But the brilliance of Aquarius is much more than just hurry and entertainment. It signals wholesale changes in our relationships, in everything from careers that take us through several or many livelihoods rather than a lifetime job with one company, to serial love relationships that mirror the stages of our soul journey. Those who are possessive, fixated on "exclusive relationships" that provide some comfort and control even if they don't bring home much love, will find Aquarius intensely uncomfortable, and may decry as the Devil's work what Aquarian people see as fluid and necessarily mutable.

In ways that most of us do not yet recognize, the brief light flashes of Aquarius, even the silly and false ones, do have the effect of uniting people, even many millions of them, in riveting moments when they all feel the same thing deeply, and are thereby drawn into communal feeling that they deeply crave. Many of us have never known the joy of being embraced by the love of many at one time, but we sense in our cellular memory that we felt it once. One day soon, when Aquarius is here to stay, our young people will not feel as terribly alone as they do now. Until we build the communities that embrace us all, the medicine people and production teams of the dawn of Aquarius will be happy to deliver temporary communities of feeling until the main show comes for a long and loving run.

FREEDOM

Freedom is the unifying element that includes all other themes of Aquarius—the engine that has driven the Aquarian impulse that began centuries ago, and gathers momentum now. But how can anyone say the thirst for freedom is "new," when "everybody knows" that freedom is a "universal goal" shared by people everywhere? Curiously, a look back through our mythic history shows that while the hunger for freedom has perhaps always been in us somewhere, it has not been a mythic theme for very long, perhaps because most of the ones who lost their freedom died in captivity. The comrades of Spartacus never idealized freedom; they just wanted to get out of Italy and go home. Jesus had no Ninth Beatitude that said, "Blessed are the imprisoned, for they shall be free."

What makes the late Age of Pisces different from these ancient events is that only in the last few centuries have the dominant Young Cultures chosen to incarcerate their criminals rather than work them to death. The Roman Empire didn't need prisons; it had warships rowed by galley slaves, and only during the last few centuries have our life spans become so long that jailbirds may now outlive their guards. Prisons have proliferated since the 17th century, and heroic breakout stories have multiplied along with them. Can anyone think of a prison that was destroyed before 1789, when the people of Paris leveled the Bastille? In the decades after the French Revolution, the clever, intrepid jailbreak became such a staple of the romantic novel that Tom Sawyer insists on an elaborate escape plan even when none is needed to free the runaway slave Jim in *Huckleberry Finn*.

Huck Finn is a breakout himself. He feels confined by "sivilization" and rules, and is determined to get free of them. Whether the story is of Huck on the river or Jack Kerouac *On the Road*, Randle P. McMurphy in the Cuckoo's Nest or the Bird Man in Alcatraz, Yossarian escaping from Catch 22 or Bart Simpson from his classroom, the longing for freedom in the United States is becoming so desperate that it is by far the central mythic theme in the culture. It has to be, given the chasm between the myth and the actuality. At a time when more African-American men are in prison than in college, and an astounding 1 percent of the population is in prison, it is hardly a mystery that the people must work so hard at convincing themselves that they're free, and almost anything—a car, a sound system, a cigarette, a can of beer—can be your ticket to freedom.

As everybody's known since the time he first got called into the principal's office in high school, there are limits to freedom. The conventional line is that unlimited freedom is anarchy; no freedom is tyranny—so we find the middle point where we obey legitimate authorities, find freedom of expression in healthy ways, and create ways to fit in and still feel free. The other shoe in this equation is the boundaries. One must not, supposedly, increase his own freedom by diminishing that of others, though this constantly happens anyway; and freedom, like the car Dad let you use for the evening, is something you're expected to use responsibly. But—and here's one difference between the Piscean Age and Aquarius—responsible to what and to whom? The word "responsible" literally means that one gives a response. And our cultural conditioning usually says that we owe responses to authority: the teacher, the clergyman, the traffic cop and the judge, the commanding officer, the supervisor, and in the end, the terrifying majesty of God, who decides whether each one will go to Heaven. Too many responsibilities. No wonder our spouses and children may feel left out.

In the Age of Aquarius it all gets so much simpler, as we dissolve artificial boundaries that divide our lives into discrete boxes, as though each of us were an apartment of several rooms that are, we hope, at least connected by doorways. Our responsibilities simplify as we shift our focus off the individual onto a community that now happily shares the responsibilities that used to weigh too heavily on just one. And the whole nuance of responsibility shifts from what it has sadly become to what it truly *is*, a way to match one's talents and dreams with the needs of the community and of the Earth. In the Age of Aquarius, we actually have only two spheres of responsibility: to the Universal Soul who has already welcomed us home, and to our communities, which include our mates, children, colleagues, and friends. While our families will continue to be important to us, they will no longer claim almost all our love, loyalty, and energy. Our increasingly independent and empowered family members will be more interested in finding the happiest and most creative ways to realize themselves. In the end our responsibilities and our freedom will be as simple as they can get. We are free and we are One, and these are inseparable. That's why the Aquarian economy works as well as it does.

CHAPTER 4

THE AQUARIAN ECONOMY

Why start this main part of the book with the economy, rather than things that must be more important, like our health, our families, and our souls? Because the first thing that almost everybody wants to know about the Age of Aquarius right now is the bottom line: *What's going to happen to my money? Will I have enough to support my family? Will I still have a job? Will the economy get better? When? How will we all get through this?*

Excellent questions, of the kind we ask when we look with Aquarian eyes to the interests of everyone. The first answer is: We will gain our security through the communities that are our true wealth. We'll build a new relationship with the natural abundance of our planet, and we'll invent new economies that we understand and know how to manage. We will no longer have to settle for mystery economies that only guru economists can claim to understand, or casino economies that are stacked against honest players.

The good news about the Aquarian economy that is starting to emerge now is that it will do a much better job of what economies are supposed to do: make sure that our legitimate needs are met, and that we have enough to live healthy, happy, and honorable lives. The tough news is that like everything else we get in the Age of Aquarius, the new economy is up to us to create. It will not be delivered to our door by experts who are kind enough to help us. We are the experts now, and our own ingenuity, effort, and teamwork will create the new economy and society that we want. The problem with Aquarius, as we'll see again and again, is that the possibilities are unlimited—but *we* will have to bring them about.

SQUARE ONE: RECOVERING FROM THE LATE PISCEAN ECONOMY

The tale of woe is so well known by now to all of us that we need not outline the failings of today's crumbling economy. The handwriting on the wall is obvious in every For Sale sign, every vanished job and diminished dream. This is why we'll fast-forward through the decay of classical laissez-faire capitalism from what was once the greatest wealth-producing engine in history, then mutated into grotesque buccaneer economies in the 1990s and early 2000s, and has suffered from 2008 a fall so shocking and complete that only those who are in total fear and denial—or are profiting as some always do from telling the desperate what they want to hear—can claim that capitalism as we have known it for the last two hundred years can be fixed with a few new laws and adjustments.

No, the system is broken, beyond repair. What must emerge now will not be some new and minimally improved version of the late capitalist economy that Benito Mussolini may have called *corporatist*, or that Robert Reich termed *supercapitalism*—that is, classical "free market" capitalism operating free of all restraint, with ruinous effects on both our economies and our dreams of creating democratic institutions.[23] Nor will the late capitalist economy be replaced by an equally disempowering socialist model that exalts mediocrity rather than merit. The time has come for our collective imagination to create what no one's individual imagination, however powerful, possibly can. Whether we call our new economy communal, a quantum economy, or something else, it is certain to be more local, and more actively and broadly participatory, than the economy that has just failed.

While we will look at some economic facts and figures as we go along, the core reason why we won't dwell on them is that the problems that have brought our economy to ruin are not merely systemic or technical. Now, as the dust of what used to be our economy settles and we begin to grasp the immensity of the damage, we have no choice but to see through the core idea that has always fueled the theory of classical capitalism. Much as American tycoons always believed, or seemed to, that there was something purposeful, even divinely timed, about *The Wealth of Nations* and the Declaration of Independence both appearing in 1776, as though to affirm the new North American states' destiny to become the wealthiest of nations, it also seemed not just optimistic, but objectively *true* that Adam Smith's basic principle had always made the great nations rich, and would generate even greater wealth now that it was articulated and clearly understood.

Yes. What made the wheels of profit run was the "enlightened self-interest" of fortune seekers who would be clever in pursuing their schemes, but who, even if not angelically ethical, would have the modesty and common sense to know when enough is enough, and would not be greedy enough to kill the golden goose and bring ruin on everyone. And so, it was believed until now, the best policy was for governments to leave well alone and have faith that the market has a wisdom of its own, will correct itself even if no one quite understands how, and will somehow keep the whole machine booming, or ready to boom again, even when some who are unlucky go bust.

But no more. The crisis of 2008–2011 is triply unnerving because it shakes our entire belief in both our goodness and our intelligence as human beings who can trust ourselves, and trust each other, to create consistent prosperity for most, if not for all, and can keep it all flowing not just for the first ten generations, but for another ten and many more. We have seen now, to our grief, that when the self-interest of the hunters is not enlightened but fervid, and the rest of the tribe is asleep, money is only one thing that will be lost.

Does this latest calamity, this product of spectacular greed, arrogance, and the fever that infects men when the stakes of the game are sky-high, prove yet again the fear-bound premise that "human nature" is corrupt and vicious? No. But it does prove how the Piscean Age, like all the other Great Ages, has shown the kind of *human behavior* that we can expect as each Age comes to its end. As we've seen, all the Great Ages from Cancer through Aries began with new ideas and discoveries that heralded their best possibilities, then flourished through phases of growth and structure, then calcified into the routine entropy and the empty protocols and rituals that creatures of habit live in when they are determined to hold on to what they have rather than risk anything new. How does this apply to the Piscean phantom economy that is in its last agony now?

GIVING AWAY THE STORE: HOW THE PISCEAN ECONOMY GOT TO BE SO TOXIC

The dire events of 2007–2011, strange as they look from the usual economic perspective of policies and numbers, make perfect sense within the context of history and astrology. The financial calamity of the early 21st century, and the climate of fraud and folly that made it possible, are in fact exactly what we could expect at the end of the Piscean Age. If you'd like to skip through a few esoteric-looking pages before we get to more familiar money terms and numbers, you can go ahead to "Betting It All on Doom."

Pisces, ruled by the dark, mysterious lord Neptune, is the most spiritual of all signs, and also the most mystical and deeply compassionate. It is appropriate, then, that the beginning of the Piscean Age in the second century BC was a time when social ideas of human equality and liberation, religious forces of pantheism, and messianic prophecies of a universal teacher coming to free and save all mankind, entered the stream a century before Virgil wrote of a new "glorious age . . . [who] shall rule the world that his fathers' virtues have set at peace."[24] These cryptic lines from the Fourth Eclogue, envisioning a new Prince of Peace about to be born, have often been said to prophesy the birth of Jesus.

Pisces rules theatre and dance, and arenas of the imagination—in places both sacred and profane—where atmospheres of mystery are created by artful arrangements of light and fragrant smoke, color and fabric and sound that can fuse all present into one heart and soul united by the same mythic experience. The downside to all this enchanting, magical illusion is that Pisces rules all manner of altered states of consciousness, in everything from mystical vision, shamanic travel and meditation, to dreams, drugs, and delusions. Thus the unevolved, needy Pisces type can be a perpetual victim and energy vampire, the artist of addiction who gets stuck in every available substance and then is deceptive about it. He is also the wishful thinker who conceives the most fantastic, gorgeous dreams, but can't seem to start himself toward realizing them. It is only to be expected, then, that the combinations of technology and propaganda that exist now at the end of the Piscean Age have created fantasy images so brilliant and seductive that millions who will believe anything now live in the enthralled narcosis of a continuous waking sleep.

Welcome to the end of the Age of Pisces. If the sleep of reason produces monsters, as Goya named one of his paintings, it also invites Ponzi schemers, inside traders, addicts, emotional vampires, co-dependents, denialists, delusionaries, and the whole menagerie of deceit who proliferate at Neptune's negative pole not because our imaginations are overactive, but because they are not being used at all. The inescapable result is late Piscean corporatism, which concentrates immense wealth in fewer and fewer talons while the many live in despair, so disempowered and dumbed down that they have never sensed the forces of mind and will that lie within them, and are unable to help or free themselves or their loved ones, much less their communities and their planet.

THE GREAT CORPORATIONS, AND THE NATIONS THEY OWN, AS LATE PISCEAN ORGANIZATIONS

The qualities of the corporations that have led us to unprecedented prosperity, followed by incalculable disaster will help us define, by contrast, the Aquarian economy:

1. The Piscean corporation is as *hierarchic* as any church or army, concentrating all decision-making and power in a few tiers, even a single tier, of executives at the top.

2. It is a *competitive* dog-eat-dog struggle for survival, in which aggressive firms create a *pervasive culture of fear* in which executives learn to trust no one and covet everything.

3. It is *secretive*, having moved far beyond the protective security that Winston Churchill described—in time of war, truth is escorted by a bodyguard of lies—to the premise that information has power when it is hidden but loses power when it is shared.

4. It is obsessively *fearful of scarcity*, seeing planetary resources as finite, so that the company must grab what is left before it vanishes, or, even worse, a competitor gets it.

5. It is *all-consuming*, seeking like Neptune's ocean to dissolve everything into itself. It not only aims to seize resources, as banks have done in the bailout robbery of late 2008.[25] It corrupts and thereby controls governments.[26] It has grown relentlessly since 2001, when 51 of the hundred largest economies on Earth were multinational corporations, to such power that it manipulates the boom-and-bust cycle at will, invariably to its own profit.[27]

6. It is deceptive and *delusive*, using the most narcotic, seductive tools of modern media to reduce entire societies to what Tom Robbins called "a vast herd of homogenized consumers, individually expendable, docile, and beyond basic job skills, not too smart."[28]

BETTING IT ALL ON DOOM

The result, in 2008, was the only outcome that was possible in a climate of greed and risk-taking that was no longer merely predatory, but self-consuming. The big sharks wolfed down the gold and ground the last of the seed corn into the Taco of Doom, devouring their companies, stealing from clients and employees, playing the game minute by minute in such a rabid intoxication with the thrills and the odds, the numbers flashing in colored lights on the scoreboard, that the last thing anyone had time to imagine was that there might be *consequences* to what we were doing to the lives of our people and our planet.

One expects the shark to strike, eat what he needs, and swim on. That is how the landlord of the ocean has always played his fearsome but necessary role. But when the shark tries to eat everything all at once, and then seeks a place to hide, some cartilage in the crown has slipped. It can hardly get plainer than it is now, as economies disintegrate and people everywhere wonder where to put their money, what's left of it, that the Great White economy of 2004–2009 is a sinking ship that the owners and rich passengers are beginning to desert, as they move into new cities for the super-rich now being built in Florida, Dubai, and other places. *Trendwatching.com* coined the term "Nations Lite" to describe these extreme upscale enclaves as "a light version of a society or country, like a Diet Coke, stripped of annoying features like crime, bad weather, and excessive taxes. Which leaves the good things like sun, nice villas and glittering shopping malls."[29] Among these new "countries" are huge luxury ships that will stay at sea almost all the time like fabulously appointed Noah's arks, stopping only to provision themselves at secure ports, well away from the turmoil on the land.

How did the unraveling all begin? As a classic example of deception and fraud at the end of the Age of Pisces, a quiet item that no one noticed at the time has had, and continues to have, enormous consequences. There was not a peep from any quarter in 1999 when United States Treasury Secretary Robert Rubin—a former investment bank executive—led the repeal of the Glass-Steagall Act, the firewall legislation passed in 1933 to prevent speculative excesses like those of the

1920s by prohibiting commercial banks from making the daring bets that make both the risks and the rewards of investment banking much greater. As soon as Glass-Steagall was no more, commercial banks and insurance firms began trading in *credit default swaps* (CDS), which were pioneered by J. P. Morgan in 1994.

The beauty of a CDS was that it had the profit potential of investment instruments, but was officially classified as "insurance" because its purpose was to protect lenders from default on loan repayments from other companies. Thus credit default swaps, and the derivatives that were also tied to the value of an "underlier," were not subject to the same governmental regulation as conventional investments.[30] When banks first began using CDS deals to hedge mortgage-backed securities in 2004, it was only a matter of time before the gambling fever of ever more complex investments would inflate the housing market into a bubble that had to explode. The only question was when.

Amazingly, danger signals proliferated as early as 2002, when investor Warren Buffett used the term "time bomb" to describe the complex investment instruments of the 1990s, and referred to derivatives as "financial weapons of mass destruction."[31] "Credit-default swaps," declared George Soros in May 2008, "now make up a $45 trillion market that is entirely unregulated. . . . The large potential risks of such investments are not being acknowledged."[32] Here's a fun way to imagine the immensity of this figure: Divide $45 trillion by 733,422 (2008 years × 365.25 days), and you get $61,356,217—that is, $61 million for every day since Jesus was born. And the actual figure could be much bigger.

Will we ever know just how much money was invested and lost in this phantom market? Not likely. But the numbers really don't matter, believe it or not. What does count is the sheer delusional madness of the scenario in which we find ourselves, so eye-widening that our grandchildren may look back at us and wonder, *what were they thinking?* Just imagine. Of all the people living on Earth, a tiny pocket of a minuscule portion of one percent, all of them persons of immense wealth, essentially bet galactic-scale sums of money on the default of everything. This is unprecedented in our history. The dream killers did not just walk the talk of destruction by putting their money where their aims were. They nailed to the table a heavier bet on doom than anyone has ever placed. Has there ever been, in all our experience, a schematic of doom as toxically, pathologically strange as this, as utterly negating of happiness, and of life itself?

It is all changing now. We may not be sure what the future will bring, but we know what is already disappearing: the corporate paradigm of hierarchy, exclusivity, and secrecy, with no responsibility to anyone but shareholders, and to each robber baron's own money launderer, travel agent, bookie, and bodyguard. What will replace the late corporatist pirate economy? Aquarian ideas that wealth has a communal purpose, and true economic growth and rest resembles a grain field more than a battlefield. We'll look now at some core ideas of the new Aquarian economy, and at specific approaches that people are already using to create more workable and sustainable new ways to do business.

TEAMWORK AND SWARM INTELLIGENCE

The innovation comes, as always, from the private sector, which has to meet a standard of quality and performance in order to survive. And some companies aren't just getting lean from outsourcing jobs overseas. No, some industry leaders are experimenting with models of flexible teamwork that empower workers to be creative and resourceful, so that they hardly need managers, and the old hierarchies, especially at the middle management level, can be streamlined. When a firm needs fewer managers and fewer tiers to put them in, rather than fewer line workers, it's on its way to Aquarian equality and teamwork.

The seminal principle is called *emergence theory*. Its main premise is that if an environment has a certain number of elements interacting within a certain set of rules, they'll tend of behave in the same patterns—but they may also form new actions and combinations that will cause new rules and relationships, even new elements, to *emerge* spontaneously. The more complex the system is, the greater the possibility that something unexpected, something beyond the sets of rules that were there before, will appear and change the rules, so that some of the elements can act—can *choose to act*—in new ways.

How does this apply to businesses and other organizations? By proving that departments, even whole companies that have been designed to operate under certain sets of rules, may still be flexible enough to accommodate new creative decisions that individual workers can make autonomously in response to unexpected, fluid conditions. As David Chalmers explains, "Emergence is the phenomenon wherein a system is designed according to certain principles, but interesting properties arise that are not included in the goals of the designer."[33] These "interesting" properties are crucial. They mean that the unpredictable is no longer a lurking danger—as it is when a hierarchy is "big on control"— but is a valuable creative resource that can now be used to invent better ways to do things.

One of the most influential articles linking emergence theory to business operations is Eric Bonabeau and Christopher Meyer's "Swarm Intelligence," the product of 20 years' research in the efficient work habits of social insects. Ants have simple rules that they follow in bringing food efficiently along an established route from the food source to the colony. Yet if the food source is moved or the route blocked, the ants immediately adapt to find a new food supply. There seems to be no conferencing among the ants, no call to the main office for instructions. The ants just move, applying the advantages of "robustness, flexibility and self-organization" to the new task at hand. Honeybees operate in a similar way, performing the same task in the same way until they see that it's now time to switch, on no authority but the individual bee's initiative to do something else.[34]

Bonabeau and Meyer list practical examples of how Hewlett Packard and Southwest Airlines are using swarm intelligence principles to devise better methods, respectively, for routing telephone traffic and cargo, and how Northwestern University has developed better methods for repainting fleets of trucks under changing seasonal conditions. The ultimate outcome, the authors predict, will be self-organizing work groups that can pool their intelligence and creativity to invent on the spot, without a manager's authorization, the best new actions in response to rapidly changing markets and field conditions.

Are we now about to perceive management itself as a useless relic of the late Piscean hierarchies, as a kind of pointless padding that grows in more and more layers between the visionary boss at the top of the firm and the workers on the floor? Is management obsolete? It's too early to tell, as complex business systems still need skilled designers and communicators to make and articulate the ground rules. But we do know now that work teams can be trusted to self-organize and reach good decisions, and that the collective intelligence of the group may be more valuable to the firm than the leadership of executive officers and the special skills of technical experts.

The new paradigm that has been the talk of the shop floor and the office cubicle village, and the terror of management hierarchy, is James Surowiecki's book *The Wisdom of Crowds*, which argues that "under the right circumstances, groups are remarkably intelligent, and are often smarter than the smartest people in them."[35] Surowiecki's theory is that large groups of "average" people are uncannily more accurate in their collective ability to solve specific problems than experts who are individually more brilliant and knowledgeable than anyone in the "average" sample group.

Surowiecki claims that for best results, "wise crowds" must meet four conditions: (1) diversity of opinion among the group's members; (2) each member's independence from the others; (3) decentralized structures and work rules; and (4) a good way to gather the group's opinions into simple option lists for clear, quick action. These ideas have been adopted by hundreds of companies who see that they'll get the best out of their people by trusting them to work smart, and empowering them to get better. No one's calling it Aquarian Business—yet—but they may as well.

For line workers, who have known all along what they're doing, this acknowledgment of their abilities is long overdue. For managers who see loss of control as a leap off a cliff on a prayer that is too short and a bungee cord that is a little too long, wise crowds look like an invitation to chaos. But there's no getting around it—chaos theory, as Sam

Foster explained, is the very foundation of emergence theory, as its swirl and random collision of elements leads to "the nonlinear evolution of chaotic networks."[36]

Whew. Scarier and scarier, for some. It's one thing to imagine that "reality" may not be as linear as we'd thought. But do we now even have to accept that order itself has become an antique? Not really. All that's needed is a willingness to consider that order and chaos may both have their virtues. Unlike rigid patterns of order, chaos does have the advantage of offering unlimited creative choices to those who are willing to surf them. The tighter the order, the less flexibility and breathing room it has. The wilder the chaos, the greater the freedom—which is, in itself, an Aquarian value so attractive that it will be, if nothing else, a useful talking point when one is recruiting younger staff.[37] Under such conditions, who knows what challenges may ensue for those who've always controlled everything from the top? As horribly awkward and unfamiliar as the sensation may be, *the hierarchs may have to learn to tell the truth.* Talk about a learning curve!

TRUST COULD BE BUSTIN' OUT ALL OVER

The dangers of stonewalling when it's time to tell the truth began coming swiftly to the fore in 2004 in lawsuits against firms that face, or have already suffered, severe penalties for concealing irregular financial actions, and even for failing to report on, and recall, a product that is potentially unsafe. New York State sued British-based pharmaceutical company GlaxoSmithKline for failing to warn the public that the anti-depressant Paxil may have harmful side effects. The ensuing publicity triggered, as journalist Alan M. Webber reported, a flurry of comment in business pages and corporate boardrooms about whether all the obsessive secrecy is useful, or now an open invitation to disaster.

"Only fools stifle truth," Webber wrote, "especially since nothing really stays under wraps."[38] Other business writers and company executives have begun to agree that, given the dilemma of either telling the painful truth or being exposed as a crook and fined for falsehood, it's better to go proactive, bite the bullet, and ask earnestly for forgiveness. The alternative—whopping fines and a deadly loss of customer loyalty and trust—is enough to make honesty, however homely she has always appeared to the corporate culture, look positively sexy for the first time. "Sunlight is the best disinfectant," wrote Theodor Baums of Goethe University on the recent scandal that Deutsche Bank now has to weather over the secret payment of excessive bonuses to bank executives.[39] What will come next? Will a pandemic of honesty endanger corporate secrecy everywhere?

The usual paranoia is under threat from another flank as well. CNET News reported that by using the revolutionary *open source* method of software development, entrepreneur John Roberts succeeded, in the unheard-of span of only five months, in attracting $2 million in outside investment and launching his new CRMSugar company.[40] Under the old closed-source rules of established firms like Microsoft and Oracle, CRMSugar's startup could have taken years.

What is open source, and how does it help entrepreneurs start new software ventures? Where does it get the swashbuckling panache that makes it so appealing to young code writers who love to break rules? Open source makes software code writing a transparent, collaborative way for programmers to assemble their new codes from components that are freely available online, and enlist in the effort "volunteer programmers [who] not only help develop the product, they also create a pool of potential customers for starting companies. In return, programmers develop new skills and get free software."[41] For those married to old cloak-and-dagger games of guarding trade secrets, John Roberts and others like him may seem at first to have a few pixels loose. By making their creative product an open book to anyone who's willing to study their code and improve it, aren't the open source entrepreneurs taking a risk that someone who likes their code will just steal it?

Yes, of course. And no, not really. The gamble that the open source rule breakers and investors are willing to take is that good code is good code, period. And when customers and backers see our code is great and we can be counted on to write more of it, the risk that we'll get nicked by a few pirates is outweighed to the tune of tons by the ways that open source lets us create new software faster and cheaper than closed-source companies can. Our new products start an exciting buzz even as they're being written, and we attract top new talent we might never find if we went the old wig and trench coat route of having tight-lipped headhunters scout the best code writers in the dead of night.

Too good to be true? Of course. Legal snags are inevitable for open source entrepreneurs who fail to "get the proper licensing and identify all the open source code with proper documentation," said Doug Levin, CEO of Black Duck Software, whose code automates the job of separating open source code from proprietary source code. But if investment in Black Duck is any indicator—$5 million in a single week of new venture investment—then someone is betting that open source has a future, and that it's coming fast. "Open source," Roberts says, is just a more efficient, effective software business model. . . . It's a shift, a movement reshaping the dynamics of a modern software company."[42] It may not be long before open source reshapes more than just software creation.

EQUALITY COULD SAVE YOUR LIFE

So far, we've seen how Aquarian values of empowerment, teamwork, and transparency may have begun to transform the most entrenched principles of capitalist enterprise. Could actual *equality* be on the way? As reported by Marek Kohn, a growing body of new research points to the increasingly plausible theory that an unequal society is an unhealthy society—not just metaphorically, but physically. It is getting clearer now that the killer in modern industrial societies, with their extreme variations in professional and social status, is not hamburgers, cigarettes, or high-pressure work styles, but inequalities of social status that can damage a person's self-esteem, and his health along with it.

This new focus on the deadliness of inequality is based on the research of British social scientist Michael Marmot, author of *The Status Syndrome*, whose team studied relationships between departmental ranks and death rates among Whitehall civil servants. The studies showed that death rates from heart disease were four times as great in the lower ranks of the civil service than at the top. When weighing other variables, the team found that "only about a third of the effect vanished when account was taken of the usual lifestyle suspects such as smoking and fatty food. This influence upon life and death affected everybody in the hierarchy, according to their position in it. Differences in wealth were an implausible cause in themselves, for most of the civil servants were comfortably off and even the lowest paid were not poor. The fatal differences were in status."[43]

"What goes for Whitehall," Kohn reports, "seems to go for the world. In rich countries, death rates appear to be related to the differences between incomes, rather than to absolute income levels. . . . Although the findings about income inequality are controversial, the broad picture is consistent; and remains so if softer criteria than death are measured, like trust or social cohesion. Inequality promotes hostility, frustrates trust and damages health."

"Inequality kills," writes Richard Wilkinson, another leading researcher in the field, whose studies led him to the same conclusions as the Marmot team: that "unequal societies are unhealthy societies. They are unhealthy not just in the strict sense but in the wider one, that they are hostile, suspicious, antagonistic societies."

"Controversial" is not the word for these ideas, so antithetical to traditional hierarchic beliefs. For now, the main question is whether, and how, these explosive ideas about the lethal effects of inequality will get to those who are most affected by them: the ones in the middle of the food chain, who are least likely to notice, much less act on, the actuality that the low life is not just a bummer and the blues, but a quick ticket to a tag on your toe.

No surprise here. Great social changes have almost always been triggered by educated middle classes who knew what was going on and could organize in response to it. But this will shift too, as the main engine of change is not the workplace or the marketplace, but the *thoughtplace* of consciousness that unites all human beings. As the awakening spreads, they'll resonate at once with the Aquarian realization that society's least exalted segments, already streetwise and tuned to the grapevine at the immediate level of their neighborhoods, are the ones who are closest to the Aquarian spirit of community.

For them, the Aquarian adjustment will in fact be the easiest. They've always known that near is dear and the street can't be beat. Once they also see the value of education, and start forming teams as well as gangs, the chemistry of their resourcefulness and creativity will yield some of the most brilliant community impact stories of the years ahead. Those who live at the level of actual needs rather than fake gotta-have-its, and are skilled at taking care of their own, are already operating by the rules of the Aquarian economy. They've got the economies of scale nailed. The entrepreneurial ideas will come.

THE AQUARIAN ENTREPRENEUR

It couldn't be plainer than it is now that the future belongs to the birds who are small and quick, no matter how impressive their ancestor the dinosaur looks as he thrashes and roars for the respect that runs from him now. The new entrepreneurs of the Aquarian Age will be little interested in creating, much less joining, Fortune 500 firms that need capital from, and pay most of their profit to, a handful of investors who are uninterested in the freedom, equality, and empowerment of others. What will Aquarian entrepreneurs do?

Rather than start one company and try to grow it for a lifetime, they'll start a series of small ventures, each one built to tackle a specific problem or serve a specific need. They'll profit from doing a few things, even only one thing, very well.

They'll earn a small profit share from each of several companies, instead of trying to control only one, and they'll network to get rich from several revenue streams.

They will not seek to "grow or die," for they know that growing bigger only slows one down, and limits his options.

Their companies will be teams of like-minded friends who share the same spiritual and social values, rather than hierarchic structures of soul strangers who have nothing in common beyond a desire for more money and higher status. Aquarians will hire people whom they believe capable of friendship as well as good work performance.

They will be far more community-conscious than corporatists have been. Their support of social and environmental projects, and cultural organizations, will often be anonymous.

They will seek, as they do now, the backing of socially and environmentally progressive investors. Aquarian entrepreneurs will not surrender both ownership and ethical principle to spiritually regressive or inert backers. Will it all be laughably easy? On the technical and financial plane, it probably will. On the spiritual plane, it will be more complicated, and the Faustian tragedies of the early 21st century could be about brilliant and rapidly successful young people who get thrown into their lap a bigger and brighter bag of temptation than anyone has ever opened.

GOOGLE GOES NOVA

Lawrence Page and Sergey Brin started what is in many ways a classically Aquarian company, the master search engine, Google.com. We can run the story by the numbers.

Act 1: The Creative Spark. Two friends who want to make a difference in the world start the best company of its kind, using superior electronic equipment and software skills to create the finest search engine ever. They build their company as a small and efficient team rather than a hierarchy. They enjoy a surge of early success, overtake established companies, and attract admirers.

Act 2: Complications and Temptations. Google.com becomes the most successful search engine of all, and attracts the ultimate Great White in the cyberocean, Bill Gates. Before their 2004 IPO, Page and Brin drop in a *Playboy* interview some information that is not in their prospectus, then remedy the gaffe by adding to the prospectus not just the relevant part of the *Playboy* interview, but the whole thing. The prospectus declares that all Google's shareholders can expect is an honest return on their money, and the cachet of being part of a hip, progressive-minded company. Shareholders will not be able to gain control of the company, or replace the founders. Page and Brin say their watchword is "Don't be evil," but otherwise give no hint of what they'll do with the capital they raise.

Act 3: Rich Enough for Hubris? Determined to offer Google stock to anyone who wants to buy, the boys use a "Dutch auction" method that prevents Wall Street banks from gaining control of the sale, while making it easier for individual investors to buy. For weeks, the launch plan goes up and down, in and out, here and there, and every which way but on. Some writers, apparently put off by the sheer weirdness and complexity of the sale process, caution against buying Google. But investors like the gamble, quickly driving the share price from $82 to just over $100, raising $1.67 billion on sale day, and giving the company a total value of $27 billion. All Page and Brin will say about their style is, "We try to use elements from different companies, but a lot of it is seat-of-the-pants stuff."[44] This is certain, of course, to reassure the people in charcoal pinstripes. But in the end, Google's unconventional moves work. "The idea behind this type of IPO," the *International Herald Tribune* observed, "is to allow online bidders to determine stock's offering price, thereby zeroing in on the sweet spot where supply equals demand. By setting a real price less susceptible to manipulation, Google wanted to democratize the process and diminish the hegemony of the investment banks."[45]

Act 4: Aftermath. Only time will tell if Google will be an Aquarian enterprise in its maturity, or only in its youth. Page and Brin won't be the first young entrepreneurs of our time to have to decide whether they'll let their loose Aquarian team turn into a stiff Piscean hierarchy. Some of the coming stories will be tragedies worthy of Sophocles. But some will be the kinds of Aquarian comedies in which the Trickster wins his own freedom, and liberates countless others too.

SOLIDARITY ECONOMY: GROWING THE WAY NATURE GROWS

In the mid-1960s, British Finance Minister R. A. B. Butler proposed another in the long parade of ideas aimed at solving one of life's most persistent headaches for those who try to manage economies: What do we mean by *growth?* How do we sustain it, and when it slows down, how do we stimulate it? Butler proposed moderate 3 percent growth, reasoning that growth at less than 3 percent a year was stagnant, while 5 percent or more a year would overheat the engine, producing a boom that would be exciting until it went bust. J. P. Morgan had the same idea, wanting to avoid the instability that led to the Panic of 1907 by creating a Federal Reserve Bank system that would keep currency and the whole economy stable.

The plain actuality, though, is that *continuous growth is a pipe dream,* as unworkable in an economy as it is in nature. Just as an animal that only grows, but never rests, can only get so big that it dies of morbid obesity, an economy that will not rest can only crash, and the longer it tries to grow too fast, the harder it will fall. In the cycle of nature things wax and wane, expand and contract. That is how it works. Once we see continuous growth as inorganic and unnatural, we can design intelligent, modest economies that live in growth-and-rest cycles, like everything else, so our economies can inhale and exhale normally, and we can say goodbye to boom-and-bust.

Nature's growth-and-rest cycle is by no means the only thing about the emerging new economy that is already getting much closer to the Earth. "What kind of economy," asks James Howard Kunstler, "are we going to live in if the old one is toast? . . . [I]t will have to be based on activities productively aimed at keeping human beings alive in an ecology that has a future. . . . To be specific about this new economy, we're going to have to make things again, and raise things out of the earth, locally, and trade these things for money of some kind that we earn through our own productive activities."[46]

What "money of some kind?" By April 2009, communities large and small in the U.S.A were printing and using more than 75 local currencies such as Ithaca Hours, in use since 1991; and Massachu-setts' BerkShares, created in 2006 for "citizens working in their own communities, region by region, to create the kind of systemic change that will lead to sustainable economic practices—practices that foster ecologically responsible production of goods and a more equitable distribution of wealth. . . . BerkShares are about building community while building the local economy."[47]

The Detroit Cheers, a company scrip now in use again, was first used in the 1930s to help a city economy that was reeling from the effects of the Great Depression.[48] The other activist measures that friends and neighbors are taking now to help each other through hard times—government and community projects of "production for use" (not solely for profit), grassroots public works projects, self-management and community ownership of production facilities, counter-economies, sitdown strikes and the occupation of factories by workers, "home defender" teams mobilized to block evictions of families from foreclosed homes—were all used with different measures of success in the decade and more following the Crash of 1929.[49]

What is different this time? Not just better cell phone technology that the Association of Community Organizations for Reform Now (ACORN) uses to call hundreds of eviction stoppers by text messaging and Twitter. And not just barter—it doubled on Craigslist in the year ending April 1, 2009.[50] What has been new since 2009 is that a dozen new organizations such as the National Coalition for the Homeless and Take Back the Land are working at various volumes, from quiet subtlety to open defiance, to jam foreclosures and move the newly evicted into foreclosed homes. This is no mere stopgap, to be abandoned as soon as things ease up. An Aquarian fight for freedom is underway, and the usual metaphors apply. Cheri Honkala, of the Poor People's Economic Human Rights Campaign in Minnesota, calls her group's effort a "modern-day underground railroad."[51]

Something new and potentially very impactful is stirring when communal activism joins proactive, progressive small business in synergies like San Francisco's Business Alliance for Local Living Economies (BALLE), which linked with Small-Mart in April 2009.[52] And when the Yachil Xojobal Chulchan farmers' cooperative in Chiapas, Mexico aims not only to get better prices for local coffee growers, but to create their own schools, health clinics, and trade alliances, and ultimately to build an autonomous society.[53] Like their fellow activists in South America, they are committed to *horizontalidad*.[54] This and other principles of "solidarity economics" began to develop in Latin America from the 1980s as crushing debts and structural changes imposed by the International Monetary Fund forced many communities to get braver and more ingenious.

Economia solidaria spreads at Aquarian speed. In only three years, from its Encuentro of eight nations in Brazil in 1998 to the World Social Forum in 2001, the Latin American Solidarity Economy Network grew to six times its size, becoming the 47-nation Global Network of the Solidarity Socioeconomy. This last word is revealing, as it envisions an economy as holistic, vitalized by the social, cultural, and spiritual aims that people hold when they live in reverence for the Earth, in "self-organized relationships of care, cooperation, and community." Thus, wrote Ethan Miller, "solidarity economics rejects one-size-fits-all solutions and singular economic blueprints, embracing instead a view that economic and social development should occur from the bottom up, diversely and creatively crafted by those who are most affected."[55]

Thus solidarity economies resemble in many ways the Earth-friendly tribal economies of the Old Cultures in which our ancestors lived. They employ local people and teach them the skills that the grandfathers and grandmothers know. They buy their materials from local suppliers and make what their local community needs, using methods that preserve health and home. They treat their workers as friends and encourage their creativity, so their shop turns out beautiful work, and sells it at the local weekend farmers' market and craft fair. They buy their fresh produce for the week, locally made beer and wine, clothes and footwear, glassware, pottery and lamps, and other works of solid, conscious beauty that they really need. They produce enough to serve their community's needs, plus a little more to trade in other places nearby. And when they provide a service so useful that they have to get bigger to serve communities besides their own, they still measure their success in the happiness they create. An economy, after all, is a state of mind.

QUANTUM ECONOMY

Centuries from now, the economies of the early Aquarian Age will be unrecognizable to our descendants, who will have learned alchemies of manifestation, and arts of intentional economies, that we can only begin to imagine now. Imagine how our lives will be when an economy is no longer a mystery no one understands, working through "market forces" that no one can shape or control, and is instead a simple system that everyone creates together in a spirit of shared responsibility. Imagine a society so intuitive and telepathic, and an economy so transparent, that the young will have to look in old writings to find what people used to mean by "trade secrets"—or secrets of any kind—and why meetings happened "behind closed doors."

Welcome to the quantum economy, based on the fundamental principle that we live not in a universe of solid objects, but within mobile, mutable structures of energy. As each atom has a few or several dozen sub-atomic particles centering or whizzing about a sphere of empty space, one does not have to be Carl Sagan to perceive that "Matter is composed, chiefly, of nothing," and that what appear to us to be material substances are in fact arrangements of energy that are in constant motion. Thus the old materialist belief that an economy is a *re-ality* of making and exchanging *things*—including labor as a commodity—is false. The truth of any economy is that it works through exchanges of *energy*, for which apparently solid objects are in fact only the material markers.

As we get skilled in the arts of intention and attraction, we'll understand that economies are states of manifestation in which individual energies combine to create a collective result. It must follow, then, that the most valuable resource each one has to sell is not skill, time, or labor, but energy, so that as we amplify our frequencies of energy and team them with the resonances of others, we can build and move new transformative forces in versatile synergies that are far beyond the limited creative range of those who look for jobs instead of creating them. The quantum economy will dare us—and compel us—to think bigger and get smarter, to see ourselves as Shakespeare once did, as beings who are "noble in reason, infinite in faculties." When we do, there will be no limit to what we, and the other highly evolved beings with whom we link in synergies, can do.

Thus the Aquarian economy will be, and is already becoming:

1. *synarchic*, rather than hierarchic. It spreads decision-making through teams working in equality. New models of swarm intelligence, which give workers more freedom of action, bring encouraging results, and promote more compact, efficient organizations.

2. *transparent*, rather than secretive and deceptive. New Aquarian teams work openly. The Internet, SMS, and other technologies that are used for activist teamwork are only the early tools of the new transparency, and its urge to move fast.

3. *empowered*, rather than passive and fooled, as we abandon toxic pharmaceuticals, genetically-modified foods and corporate media, and create farmers' and artisans' markets, and barter. We buy food locally. It tastes and works better.

4. *communal*, rather than exclusive or divisive, created by builders of community who focus on what they want, and what they have in common.

5. *abundant*, rooted in the Earth-loving knowledge that scarcity is a mere opinion when human communities serve and revere nature's limitless capacity to renew herself.

AQUARIAN PROFILE: KJAER GROUP AND THE GREAT PLACES TO WORK INSTITUTE

One new Aquarian trend is the radical notion that a company's value and success can be measured in the job satisfaction and happiness of its employees. The team that surveys and reports the happiness quotient of employees is the Great Places to Work Institute, founded in San Francisco in 1991 by Amy Lyman and Robert Levering, who wrote the 1984 book *The 100 Best Companies to Work for in America*. The authors diverged from the usual company evaluation methods by making sure to focus on small firms as well as big ones, and emphasizing "personal practices" along with salary and benefits. At the start of their work, Lyman and Levering had the interviews and anecdotes to show whose employees were happiest, but had no hard data on possible correlations between smiling workers and smiling investors, who might expect a higher rate of return from cheerful people than from stressed, disgruntled ones. But the numbers began to take shape and look good when the GPWI became a global research and managing firm that since 2003 has announced annual awards for the best places to work in the European Union.

The data are impressive. They show that "an investment made in all of the companies on the best 100 list in 1998 and then plowed back into the new list each year would have earned 15.21 percent annually, compared with 3.81 percent for the Standard & Poor's 500-stock index."[56] Getting on the best companies list also helps companies keep their employees longer and attract twice as many job applications as firms that didn't make the list. The Institute's annual nomination process for Europe samples the views of over 120,000 employees and managers in 14 countries on such criteria as trust, workplace camaraderie, mutual respect between managers and staff, and each company's "people score," as GPWI believes that in the most productive workplaces, workers "trust the people they work for, have pride in what they do, and enjoy the people they work with."

The Kjaer Group of Denmark, winner of the 2004 award for Europe, goes out of its way to make the job light as well as efficient. Company president Mads Kjaer has been known to wear a flower print dress and long blond wig when presiding at the annual Elephant Awards for those who've made such outstanding contributions as the Laughter Club, based on a concept that's no-brainer at Kjaer: that a good laugh can lead to a good effort. The Kjaer (pronounced "care") Group has 59 employees at its headquarters in Svendborg and 140 overseas, mostly in Africa, where the company sells rough-terrain vehicles and transportation services to international agencies, including UNICEF.

Kjaer attributes its high level of worker loyalty and good will to a company culture in which all views are respected and encouraged, and to such other benefits as home work stations, flexible schedules, and an inhouse squash court and massage service. While not actually calling itself an Aquarian company, Kjaer is certainly behaving like one, basing its corporate friendship culture on the values of trust, empowerment, equality of respect, teamwork, and honesty, and the recognition that the company's most valuable resource is the creativity of its people.

CHAPTER 5

THE AQUARIAN REVOLUTION

Thomas Jefferson had some breezy opinions about forceful disobedience when he was living in Paris in early 1787. He had replaced Benjamin Franklin, a very hard act to follow, as American ambassador to France. In a letter to James Madison, who was then up to his widow's peak in the intricate business of designing the American constitution, Jefferson wrote, " . . . a little rebellion now and then is a good thing, and as necessary in the political world as storms in the physical. . . . It is a medicine necessary for the sound health of government."[57]

As always, Jefferson was precise in his choice of words. *Rebellion* literally means "fight back," against an assault by authority against one's home, money, or liberty, as in the example that prompted Jefferson to write. The grievances of American farmers led by Daniel Shays escalated in the autumn of 1786 from polite protest into rebellion when the American government refused to lift excessive property taxes, poll taxes that prevented the poor from voting, and other abuses of the principles for which Americans had fought for their independence. Shays' Rebellion would not be the last time that less affluent Americans would fight against being denied a fair shot at the pursuit of happiness.

To Jefferson, Shays' Rebellion was a success. The leaders were jailed long enough to bring them back down to room temperature, but none were executed, and the conditions that moved them to an *uprising*—a classic Piscean word, claiming hierarchy of rulers over citizens—were corrected, so that no more violent action was needed. By Jefferson's lights, Shays' Rebellion was exciting because it showed that American democracy was working. Smug, elitist officials were shaken into compliance with the people's rights, injustices were rectified, and the judges who tried the rebels wisely chose to soothe the people's fury rather than inflame it again, and issued lenient sentences. A little rebellion had made a full-scale revolution unnecessary. The medicinal effect of a little rebellion would be on Jefferson's mind again in the years ahead, when he'd witness the cataclysm of 1789 in Paris. There he witnessed events that showed how horrific the people's rage can get when a little rebellion fails to bring a change, so that before long the new autocratic master, Napoleon, remarked that "Revolution is an idea which has found its bayonets."

We've already glanced at revolution as an Aquarian principle. The word was first used in English in Chaucer's time to mean the motions of celestial bodies in their orbits; then from the 1600s it came to mean the kind of political upheaval that shook England in 1648, when Puritans toppled and executed the king. Revolution came more gently again 40 years later, when barely a wisp of snuff was stirred as James II sailed into exile, and William of Orange strode in. The 1688 revolution was called "Glorious" because hardly a drop of blood was shed. It was a perfectly civil affair. So no one remembers it. What they do remember is 1648: the butchery of Oliver Cromwell, three years of civil war, and the beheading of Charles I. People remember bloodshed.

Why all this history, and why does it matter now? Because the powers that be are asking themselves those eternal questions again: How much freedom will we allow our people to have? Do we give them so much of it that they disrespect authority, forget civic duty, and even swing into anarchy? Or give them so little that we stifle their hope and energy, force them underground into black markets and shadow societies, even strike a spark that leads to revolution? How do we steer safely between the two, and *how do we keep control?* You already know which choice—too much freedom or too little—governments in the "developed" world and wealthy elites in white-knuckled regimes like Saudi Arabia are embracing with all their strength. When times get tough, control tightens.

In the minds of billions of people on our planet, revolution is long overdue because patient, persistent effort to bring relief from oppressive conditions either gets us nowhere or seems to bring the opposite of what we want by making things worse. This may be why people dream and talk of revolution as though to feed their fantasies of the change that all our struggle fails to bring. Count 'em. The sexual revolution of the 1960s. The information revolution and its love child, the Internet revolution. The green revolution in agriculture. And the revolutions that advertisers claim their drinks, clothes, and music are sure to trigger in your life. One would almost get the feeling that we think all avenues of healthy change are blocked, and this is why metaphors of revolution appeal so much.

We need not look in detail at all the political and social constipation of controlling elites who've become so shrink-wrapped in their insecurity that pressure, not outright violence, can now bring change. When the intention of the Aquarian revolution is clear and firm in the mind and the heart, the feet will step lightly to meet it. How will the action and style of revolutionary change in the Aquarian Age be different from what we've seen before?

CANDLES AND BREAD

To answer this, we can look at the causes of revolution as we've come to see them from the abortive Bolshevik revolution of 1905 until now. The seminal book, still widely studied since it first appeared in 1938 in an era of right-wing revolutions in Germany, Italy, Spain, and Argentina—and the terror of Stalin's show trials—was Crane Brinton's *The Anatomy of Revolution*. It proposed seven "tentative uniformities" in economic, political, and social conditions common to the English Puritan revolution, the American and French revolutions of the 18th century, and the Russian revolution of 1917.[58] Brinton's ideas, presented as a guide for spotting and averting trouble in the 1930s rather than as a set of tools for those wanting to bring a revolution about, were further developed by James Chowning Davies in 1962 in his "J-curve theory of political revolutions."[59] Davies' premise was that when "rising individual expectations" and "perceived wellbeing" follow the same gradually improving trend, societies remain stable—but if perceived wellbeing keeps falling as individual expectations continue to rise, so the downward curve becomes more and more pronounced, and people "subjectively fear that ground gained with great effort will be quite lost; their mood becomes revolutionary."[60] Tea Party, anyone?

So—if Brinton and Davies are correct in outlining the conditions that must apply when a revolution is going to come, then which societies are on the brink of revolution in the early decades of the 21st century? Is the United States now boiling toward a bursting point at a time when more wealth is concentrated in fewer hands than at any time since 1928; when bailout legislation passed in a panic has transferred massive amounts of money to investment banks; when millions of homes are foreclosed and unemployment on the rise; when habitual war exhausts the country's treasure; when the legal principles of habeas corpus and posse comitatus are suspended not in response to an emergency, but as ongoing policy; when police agencies are allocated to covert surveillance, public intimidation, and the limiting of citizens' constitutional rights to free speech and free assembly?

The answers depend on what we choose to believe, at a time when Aquarian impulses toward change are masked under dreamy Piscean deceptions that each country maintains through controlled media. How turbulent is life in the Uighur communities in China's interior, and among farmers and urban workers resisting governmental corruption and control? We saw nothing about it amid the gorgeous spectacle of the 2008 Beijing Olympics. How many indigenous people were killed by corporatist agents and Peruvian police in the Amazon jungle in the spring of 2009? We'll never find out in *El Comercio de Peru*, any more than we'll learn from the Mehr News Agency what really happened in and after the disputed Iranian election of 2008, or we'll get from Italian media—90 percent of it owned by press lord Silvio Berlusconi—more than celebrity cleavage and game shows.

Whether one is a "conservative" aiming to maintain the status quo, or a "progressive" who wants change, both sides remain caught now—in the transition between Pisces and Aquarius, and in their respective zones of the old Piscean paradigm. While one side holds to delusions and denial reinforced by religious and patriotic images, their equally self righteous opponents, addicted to dualistic condemnation and conflict, anticipate "full-fledged violent revolution" brought by "28 years of conservative misrule."[61] Al Jazeera and The Real News network, stuck in metaphors of conflict as the lifeblood of the drama, call their news reports about Peru's crisis "The Battle of the Amazon."[62]

Neither side is yet ready to consider that the same old struggle and fury will only bring us more of the same, only more painful. The Aquarian solution, scary because it hasn't yet been tried, can bring happy, lasting results if our *intentions*, rather than clubs and guns, create the change. One needn't be Dr. Wayne Dyer to know that what we focus on grows, and what we damn, we empower. Nor does one need to be David Spangler to see that images of a battle between "good" and "E-word" aren't just outworn, but dangerous, and that we'll never solve our problems as long as we're addicted to conflict. "Instead," Spangler writes, "we need to think the way a caterpillar thinks as it transforms into a butterfly. The cells that formed the old structure of its body are not enemies to be defeated and cast out by the new shape; they contain the very life force and substance from which the new will be built once they surrender to the alchemical miracle of metamorphosis."[63] These ideas are not new. It's been half a century since Martin Luther King, Jr. delivered the same point: "Darkness cannot drive out darkness; only light can do that. Hate cannot drive out hate; only love can do that. Hate multiplies hate, violence multiplies violence, and toughness multiplies toughness, in a descending spiral of destruction."[64]

Is any kind of "revolution"—even the Aquarian dream of worldwide liberation into social equality and universal freedom—even remotely possible amid today's conditions of mass delusion and iron control? The simple answer is yes. The kettle of revolt began to boil in Paris in 1789 when the price of candles went up, and poor people had two choices at night: either sit at home in the dark or go out in the street and join the ranting under the lampposts. A few weeks later, when the price of bread went up too and the poor had the intolerable choice of either watching their children starve or taking action when there was nothing left to lose, the pot boiled over on the first Bastille Day.

The slipperier answer to the question of whether revolutions are likely now is another question: which kind of revolution are you talking about? The "real" kind that brings a change in the society's rulership and government? Or the made-for-TV kind that seems to happen almost every year, now that revolution has become, for the first time, a showbiz medium with its own stirring images and new rules?

VIVA LA REVOLUCION!—BROUGHT TO YOU BY . . .

. . . the Age of Aquarius, when anything and everything is entertainment. One thing that makes ideas and impulses of revolution unique in our time is that images of upheaval stream so bright and fast through our consciousness that it can be hard to tell which ones are welling up from a people's hunger for justice or just for rice, which are concocted by spooks and financiers who want to topple old enemies, irritate rivals, and attract new clients, and which are just pressure relief valves aired to reassure viewers that you don't have to get up in arms because, look—all these other people out in the streets in Athens and Rangoon, and Beirut and Teheran, have got it *much* worse than you do.

Thanks to the miracle of television, we now have in the mythic gallery of our memories more compelling images of heroic resistance—sometimes spontaneous ones, not footage crafted by D. W. Griffith and Eisenstein—than we've seen at any time in our history. People everywhere can see live, as it is happening, one man in Tiananmen Square blocking a column of tanks. Boris Yeltsin standing on top of another tank, defying a coup against the Russian Federation. Berliners knocking down the Wall. Thousands of people waving their green banners in the streets of Iran and, as though sent from central casting, a young woman as beautiful as an angel who has been murdered by the Basij.

What would the socialists of Budapest, Berlin, and Dublin in the 1840s, and Bolsheviks of a century ago, not have given for such icons of fire, which would surely have ignited all of Europe into a cyclone of righteous fury? And yet . . . the more these unforgettable images multiply, the more they have seemed, at least until January of 2011, to inspire not protests, but posters to sell online. So is revolution all but impossible now, as seductive, entrancing electronic media soothe viewers but don't stoke them, as governments control what their people see, and more of us see old "revolutionary" images—Iranians marching against Mohamed Mossadegh in the CIA's "splendid little coup" of 1953, Iraqis pulling down Saddam Hussein's statue—as fake events, fabricated here this morning for airing overseas on the evening news?

As the zodiac sign of Aquarius and its ruling planet, Uranus, are both closely related to electrical energy and its art forms in electronic media, it is impossible to imagine politics in the Aquarian Age without mass media. This is triply true in the first decade of the new millennium, as new communications gadgets and digital networking tools appear every year, and at every public event people on both sides of an issue can get a crowd of their people there at once, capture images of whatever goes down, and relay it anywhere immediately. The best place to begin looking at the new electronic politics of trick or tweet is in today's most active laboratory of change, and the first studio to televise a revolution.

The Venezuelan referendum of August 15, 2004 was seminal. The vote appeared to have been sound and honest. The United States government, while not all pleased, announced that Venezuela's people had spoken, and their choice was to be respected. In an immense turnout of voters, Venezuela's newly empowered urban poor defeated a move to recall President Hugo Chavez, who is adored by the lower orders but hated by *hacenderos* who comprise 3 percent of the population, but own almost all the land. The wealthy elite feared that Chavez, a friend of Cuba's Fidel Castro, would turn the country into a socialist bedlam. So far, on a continent that has seen notably violent clashes between old money and new impatience, Chavez's time as president, even with an aborted coup and now two failed attempts to vote him out, has been remarkably free of bloodshed. His bumpy success, some by design and some by luck, is a textbook case in how Aquarian revolutions work.

Chavez was first elected in 1998. The centerpiece of his "Bolivarian" program was to redistribute his country's oil profits, first by doubling royalty taxes that oil firms pay on new oil discoveries. Chavez also "enacted the *Ley De Tierras*, which provided for unused land to be given to the landless; he instituted free health care and public education to all; he backed a new Constitution that enshrines rights for women and indigenous peoples; and he lowered the inflation rate."[65]

Dangerously loony stuff. No telling where it could lead. So on April 11, 2004 Chavez's enemies, with U.S. military help, stormed the presidential palace, removed Chavez, and installed a "president" who lasted two days, until a counter-coup restored Chavez to power. All of this was captured by a film crew who then produced *The Revolution Will Not Be Televised*, a documentary that galvanized support for the Chavistas in Venezuela and abroad. The filmmakers, caught in the presidential palace when the counter-coup broke, had no idea what was about to happen. But they were ready. The lesson for Aquarian revolutionaries: *Be prepared. Riveting images can come from anywhere, anytime.* Shoot them really well, and the other kind of shooting may not have to happen.

Outmaneuvered on their first try, the *hacenderos* then proceeded, again with help from the United States, to force a referendum to recall Chavez. Sure they would win, the anti-Chavez forces were happy to accept election monitoring by the Organization of American States and former U.S. president Jimmy Carter, and a computerized vote audit plan. An astounding 95 percent of the people voted. The *hacenderos* screamed "Fraud!" when they lost, but so far they have had to abide by the rules they accepted. So another of the essential tools is plain enough: *Get respected, impartial observers and a way to verify the results.*

The drama between Chavez and his foes has continued since 2006, when he won another term—and another chance to see if he, like Castro, can survive the thousand dirty tricks his enemies in El Norte will invent to destroy him. Chavez, a former paratroop commander who failed to seize power in a coup of his own in 1992, now claims to do what he can to communicate openly. No American president has ever fielded all questions, many shrill and hostile, in a four-hour press conference; but Chavez did after the referendum, when passions were raw and high. He is committed to power by peaceful means, affirming that "Violence can only be ended if . . . all human beings have access to the fundamental human rights, including education, housing, work and health."[66]

No one can tell yet whether Chavez will survive, whether he will be corrupted into a dictator, and if his sweeping reforms will continue, or crash. All we know is that Venezuela's great poor majority is happier and more hopeful than they have ever been, empowered into a team-work that is rare among those who normally don't focus on anyone's misery but their own. "The very poor," Medea Benjamin reported from Caracas, "now can go to a designated home in the neighborhood to pick up a hot meal every day. The elderly now have monthly pensions that allow them to live with dignity. Young people can take advantage of greatly expanded free college programs. And with 13,000 Cuban doctors spread throughout the country and reaching over half the population, the poor now have their own family doctors on call 24 hours a day—doctors who even make house calls. This health care, including medicines, is all free. . . . The poor are now not only recipients of these programs, they are engaged in running them. They're turning abandoned buildings into neighborhood centers, running community kitchens; volunteering to teach in the literacy programs, organizing neighborhood health brigades, and registering millions of new voters."[67]

This is how the Aquarian Revolution looks: broad in its base, organized at the grass roots and motivating empowered teams to spread the word wider and galvanize more help. And Venezuela has inspired others nearby. In 2005 the populist Evo Morales became the first president of Bolivia to come from the dark-skinned *indios* who have always been the majority, but never the rulers. Rafael Correa was elected president of Ecuador in 2006 and re-elected in 2009, when he aligned Ecuador with what is now a Bolivarian Alliance for the Americas. In

El Norte capitalists are not amused, and some may have wondered if Correa selected his vice president for the annoyance value of his name: Lenin Moreno. As of 2011, Chavez has been in office for 13 years. He and his allies enjoy greater influence in Brazil, Paraguay, El Salvador, Argentina, and other countries emerging from the shackles of debt to the World Bank and International Monetary Fund, and now build new prosperity and prestige from trade alliances with new European and Asian partners.[68]

Time seems so far to be on their side, as they use cutting-edge Aquarian methods against adversaries who are stuck in old Piscean postures. And South America is not the only place where Aquarian revolution is cracking hierarchies and sending currents of change through what used to be grim, captive underclasses. It's also happened on the other side of the Cold War—and each time, *peacefully*—in the Czech Republic, Germany, Poland, and Serbia, and in the former Soviet republic of Georgia.

ROSE-COLORED MASSES: HOW TO USE MODERN ORGANIZATION, MEDIA—AND A BILLIONAIRE

Mikheil Saakashvili, "the year's most successful revolutionary" in 2004, was 35 when his "Rose Revolution" toppled the corrupt regime of Eduard Shevardnadze. Some of his tactics were similar to those who worked for Hugo Chavez. Saakashvili brought in experts from foreign NGOs, invited the American Bar Association to supervise selection of new Georgian judges, and got money from billionaire currency trader George Soros, whose Open Society Project trained Saakashvili's team in non-violent protest and publicity. Saakashvili used Georgian media's antagonism to the old regime by enlisting them as active partners in "open government." He got dense coverage of the dramatic scene his partisans staged when they occupied parliament to protest a blatantly fraudulent election, and the ABA-administered judicial exams were broadcast on live television.

From the start, Saakashvili's movement was committed to non-violence, no matter how great the provocation. "The temptation to use force is huge," he said—"But once you cross that threshold, you can never go back."[69] In fact, much of the new government's success came from their patience in winning over the military and police forces. "The smartest thing Saakashvili did," David Ignatius notes, "was to woo the Georgian army and police. His followers showered the troops with roses, paid visits to their families, invited them to share food in the chilly streets outside parliament. When the soldiers were ordered to attack the protesters, they refused—and the revolution triumphed."

Saakashvili has been second-guessed by those who see him as an inept creature of foreign governments and big money. He is harried by a Russia determined to arm and aid the autonomous districts of Abkhazia and South Ossetia even as Saakashvili tries to unite them with Georgia. Saakashvili does what he can to see his program through. His anti-corruption campaign aimed to replace 19,000 police officers and thousands of tax and customs officials, on the premise that "Once you start reform, you have to do it all." He has no illusions about job security. He estimated that the people of Georgia would tire of his policies and throw him out after one five-year term, and this would prove that Georgia is "a normal country." He was re-elected in 2008.

The peaceful Rose Revolution—and the Orange Revolution that followed in Ukraine—are far from normal. Both have been discounted as puppet shows pulled off by American agents for the sake of embarrassing Russia. Time will tell if Georgia and Ukraine were only arenas for cynical moves in the Great Game—or achieved what will soon be normal: a peaceful transfer of power by people who express their political will by throwing roses, not bombs, and master Aquarian tactics of friendship and communal activism.

THE AQUARIAN REVOLUTIONARY'S TOOL KIT

In the centuries since printing presses made ideas easier to circulate and read, and soon led to a much bigger middle-class readership for novels and newspapers, what's been one sure sign that revolution is in the air? The number of books published about it. They come in waves in volatile decades, so naturally, in 1968, Kwame Nkrumah's *Handbook of Revolutionary Warfare* taught the lessons of guerrilla war and liberation in Ghana to other Pan-African revolutionaries, and a year later, Tariq Ali's *The New Revolutionaries* took the same ideas global, into international organization and propaganda.[70] Between five and 6.5 billion copies of the "Little Red Book" of *Quotations from Chairman Mao Tse-Tung* were printed from 1964 to 1976, and the Rolling Stones' "Street Fighting Man" (1968) echoed a year later in "Revolution" from the Beatles' *White Album*.

The same thing is happening now, but with a big new difference, in the first turbulent decades of the 21st Century. The American election of 2008 brought forth *Revolution: A Manifesto*, Congressman and presidential candidate Ron Paul's blistering attack on both the U.S. political parties and their abandonment of constitutional principles to corporatist entities like the Federal Reserve; and Naomi Wolf's *Give Me Liberty*, a casebook of success stories based on the revolutionary idea that when "an army of citizens, supported by even a vestige of civil society, believes in liberty—in the psychological space that is 'America'—no power on earth can ultimately suppress them."[71]

A year later, the pamphlet *L'insurrection qui vient* (The Coming Insurrection) sent such a *frisson* of alarm through the French establishment that people suspected of being on the anonymous "Invisible Committee" of authors were detained and grilled by the Paris authorities. And no wonder. This little bombshell, compared by some to Thomas Paine's *The Crisis*, applied the results of the 2005 Paris riots and the national strikes in Greece a year later to support the chilling premise that the surest way to beat the predators at their own game is to use theft, sabotage, refusal to work, and "the elaboration of collective, self-organized forms of life" to bring down for good a power structure that is too corrupt to be reformed.[72] Perhaps even more troubling to those who fear *L'Insurrection* is its obvious comfort with chaos. It does not present a set of reformist ideas, as traditional manifestos always have, and sees no need for such goals, as the new cohering force—an energy rather than a form or structure of order—will be whatever evolves spontaneously, what *emerges* uncontrollably from unpredictable and fluid conditions.

How to invite the kind of emergence one wants? With the new element that is easy to get and use, can draw thousands together in minutes in the same physical place, and get millions on the same virtual page instantly. What 2004 had that 1968 didn't was the Uranian factor of the technological hive mind that doesn't require anyone to be near a TV or a land telephone, but leaves them free to send and receive anything anywhere. The speed of it all has been uncanny since the watershed moment of summer, 2004. One new gadget that proved very effective at the national conventions of America's major political parties was a simple cell phone service that allows a subscriber to direct hundreds, even thousands of fellow subscribers instantly to places and situations where they are needed to conduct peaceful protest, or to witness and help deter those who are trying to suppress it. Called TxtMob, the service was created by the Institute for Applied Autonomy—there's an Aquarian name!—to blast messages instantly to everybody who uses the service.

"'There were . . . a number of interesting uses that the system got put to . . .' said John Henry, TxtMob's developer, in an interview with *Wired*. 'Police did arrest one protester, and there were not a lot of people around. Someone saw it happen, [sent a TxtMob message], and a hundred of that kid's friends were on the scene in minutes . . . to make sure' the police acted correctly."[73] The applications of TxtMob are virtually unlimited. Whether one is a revolutionary or not, it is clearly a new system that works on Aquarian principles by linking a few people, or many, instantly under rapidly changing conditions.

Since 2004, social networking sites, Twitter and whatever new digital technology appears before you finish this page, have made TxtMob look as quaint as semaphore flags. As current technologies could prove obsolete by nightfall, we look here at only a few recent examples. The best-known political success story of 2008, likely to be copied as a strategy for integrating new media in seamless new synergies to brilliant effect, was the Barack Obama campaign. Called "The YouTube Election" and "The Facebook Election," it was also an *Aquarian* election, and not only because it used new electronic technology. It was also clearly synarchic, not hierarchic, in broad-based, innovative fundraising.

It also spelled the end of "old media." It replaced reportage by "the boys on the bus"—the all-male media elite whose access to candidates between campaign stops had always been the main source of quotes from the contenders—with source images captured anywhere, any time by amateur "citizen journalists." Their footage, shot on a cell phone tonight, could be viewed the next day by millions as a "viral video"—another new phrase from an election that seemed to generate a whole new lexicon.[74] The old divide between reporters and readers, professional newsmen and viewers, seemed gone for good in an environment more interactive than anything ever seen before. If anything, the trend has picked up speed since November 2008, thanks to the truly revolutionary power of Twitter.[75]

Another example of Aquarian grassroots activism at work is the heady saga of *Outfoxed*, Robert Greenwald's documentary about the Fox News Network, which by 2004 had become a virtual advertising agency for the U.S. Republican party. Attempts to distribute the film through the usual channels met the predictable resistance, until the co-producers, MoveOn, and the Center for American Progress, allied with Common Cause, launched a campaign to duplicate and screen *Outfoxed* as widely as possible at art film houses, in private homes, anywhere that could stoke a buzz. The results were stunning. The dubbing decks could not keep up with the demand, as 100,000 video and DVD copies of the film were sold almost overnight, and *Outfoxed* became the almost unthinkable product: a low-tech film that is made on a shoestring and jumps *up* the distribution ladder from homes and offices to theatres in more than a dozen big cities. This is the kind of thing that can happen when like-minded networks combine and use everything they've got to create a groundswell.[76]

And these new ad hoc networks are not just joining together for a one-hit blitz. They are also building organizations that will continue to work together for new objectives. This is another major departure from the May fly activism of the 1960s, which thought mainly of the happening at hand without looking beyond it, and achieved as much lasting impact as a chess player who thinks only one move ahead. The new Aquarian activism, while it loves to party and celebrate, is constructive in literal terms, *building* something meant to have staying power. This clear intention to build something is what Jose Ortega y Gasset saw as missing in abortive revolutions when he wrote in *Revolt of the Masses* (1932) that "Revolution is not the uprising against existing order, but the setting up of a new order contradictory to the traditional one."[77] Even if the new order is only loosely bound and autonomous, the intention to create communities, to feel with all our senses what they look and sound and move and taste like, is essential if we're going to manifest them.

BUILD COURAGE IN NUMBERS— AND WITH LOVE

"Never show fear," Mikheil Saakashvili said.[78] This is easy to say—if one has the nerve of Boris Yeltsin jumping on top of a tank, or of the anonymous Chinese who stood in front of another tank in Tiananmen Square. Few of us have that kind of solitary courage—but fortunately, we don't all have to. The saying that "there's safety in numbers" is not just a practical proverb. The simple fact is that fear separates us, making each one feel that he or she is alone and helpless. Love unites, enabling each one of us to feel that that the strength of the whole team or community is flowing through us.

This, naturally, is why those who intend to bring about change arouse the uniting, galvanizing force of love, while those who want to block change stimulate instead the isolating, freezing note of fear. H. L. Mencken was one of those who saw, in the Red scare of the 1920s, how amazingly resourceful and ingenious the power elite would be in devising endless distractions and scares to keep us ditsy and nervous. "The whole aim of practical politics," he wrote, "is to keep the populace alarmed by menacing it with an endless series of hobgoblins, all of them imaginary."[79] The same note sounds constantly now, as officials issue daily orange alerts to turn their people into Spartans, engaged at every moment in war and preparation for war. As there is so much running of the fear frequency now, we'll look at few simple ideas to help us stay out of fear.

FEAR MANAGEMENT 101

Acronym 1: *False Expectations Appearing Real.* Most of what we fear is a phantom. When we are in fear, we must *feel* the thing that induces fear until we own it, and it dissolves. There is a practical reason why courage comes from *coeur*, the word for heart.

Acronym 2: *Forgetting Every Available Resource.* Fear isolates us, and can make us think we're without resources. Not true. We're loaded with resources:

> We are *quick and clever*, and that's why, like tricksters, we can play the revolution at the tempo of comedy, which is always fast. The people are swifter and far more creative than their governments. Therefore we can play the lead in events that must occur. We are the ones who cause the house of cards to slide apart more easily than anyone dreamed. The true art of the transition will be in whispering "love" with just enough breath to move one card, then another, letting them all float into a new alignment that brings the new as gently as possible for the highest good of humanity and Mother Earth.

> We are *compassionate*, so we can *feel the other person's fear.* The authorities are even more frightened than we are, which is why they're trying so hard to transfer their fear by scaring us. The more we feel compassion for their fear, the less we will buy into it.

> *We have each other.* As new linkages grow, like-minded people build communities that are lateral rather than vertical in their energy flow. This transition from hierarchy to *synarchy* (power exercised jointly by equals) has already begun. The Internet is our main resource in this transition, but, powerful as it is, it is still only a mechanical tool for the moment, until we develop from within the intuitive power of the global hive mind.

> We are engaged in *spiritual revolution*, as Aung San Suu Kyi of Burma insisted when her supporters are tempted to use forceful means to free her from house arrest. As she and other teachers of

non-violence know, the outer changes will come when the inner changes have been made, and people who are moved by love rather than fear will not need to destroy oppression. They will dissolve it. In the end, when the critical mass of awakened human beings brings about a change to mass spiritual consciousness, we will perceive that government is to community what a dinosaur is to a turtle, whose modest, homely tenacity has made him a universal symbol of wisdom. Gigantic powers that solve nothing and interfere in everything will wither away from lack of attention and serious regard.

Love conquers all. Jesus said "Love your enemies"; Confucius said "answer harm with goodness." The only problem with love as a revolutionary resource is that inconstant human beings often give up on love before it has a chance to work. One good thing about the Aquarian Age, though, is that the sign of Aquarius is "fixed," meaning that it fortifies the perseverance of those who can stick with an aim and carry it through. Thomas Edison had that kind of fixity. Just before he perfected the incandescent light, he wrote in his lab notes that he had just discovered the 10,000th way not to invent the light bulb. The only question now is whether human beings will invest the same faith and effort that Edison had in illuminating the human mind and bringing about a new Earth.

One of those who saw love as the key to revolution is among the ones we're least likely to guess, as we naturally think the masters of love on our planet are Jesus and Mother Theresa, ecstatic Sufis, and Tibetan monks who live in continuous elation. "At the risk of sounding ridiculous," Ernesto "Che" Guevara said, "let me say that the true revolutionary is guided by feelings of love."[80] Small wonder that he, like Jesus, appeared dangerous to those who feared freedom most. But the time is coming soon when we will all speak of love the way we do the about the air we breathe and the water that purifies us, with the certainty that those around us will wonder why we are affirming what everybody knows.

THE IRON RABBIT ROARS

A Chinese lunar Year of the Rabbit began on Feb. 3, 2011. Many astrologers and other observers expected that like most rabbit years, coming as it does between dynamic Tiger and Dragon years, this one too would be relatively mild and placid, a kind of rest interval between the stresses of 2010 and the powerful currents of transformation coming in 2012.

Not quite. A funny thing seems to have happened on the way to the briar patch, as Earth heaved with earthquakes and civil unrest. Revolutions toppled corrupt regimes in Tunisia and Egypt, and other dictators and kings in the Middle East were under attack. Labor actions grew bigger and hotter in Europe. In the United States, workers and their allies in Madison, Wisconsin, then in other states, resisted moves by governors and their corporate owners to kill labor unions by taking away collective bargaining rights. The fight seemed to gain creative momentum almost every day as firefighters closed their accounts at banks that had supported Wisconsin's governor, and citizens launched initiatives to recall Republican politicians, boycott companies, and set up state banks and thereby free their monies from commercial banks.

Everything was in play, for 2011 is an *iron* rabbit year, when ordinary human beings can join forces in great numbers to achieve extraordinary things, pull them off much faster than anyone ever dreamed, and do them in ways that are no longer local and limited, but viral and global. When students in Cairo and teachers in Madison, Wisconsin are acting in solidarity across national and cultural borders, and even across barriers of bigotry and fear that controlling elites have erected to keep the Muslim East and the Christian West divided and powerless, then something has shifted mightily in the social and political realms, and in our whole field of consciousness.

Not only this, but early 2011 is only the beginning of what is likely to be an Aquarian revolutionary phase of seven turbulent years, followed by seven integrative years. From 2011 to 2025 we'll see two planet transitions of extreme importance, both involving the "outer" planets—so called because they are farthest away from the Sun—which pertain to collective human actions on the scale of mass political, social, and spiritual movements:

Uranus entered Aries on March 12, 2011, and will remain in this fiery, Mars-ruled sign until May, 2018. The essence of this combination is Change, as Uranus is the artist and trickster of Revolution, the one who brings change that is heady and exciting to those who welcome it and are brave enough to play it, and upsetting, even terrifying, to those who resist it, or think they will control it to their ends. We can expect upheavals like the ones that Uranus brought on his most recent visits to Aries:

1927–1935: The 1929 stock market crash led to worldwide depression. Revolutions and new dictatorships transformed Germany and Russia, the New Deal began in the U.S., and civil war in China culminated in the Long March. The new planet Pluto was discovered.

1843–1851: Socialist and other anti-monarchic uprisings shook the regimes of Europe and propelled new emigration to the U.S. The *Communist Manifesto* was published, and the labor movement began. The new planet Neptune was discovered in 1846.

1756–1764: In the Seven Years' War, England defeated France and emerged as the world's dominant empire. The Industrial Revolution spread and the Enlightenment began, as Louis XV failed to suppress the publication of the *Encyclopedie*.

Neptune entered Pisces in April, 2011, and after a retrograde move back to Aquarius, he will begin a 14-year visit in February, 2012. In the sign he rules, the planet of spirituality and mystical consciousness will be at his most positive and powerful, assisting the efforts of human beings to feel their common resonance in the universal heart, and to align in compassionate service toward one another and Mother Earth. Neptune last entered Pisces a year after he was discovered in 1846, and his 15-year Pisces tour embraced the growth of the Baha'i faith and the American abolitionist movement, which culminated in the outbreak of civil war on the day Neptune crossed into Aries: April 12, 1861.

How are these events and conditions that we have seen before in our planet's history now being played out again, only this time in ways that are specifically Aquarian? We can run them by the numbers, as of this writing from Cairo on March 15, 2011:

1. The struggle for freedom and control is being waged in electronic cyberspace as well as on the ground. The moves resemble a chess opening. Cairo protestors used cell phones and social media to gather their numbers. Hosni Mubarak countered by shutting down the web and mobile phone services, until a money hemorrhage of billions of dollars forced him to turn them back on. As Muammar Qaddafi jams communications among rebel forces, Western military forces consider deploying cell phone base stations on aircraft or tethered balloons, both linked to satellite communication terminals on navy ships.

2. The effort is synarchic. During and after the events in Tahrir Square, protestors and observers both noted that "There were no leaders." No badges designating any rank, no bullhorns barking instructions. Accounts of the first massive march on January 28 emphasized that the crowds moved slowly and peacefully in a state of high focus, as though linked in the intuitive swarm intelligence of a group mind.

3. For the first time in our history, the people of many countries acted together not only in solidarity, but in a creative cross-fertilization, sharing ideas, encouraging and inspiring one another. Workers in Madison were moved to see a sign from Tahrir Square that read: "Egypt Supports Wisconsin. One people, one pain."

4. There was a communal spirit of inventive, spontaneous teamwork throughout Cairo, as local people organized neighborhood watches to protect buildings and blocks from security police provocateurs. For the first time, garbage cleanups got done not just in Tahrir Square, but in many other places. Muslims formed cordons around Coptic churches. There was no program for this. It just happened.

5. And when people are collaborating creatively as equals, celebration and comedy tend to occur, even amid intense and sometimes violent conditions. This was the case especially in Wisconsin, but also in Egypt. Naturally. In its classic scenario of Boot the Boss, in which people who are powerless but clever defeat authority who is strong but slow, comedy is innately revolutionary.

We have no idea where all of this will lead, only that it will continue to unfold. Our best posture is one of resourceful courage in surfing unpredictable, even chaotic conditions, and improvising as we go. "We don't have parties," said one organizer of the revolt in Libya. "We don't have a constitution, we don't have political organizations, we don't have an effective civil society. We have to create a completely new state and we have to do it in the middle of a war and revolution."[81]

But we will, in time. As of March, 2011, the Aquarian Revolution is no longer only wish or theory. It has begun.

AQUARIAN PROFILE: STAINLESS STEEL MOUSE

It's plain to all freedom-loving people that the Internet is, depending on how you look at it, either the battleground for freedom, or the means by which love workers will achieve freedom without battle. One way or the other, some of us, at least, must know how to use what is obviously the Aquarian network, the most powerful instrument of freedom since the printing press. Just as Gutenberg's invention promoted the modern era through new literatures in vernacular languages, and created an immense new readership for works of science and history, philosophy and poetry—and thereby freed the European mind from kings and churches who had long controlled their people by keeping them illiterate—the Internet is a door to wonder or calamity. Bloggers are either the pit crew of the revolution or an affront to what used to be professional media, depending on one's point of view.

For those who love to surf it, the Internet is a portal to liberty that allows anyone to find or publish anything at once, form networks and alliances overnight, and engage millions of people simultaneously in activism, ceremony, meditation, and transformational events that aim at nothing less than liberating the consciousness of all humankind instantly, in a single incandescent moment of shared intention and all-embracing love. All embracing chaos, that is, reply those who fear the Internet as a doorway to anarchy so dark that it looks like the mouth of Hell, where grinning devils with pierced noses and vermillion hair wait to torch us, devise unspeakable hobbies for our children, and teach us how to design ugly clothes and get medicines from who knows where for practically nothing.

The Taliban banned the Internet as contrary to the Qur'an, while the terms of the struggle for control of the web—and with it, communications—have shifted in the United States since the epic clash of 2000–2001 between Microsoft and the U.S. government for a purse so big that all the zeroes won't fit on your calculator. It remains to be seen whether Bill Gates will swallow the American computer industry, and then presumably reboot himself; and how the feds will track and tax business transactions conducted over the web, so that they can gain control of the Internet without appearing to do so. The hottest sector of the web control contest is now south and east Asia. For years, until its growing economy forced it to open up, India tried to control the Internet indirectly by requiring anyone who imported computer equipment to follow complicated and costly rules. Japan, deliciously subtle as always, impeded the wildfire of the web years ago by setting the licensing fees of service providers so high that ISPs had to charge customers the equivalent of $100 a month. Market forces soon kicked in, of course, and convinced even the Ministry of Communications in Tokyo that only a person of doubtful sanity would try to stop the Japanese from using the gadgets they love.

This leaves you know who: the People's Republic of China, pulled in opposite directions by authorities who want to keep the country chained to socialist orthodoxy, and educated young fire dragons who long to go where they want, make lots of money, live in chic cities, hold elections that give parties other than the communists a chance, and even take over the whole Eight Jewel Duck and start a democracy. Tension has been building underground ever since the horrendous events in Tiananmen Square in 1989, then burst into guerrilla trickery a decade later when hackers began to move like lightning from one website to the next, broadcasting messages of liberty before vanishing into Shanghai and the night. They became the most thrilling freedom blaster scenario of 1999, and inspired cybertricksters everywhere to learn how to link up, log on, let fly, and clear out.

For nervous men in Mao jackets, the most terrifying new possibility had arrived: the use of the web for digital guerrilla warfare that needs no physical explosives, but uses words, music, and video to fire freedom flares that millions can see before the police even smell the smoke or hear the laughter. Even worse, hackers could use even the government's own computers to launch their barbs and tell the whole country which local party official was on the take and in the henhouse. China was suddenly a much less predictable place.

By 2005, China had more Internet users than communist party members. A fifth of the 80 million people who use the web in China make almost daily visits to bulletin boards that have become forums for political protest and tools for pulling a team or a multitude toward an abuse that needs to be seen and solved. In 2003, after the parents of a young man who had died in police custody placed on the web a petition that one of China's most progressive newspapers picked up and posted on the nation's largest news portal, thousands of comments hit the boards at once, and started a surge of protest that led to the trial and conviction of police officials and the government's dissolution of the arbitrary and deeply hated "custody and repatriation" system.

"[D]espite authorities' persistent efforts to control the Internet," writes social activist Xiao Qiang, "the rising tide of online opinion is a fact of life in Chinese society now and will continue to play an influential role in expanding the space for free expression and even in creating social change. The transformative effect of the Internet has already set China on an irreversible course toward greater openness and public participation in its social and political life."[82] From such a heady brew of possibilities, heroic new faces must emerge. Perhaps the best known is the woman known as Stainless Steel Mouse.

Liu Di, 29, returned to her post-graduate courses at Beijing Normal University after a year off from her studies as a guest of the Chinese government at Qincheng Prison, where she spent her time in solitary confinement. Had she earned this sentence in the usual way, as a member of a drug ring or a terrorist group plotting to make exploding bicycles? No. She was an outspoken blogger who had complained online about laws restricting Internet cafes, and other government limits on freedom of expression over the web. And she had posted on her blog a satire on the Communist Party that was much funnier to her many new readers than it was to the Internet police force in China's Bureau of State Security Protection. With a total staff of over 30,000—one officer for every ten of China's estimated 300,000 bloggers—the Internet police are clearly a signal that Beijing means business when it comes to cracking down on dissent and disrespect over the web.

Liu made it plain in her writings that she was not trying to start a movement, but was an ordinary person with a desire for freedom. This may be why she gained so much support from others who saw themselves in her that the government responded to pressure on her behalf and released her. She's back at her blog, working away again, offering the quiet suggestion that more freedom will not kill anyone, and may even make their lives a little happier. "Ignore government propaganda and live freely," she writes.[83]

We don't know yet how many tens of millions of Chinese high school girls want to grow up to be Liu Di. Or how they use their time at school to draft what they'll put on their blogs tonight. They will be the bringers of freedom in the years to come. They know what people in Aquarian communities everywhere are learning. Soft, sincere inspiration does it. You don't have to be a star. You just have to speak from the heart.

CHAPTER 6

AQUARIAN MEDICINE

Every country has some version of a "health care system": an arrange-ment of health care providers, medicine and equipment makers, and some kinds of health insurance and education. Official agencies may regulate the various exchanges of money for health to ensure that the "system" is ethical, and that the craft, profession, or industry of "health care" will not kill more patients than will normally be lost to human error and tough luck.

Some countries, such as Japan, really do have health care *sys-tems*. Some do not, though they claim that their health practices, laws, and business deals do constitute a system. The actuality is that since the 1600s, when physicians in Europe began to apply empiri-cal methods to their practice, the health cultures in their countries have been a struggle between traditional, naturopathic healers whose art is as much spiritual as physical, and "scientific" doctors who insist that illness is solely a physical condition, to be treated solely by physi-cal means. These include new medical discoveries that are invariably thought more effective than traditional remedies that were ancient in

Hippocrates' time. And the new medicines seem to *work*—they can suppress the symptoms of illness—at least until the deadly side effects arrive and kill more people than the drug seems to help.

Most cultures reach accommodations that balance the interests of patients, providers, and medicine makers in order to give people a menu of holistic and high-tech choices, and the freedom to shop for the best price. The scenario usually has some flexibility, allowing honest and talented practitioners a chance to work, and giving patients the right to find them. At least this has been the case until now. Today, as we're about to see, the riches to be reaped from new medicines are so immense that drug firms prefer to leave nothing to chance, and will use any means to drive out competitors, buy government officials, and otherwise ensure that their profits keep growing. The result of this is most ironic in the United States, which has long been in the strange position of claiming to have the world's best health care system, while resisting as "socialized medicine" anything that might help make health care more uniformly effective and affordable.

The bizarre secret is this: the United States does not have a health care system. Never did. In the old days there were naturopaths and general practitioners who knew a patient's name from the moment they delivered her at birth, treated almost anything, even made house calls. Perhaps in the 1960s, when the Medicare and Medicaid programs were designed and launched and no one knew how to work them for fraud and profit, there really was an attempt, by a government that felt duty-bound to help its people, to connect physicians who wanted to heal the sick with patients who wanted effective, affordable health care. It seemed like a great idea at the time, still does for those too aged or poor to have a choice.

THE ILLNESS MAINTENANCE INDUSTRY

What has replaced it, and what America has now, is not a health care system, but an Illness Maintenance Industry (IMI) that could not care a spoon of salt water—for which Straub Hospital in Honolulu tried to charge me $55.00 a milliliter when I spent three days there—whether afflicted people die because they can't afford medications, or die of poverty. Not that American IMI firms are unique in their greed at a time when Meyer Lansky, the financial wizard who got the mob into legitimate business and crafted the cash fountain of Las Vegas, might choose to acquire a drug company if he were looking for a good way to trap people and take their money. Few people other than investors have any idea how huge the profits of the most powerful drug cartels—not the cocaine lords of Colombia, but the drug barons of North America and Europe—really are.

DRUG FIRMS LEAD THE TOP CORPORATE CROOKS

"The Top 100 Corporate criminals of the 1990s" by Russell Mokhiber, co-author with Robert Weissman of *Corporate Predators: the Hunt for Mega-Profits and the Attack on Democracy*, lists six European drug firms along with 14 American companies among the 20 drug firms, medical equipment manufacturers, and health insurance providers who were nailed by U.S. federal prosecutors for price fixing, Medicaid fraud, violating of FDA regulations and other charges, and chose to plead guilty or no contest and pay their fines. The criterion for getting into the Top 100 was the penalty the guilty company had to pay, ranging from $500 million from the champ, F. Hoffman-La Roche of Switzerland, "for leading a worldwide conspiracy to raise and fix prices and allocate market shares for certain vitamins sold in the United States and elsewhere," to $150,000 that Samsung America paid for making an illegal contribution to a political campaign.[84]

The 20 firms in the "health" industry comprised by far the largest group among all industries in the Top 100, well ahead of military armaments, equipment, and systems (13), oil and food (both 10), chemicals (9), and banking and financial services (7). Setting aside the ten drug and medical firms in the middle and lower end of the list who were penalized for fraudulent Medicaid claims and FDA reports and environmental pollution, the Big Crime committed by four of the top 12, and seven drug firms altogether, was collusion to fix prices and allocate market shares in the international vitamin market.

The stakes are huge. They'd make Harry Lyme of *The Third Man* swoon, though he was a small drug swindler in today's terms. Some of those sorbates and citric acid mixtures must be as precious as diamonds, if big drug firms who are speaking German, or sound like they are, can absorb fines of $500 million, $225 million (BASF Aktiengesellschaft), $50 million (Haarman & Reimer), or $36 million (Hoechst AG), and keep going as though they've been hit by nothing bigger than a snowball. Since 2004 Bristol-Meyers Squibb, maker of Excedrin, has been juggling a whole icebag of Excedrin headaches. It agreed to pay $150 million in fines—for having manipulated its inventory to inflate earnings, thereby misleading investors—just a month after agreeing to pay $300 million in a class-action suit brought by investors who accused the company of lying about its accounting practices and its investment in the notoriously corrupt ImClone Systems.

The terms of the trouble are revealing. The charges were not that Bristol-Myers knowingly sold unsafe products, but that it *misled investors*, thereby imperiling the money of wealthy people who invest in pharmaceutical stocks. And true to the *omerta* of pharmaceutical firms, Bristol-Myers "neither admitted nor denied wrongdoing in the settlement but did agree to abide by a permanent injunction against future violations."[85]

Schering-Plough paid $345.5 million in 2004 for overcharging the Medicaid program for Claritin. One wonders how a company can absorb such a blow after four consecutive quarters of net losses so severe that in late 2004, Schering-Plough sold $1.25 billion of convertible preferred stock to pay legal penalties.[86] This spate of whopping penalties to drug companies has continued since. In 2009, year of the fake Swine Flu scare, Pfizer was hit with a record $2.3 billion judgment for having promoted unsafe products.[87]

MAKING A KILLING AT BOTH ENDS

An effective national health insurance program, like the one America's neighbor to the north uses to keep Canadians fit and mellow, would cut the profits of the IMI's unholy trinity of HMOs, insurance firms, and pharmaceutical companies. It would also reduce the stock dividends of Warren Buffett and others like him who invest in both ends of the IMI game: in tobacco companies that make people sick, and drug companies that don't help patients get well, but keep them hooked for decades on "medicines" that are overpriced, even addictive and harmful. In having now become America's most profitable industry, the IMI has become the polar opposite of the common-sense Chinese custom that kept peasants tough and the land hardy for thousands of years.

In ancient China, the physician's relationship with his patients was simple and practical. As long as a family was healthy, it would give the doctor some money, a bolt of silk, a barrel of wine, or a chicken or two every month. When someone in the family got ill, they'd stop paying the doctor. Imagine trying that now in the United States, where even the finest and most caring physicians struggle to keep their practices alive in the face of soaring medical equipment prices and malpractice insurance premiums.

What's one sure clue that the pharmaceutical companies don't really want to cure you, but only want to squeeze you for as long as they can? Consider this revealing fact: Before he became Secretary of Defense to George W. Bush, Donald Rumsfeld was the CEO, President, and then Chairman of G. D. Searle & Co. He turned the ailing firm around so impressively that the *Wall Street Transcript* (1980) and *Financial World* (1981) named him the Outstanding Chief Executive Officer in the Pharmaceutical Industry.

How did Don pull it off? Using his Washington contacts and his relentless style, he railroaded the FDA approval process for aspartame, the artificial sweetener that's been a focus for alarm among health care providers for decades now, but makes terrific money for Searle. Rumsfeld's coup was not the first time that the Food and Drug Administration forsook its mission of regulating the pharmaceutical industry. It has been corrupted since into a corporate attack dog that stands and roars when effective natural medicines try to gain entry to the U. S. market, but whines and rolls over when a powerful corporate player wants to fill the shelves with a poison like aspartame—or monosodium glutamate (MSG), another deadly powder that keeps on making people sick, and profits fat.

LIFE GETS RISKY HERE IN THE COMIC UNIVERSE

Even if we didn't have corporate crooks and denial-bound, suicidally opinionated people, we'd still be living in the comic universe, where human beings suffer not because we are wicked but because we are just plain dumb—and we are dumb not because we're mentally lame, but because like most fools, we are too smart for our own good, or too slow to pick up on clues that are so obvious a bat could see them.

The author is a prime example of how dumb we can be here in the comic cosmos. I've known for over 40 years—since not long after my first adult sight of New York, when I missed the IRT express stop at 125th St., and came up out of the next station with wide eyes, a high-decibel jacket and a cardboard suitcase at 11:00 pm in Harlem—that the wetter a place is, the more it triggers asthma, so I should probably live in a desert. So where did I live for 38 years? In the spring shower and snow bowl of Manhattan, the steam room of Kyoto, and the rain forest of Hawaii. Now that I've lived since in Egypt and the pure air of the Andes, asthma is no problem, and it seems, weirdly enough, that I get along better in a place where the air is filthy but dry than I do in places where it's clean but damp.

I wanted to be sure, though, that if I had an asthma attack in Cairo, I'd have the medicine to stop it. So I went to the Shaalan Surgical Centre. The first visit to a clinic always costs more, of course, so I paid 80 Egyptian pounds, just under U.S. $12.93, to see Dr. Akl. He prescribed the medications I'd been taking in Hawaii: Seretide (called Advair in the U.S.), a powder taken to control asthma symptoms; and Combivent, an aerosol inhaler that stops an attack, or at least slows it until one can get to a hospital. The Seretide/Advair that would have cost me $250 at Kaiser Permanente Hospital or $215 at Long's Drugs when I was uninsured in Hawaii cost me $19.40 in Cairo. The Combivent that was $89 at Kaiser or $74.50 at Longs came to $4.36. For a doctor visit and medications that would have cost me $400 in Hawaii, I paid less than $40 in Cairo—and I wasn't even registered yet with Egypt's national health insurance plan.

Somehow the companies that make Seretide in England and Combivent in France can realize an acceptable profit when their products are sold in Cairo for one-twentieth the price that a hospital or pharmacy charges in the United States. Why is the American overhead so big? What happens to all that money that someone in America gets and someone in Egypt doesn't? Is it any wonder that Americans try to buy their medicines from Canada, from the worldwide web, from anyone besides American HMOs?

As Lily Tomlin put it, we can expect that it will get worse before it gets worse. In July 2004, a documentary by Bill Moyers aired on U.S. National Public TV about the health crisis now facing "Mississippi, [where] as many as 65,000 people are bracing for the deepest cuts any state has ever made in Medicaid eligibility for senior citizens and the disabled. The cuts are so severe, critics say, that many of the state's most vulnerable are facing an unthinkable choice between buying food and buying medicine."[88] First poorer states like Mississippi, then others soon after, will find that as more and more of their people need help with health care, there will be less and less federal money to give them.

One traditionally self-reliant state has become more assertive. Vermont is "the first state to sue the federal Food and Drug Administration for rejecting a plan to import prescription drugs from Canada. . . . Reacting to intense pressure to make prescription drugs more affordable, Vermont officials had asked the drug agency . . . to approve a pilot program under which the state could contract with a Canadian company that would take orders from Vermont residents and distribute the drugs by mail."[89] The FDA ruled no, as the drugs from Canada might be unsafe. The agency's posture was clearly false. The drugs from Canada are the same ones being sold in the U. S., in the same tamper-resistant packages. The real issue, which the FDA dares not address, is the loss of revenue for American HMOs and pharmacies.

THE HELPING HAND MAY HAVE TO BE YOUR OWN

FDA or no, Americans are very resourceful. More and more Americans, working together like Aquarian teams even if they don't yet know who Aquarius is, are learning how to find effective new healing resources, form healing teams and take care of each other, and how to learn and practice self-healing. And for some of the most intrepid, as we'll see later, civil disobedience is now no longer an issue of politics, but a matter of life and death for themselves and their loved ones.

One significant development is that since the 1990s, Americans have annually spent more money on natural medicine and holistic health care than on the synthetic drugs and allopathic treatments that have dominated American medicine for over a century, ever since the Vanderbilts and other promoters of the new medical establishment and drug industry began quietly to destroy naturopathic medicine. It is revealing that Vanderbilt Medical School graduated its first class of 61 M.D.s in 1875—the year of Pasteur's breakthrough in germ theory—while the rest of Vanderbilt University was still under construction. Medicine in America was about to change from a local and natural matter to a strategic alliance between a medical establishment that would determine who could practice medicine, and a pharmaceutical industry selling for a lot more than nature ever did synthetic drugs made from the same plants that naturopaths had been using all along.

This is why today's newly emerging Aquarian medicine is nothing really new. It's a revival of natural, communal medicine as practiced in the 19th century by herbalists and "country doctors" who knew how, and often taught others how, to eat an apple a day and keep the doctor away. How to use ginger to treat most anything. How to use pennyroyal to prevent unwanted pregnancy. How to clear congested lungs with licorice root. How to use a thousand fruits and roots and herbs to prevent and treat a thousand things, and practice what Hippocrates had in mind when he wrote, "Let food be your medicine."

This all began to change in the 1870s with Koch and Pasteur, who had the idea that illness is caused by invasive *germs*. The resulting pitch from new medical establishments and synthetic drug industries was not long in coming: If you want to fight these germs, you're going to need something more than things you've been picking from the field. After all, your leaves and roots didn't prevent the germ from getting you just now, and they won't stop it the next time either. You need our crystalline powder prepared in a laboratory by disinfected people wearing rubber gloves made by the same company that makes these condoms, since we're sure you'll agree that men can be trusted to use their rubbers a lot more than women can be trusted to remember their pennyroyal.

Our pills and capsules have all the power of your herbs—in fact, our products are made from the same plants you've been using all along, but are so much more suitable for the busy lives we have now. No more years of learning how to tell chamomile from ragweed and aloe from poison oak. No more waiting for herbs to dry and tinctures to set. No more smelly pots and teeny bottles. Now you just get your doctor to write some prescriptions, get your pharmacy to fill them, and hope that what you spend on medicine in a month is less than the payment on your house. We're sure you'll agree that the convenience of it all, and the time you don't have to spend on what you don't have to know, is worth the extra expense, even if you have to spice up some dog food or dive a dumpster—careful, our bones really do get more brittle as we get older!—when dinnertime comes.

Compassionate change is unlikely, if for economic reasons alone. "The regulatory lockout of natural remedies," reports the Herbal Medicine Panel, "has crippled natural products research in U. S. universities and hospitals. There is no dedicated level of support by the Federal Government for herbal medicine research. Herbalists may apply under existing guidelines for approval of new pharmaceutical drugs, but this burden is unrealistic because the total cost of bringing a new pharmaceutical to market in the United States is an estimated $140 million to $500 million (*Wall Street Journal*, 1993). Because botanicals are not patentable (although they can be patented for use), an herbal medicine manufacturer could never recover this expenditure. Therefore, herbal remedies are not viable candidates for the existing drug approval process: pharmaceutical companies will not risk a loss of this magnitude, and herb companies lack the financial resources even to consider seeking approval."[90]

At least $140 million to bring a new drug onto the market. And that was almost twenty years ago. At least $140 million more than Mother Earth needs to arrange her herbs like green jewels on her body. And $140 million more than herbal healers from Chiron to Friar Laurence to Jethro Kloss ever had to pay to go out and pick whatever grows wild. This situation is unsustainable. This is why the central clash in Aquarian Healing will be between the authoritarian control of medicine by the unhealthy alliance of the IMI and its priesthood in the medical schools, and the determination of holistic practitioners, and people who take responsibility for their own health, to put their money where it will do them some good. Like many Aquarian forces, this movement is revolutionary, literally a "turning back" to what we used to do well. In fact, the tide has already turned.

HOLISTIC MEDICINE GOES NOVA

A *Prevention* magazine report of a survey conducted for the American Holistic Health Association noted that "an aging population and an increased sense of alienation from the health-care system are causing an increased desire for self-care. An estimated 158 million consumers use dietary supplements because these products help them attain their self-care goals. An estimated 22.8 million consumers use herbal remedies instead of prescription medicine, and an estimated 19.6 million use them with a prescription product. Similarly, an estimated 30.3 million use herbals instead of an over-the-counter drug (OTC), while approximately 19 million use herbals and OTC together."[91] And these figures represent only one sector of the holistic health field, and do not include hundreds of billions of dollars that Europeans and Americans now spend on flower remedies and essential oils, aromas, crystals, light, color and sound therapies, acupuncture, massage, *reiki* and other methods of unblocking and releasing energy, yoga, Pilates, Feldenkrais and other movement disciplines, and meditation techniques and other spiritual practices.

Indeed, one reason why so many now distance themselves from allopathic medicine is that the drug vampires, and the white-coated technicians who do their research and speak in their commercials, cannot accept and have no interest in the spiritual basis of true healing. This is not to say that some brave physicians do not question the materialist dogmas of "pure" science. Yet it is a safe bet that those who keep prescribing all the pills and sprays are not yet ready to endorse such remedies as love and intention, which can't be weighed or measured, but which may prove more effective than anything else. If the will to live and recover can be mightily fortified by the active presence and love of our dear ones, we can easily understand why so many people now avoid the hospital and go instead to the healing circles that multiply each year everywhere, especially in the U. S.

The trend began snowballing in July of 2004, as Chiron, the planet of the "wounded healer" (see Aquarian profile below) waited in the sign of Capricorn for Saturn, who embodies the "old forces" of established government and medicine, to move into opposition against him in the sign of Cancer. It is no wonder that pharmaceutical giants in Europe and the U.S.A were pressuring their governments to declare "unsafe" the herbal remedies that have begun to siphon off more than a trickle of revenue. The real question about these remedies, which have been used successfully for thousands of years, is . . . unsafe for whom? People? Or profits?

OUR ANCESTORS DIDN'T NEED INSURANCE. THEY HAD FRIENDS.

Fortunately, help is at hand. New Aquarian tools like the Hawaii Health Guide (HHG), which provides online visitors with leads to a huge assortment of health practitioners and resources in Hawaii, and is now expanding its coverage to the west coast of the United States, are among the emerging models that will soon be adapted worldwide by people who want to care more actively for themselves and each other, learn again what their ancestors knew about remedies in the field and the forest, and recognize that the best health insurance is a community of friends.[92]

The HHG is also connected to the kinds of healing circles that proliferate now, in addition to the tribes that hold festivals at the equinoxes and solstices, and the Wiccan circles that meet at the full moon, in yet another obvious manifestation of Aquarius: the abandonment of rigid, institutionalized religious hierarchies by people who seek their spiritual experiences in the fire circle, the beach, and the meadow, and celebrate anew the divinity that lives in nature and in each human heart.

One among the Aquarian healing circles that proliferate now is the Cairo Women's Group for Health and Well-Being, founded in 1996 by a group of Egyptian, European, and American women who wanted to explore holistic healing in order to develop their own skills as practitioners, and spread knowledge of alternative health care in the country that has dug up many of the old stones and bones of its past, but has not yet noticed that some of the holistic medical practices that are now unknown or unavailable in Egypt today were in fact birthed here long ago by stunningly gifted physicians.

The holistic health specialties practiced by the Women's Group include Egyptian flower essences, called Al-chemia Remedies—produced and marketed on the web by Group co-founder and coordinator Leslie Zehr—homeopathy, color, sound, and dance therapies, and other skills.[93] The Group hosts teachers such as Esther de Angelis, an Argentinean pioneer in the use of Kirlian photography to diagnose the patient's bioplasmatic energy field. No one makes any claims to heal anyone. But something must be working, as this group has some of the healthiest women this writer has seen. They will be interesting to watch in the years to come as a test case for the arrival of Aquarian medicine in the Islamic world.

Another example of how creative people can improvise, even though it's not so much a healing circle as a shared treatment, is America's growing network of more than 200 Community Acupuncture Centers. Unlike the places where you and I first experienced acupuncture, in the isolation of a small room with a single massage table or reclining chair, a CAC clinic has a large room with ten recliners, where several people can be treated simultaneously as they listen to a fountain and soothing music. This enables the acupuncturists to cut fees to a sliding scale of $20–$35 and attract people who've never had acupuncture, but feel its benefits at once and keep coming back. So the practice grows, the clients are happy, and we see yet again how resourceful Aquarian people can be when inventive minds are driven by a spirit of communal service.[94]

WHY MANY "HEALERS" DON'T CLAIM TO "HEAL" ANYBODY

The very vocabulary of healing is changing now. More and more people who seek greater well-being, and not just people with AIDS, no longer call themselves *patients* (literally meaning "sufferers"), because this implies that one is on the lower tier of a one-up, one-down relationship, can only receive better health passively from a possessor of special knowledge, and may not take the active, resourceful role of the one who heals himself.

The same awkwardness about terminology applies to those who are giving help. Health experts who are not licensed as *doctors* ("learned ones") or *physicians* (from the Greek word for "body", suggesting that the care giver works only on the material meat) can call themselves *facilitators* (who "make it easy") or *practitioners*. Words like *medium* and *shaman* are still too strangely spooky and scary in countries where most people are suspicious about "spirits," yet think they have "immortal souls" and even believe Satan exists. The right words for what healers do will come in time.

More and more holistic health practitioners now hesitate to claim that they "heal" anyone. Why? It's not that they fear being punished for making phony claims by the government and the rest of the New Inquisition (Robert Anton Wilson's phrase) that harassed or ruined Nikola Tesla, Dinshah Ghadiali, Wilhelm Reich, Harry Hoxsey, and many others whose methods were highly successful.[95]

The main reason why many healers avoid calling themselves healers is that the essence of wellness in the age of Aquarian medicine is not only physical, but also mental, emotional, and spiritual, and highly interactive too. At the core of the Aquarian health paradigm is both the freedom to choose whatever therapy one wants, and the recognition that healing is an intentional act of opening to energy that flows through a channel from the Universal Source. "Go, your faith has made you well," (Mark 10:52) Jesus said, the point being that yes, while a master practitioner or the powerful concerted intention of a sound or other healing circle may help, the firm, clear, positive intention of the one who seeks better health is everything.

MADEMOISELLE, THE TIME FOR ACTION HAS ARRIVED

This line was always spoken by Scaramouche, the *commedia dell' arte* Trickster, when trouble was closing in, escape was impossible, and the only way to save the situation was to help each other, and seek the help of allies nearby. This is why recent years have seen an explosion of health-related information on the Internet, the only communications medium that moves too fast for authorities to control. The American Holistic Health Association, cited above, now operates on its website a search service that enables visitors to find health information, services, and other resources in their area.[96]

Physicians wishing to practice outside of the conventional models are turning more and more now to new ways of communicating through the web the kinds of health strategies that can't be delivered through corporate-controlled media. The website of Dr. Joseph Mercola is particularly influential. Others are proliferating. The bravery of Dr. Matthias Rath in publishing full-page newspaper ads about the lethal criminality of the American pharmaceutical establishment may be a sign that physicians who break ranks may now find themselves much less isolated than they were only a few years ago.[97] Anyone can do it, really. All that is needed is a willingness to put in the time and effort, and an urge to act in service to others. One particularly charming site is Shirley's Wellness Café, created by Shirley Lipschutz-Robinson. Don't let the folksy style fool you. This site is loaded with useful and frequently updated material, and is a model of the Aquarian help yourself, help each other paradigm.[98] Where but on such sites are you likely to find such statements as this one, from Dr. Robert A. Mendelsohn: "I believe my generation of doctors will be remembered for two things: the miracles that turned to mayhem, such as penicillin and cortisone, and for the millions of mutilations which are ceremoniously (and totally unnecessarily) carried out every year in operating rooms."[99]

Dr. Mendelsohn has the numbers to back him up. Tables compiled from several official sources, including the U.S. National Center for Health Statistics and the Journal of the American Medical Association, indicate that in 2001, the leading cause of death in the United States was medical error, cited in a stunning 783,000 instances, followed by heart disease (699,697), cancer (553,251), stroke (163,601) and so on. It begins to make sense that malpractice insurance rates are as high as they are.[100] Terrorism accounted for 3,000 American deaths in 2001. If the political speech and media time that are devoted to hazardous conditions were allocated according to the number of people who are dying, then inept physicians and medical staff would have gotten 261 times as many airtime hours and column inches in 2001 as terrorists did, and would be getting even more now.

HEAL YOURSELF

It is up to those who seek wellness to be resourceful. Examples proliferate, now that the kinds of activism we've seen in the last chapter extend also into aggressive communal efforts by people who recognize that their health, and the well-being of their loved ones, depends on how they'll take action, and trust that their own intuition and teamwork may work wonders. It helps that Medecins sans Frontieres ("Doctors without Borders," or MSF) has responded so effectively to natural disasters and epidemics, and has worked so diligently to teach and organize communities to help themselves.

Impoverished African countries such as Ethiopia, Malawi, and Mozambique have gotten encouraging results from training local people to act as what Ethiopia calls "health officers"—that is, paraprofessionals who are not certified as M.D.s, but who are trained and licensed to diagnose and treat illnesses, and whose efforts have brought about results that are beginning to go far beyond the physical, into the empowerment of communities. While such programs are at best partial, temporary solutions—as talented health officers are soon lured away to work in Western countries, or more prosperous African nations—they are now, says Lincoln Chen of the Global Equity Center at Harvard University, the only hope for the moment in Africa, where "paraprofessional systems will have to be built throughout the continent to address this health crisis."[101]

In South Africa, MSF and local agencies have taken the effort a giant step further by teaming medical paraprofessionals and local health activists in what Geoffrey Crowley calls "a whole new approach—a grassroots effort led not by doctors in high-tech hospitals but by nurses and peasants on bicycles."[102] Now, villagers with advanced symptoms of AIDS need not settle for the cold custom of walking out of the village to die. Their loved ones can team with medical assistants and volunteers to make sure that the sick are educated, monitored, and when necessary nudged to take their meds. This teamwork promotes versatility, ensuring that each family member can act if needed as physician, nurse, and teacher. All are determined to make sure that communities take responsibility for doing what governments and corporate entities cannot or will not do.

Is the allopathic medical establishment about to wither away, replaced as the Aquarian era moves along by a new populist medical culture that features a citizen-physician on every block? Obviously not. But the common, passive notion of the "doctor as God" is likely to be one of the early casualties of a new time when helpless "patients" no longer suffer what they can't solve, but take action for their own health and the wellness of their loved ones. In time, the inspiring stories will be told, once we adjust to a new terrain in which whole communities, rather than just a few colorful, strong-willed leaders, dare to make heroic choices and get extraordinary results.

For the moment, Western-style stories of conflict and entertainment are likely to remain the dominant model, as works like Michael Moore's *Sicko* and Kevin Trudeau's *Natural Cures "They" Don't Want*

You to Know About—with its revolutionary advice that all food made by publicly traded companies is toxic and should be avoided—serve the market of people who continue to focus on what they don't want.[103] But as we get closer to 2012, we'll hear more about the brave choices that turn "ordinary" people into the most admirable tricksters of all, the ones who act to save the lives of those they love.

There's a story waiting to be told about busloads of seniors who travel from the U.S. into Mexico to buy prescription medicines, and make deals with customs inspectors on both sides of the border who know that what Grandpa Walt and Grandma Millie are doing is illegal, but look the other way and let them through. There's always a complication in the plot, as Jack Nicholson's character tries to smuggle enough drugs to start an underground pharmacy, but in the end the payoff for communal courage is better health, more powerful self-esteem, maybe even an unmarked green bottle of magic from a *curandero*.

There's a story about Stan Brock, who left a heady life as the star of a TV adventure show to start Remote Area Medical, which provides free medical and dental care by volunteer physicians at clinics organized in rural areas.[104] And the most poignant tale of all could be the true story of the American woman who had a stark, simple choice: obey the law and pay $47,000 in the U.S. for her father's cancer drug—or break the law and smuggle the same drug back from France for $1,200. Her decision, charmingly, took longer than we usually expect, as this scrupulously honest, straitlaced daughter agonized over her decision to commit a crime, then made the first of many flights that got easier once her priorities shifted. It was only a matter of time before she saw that breaking the law was hardly an issue, since the law was breaking her dad. This kind of activism, courageous and compassionate as it is, will in the end be only a doorway to the ultimate Aquarian perception that health is an individual, and communal, creative act.

The main premises of Aquarian Medicine are simple. The new medicine is communal and personal rather than authoritarian and hierarchic. It is not arcane, but open and honest. It works best in relationships of equality among friends. It is holistic in addressing all four bodies—physical, emotional, mental, and spiritual—in the human energy field. Above all, Aquarian medicine is spiritual, founded on the realization that our illusion of separation from the Universal Soul and one another is the original disease—sometimes mislabeled original sin—and that the ultimate health is in overcoming separation, and the reunion of a healthy body with a healthy soul, in a healthy intentional community.

AQUARIAN PROFILE: CHIRON

Chiron (more accurately, Cheiron) has been known for thousands of years to students of Greek mythology. Yet it's been only since 1977, when astronomers found the planetoid Chiron and mapped his unusual 50-year orbit, that astrologers and psychologists began to give Chiron special attention, and note his crucial importance in the healthy growth of each individual personality and soul.

Who started the Chiron boom? Maybe George Lucas and Joseph Campbell, who modeled the Star Wars character Yoda on Chiron. Maybe the first writers on holistic medicine, who saw Chiron as a kind of patron deity of their art. It hardly matters who launched the wave. What is notable is that astrologers track Chiron closely, and note how his position in the chart, and his relationships with other planets, indicate the health issues in the soul. C. G. Jung was the first to write in depth about the mysterious paradox of Chiron as the "wounded healer" who is matchless in treating others, but helpless to heal himself.

It is Chiron's agony that makes him one of the most poignant of all mythic figures, as he bore a wound so excruciating that in the end he was happy to trade deity for mortality, asking Zeus to grant him the blessed relief of death. The most compelling story of his birth is that when Kronos (Saturn) forced the nymph Philyra, she was shape-shifting from human into horse form at the exact moment when the god ejaculated into her, and this is why Chiron looked like a centaur. When he was born, Philyra screamed in horror at the first sight of her son and literally threw him away, piercing him from the moment of birth with a pain that few children ever know, and marking him for life as one of those solitary figures who would be, in the words used of another great soul remarkable for his wounds, "despised and rejected, a man of sorrows and acquainted with grief."

Chiron grew up a virtual hermit on a mountain in the wilds of Thessaly, shunned by humans who feared his rough appearance and by centaurs who, when sober, could smell that he wasn't one of their own. The solitude helped him become a keen observer and intuitive inventor. He is credited with having discerned the constellations in the night sky and with discovering medicinal herbs. He was even, it is said, the first to make music by blowing through the hollow branches of trees. His best instrument, though, was the lyre, which he tried to teach to Achilles, one of the many heroes-to-be whom the kings of Greece sent to learn from Chiron. It was Chiron's instruction that made Achilles one of the most skillful wound-dressers at Troy. The old master's other pupils included Peleus, Jason, Theseus, Meleager, Orpheus, Asklepius, and Chiron's favorite and fateful pupil, Hercules, who had to endure among his many other sorrows the guilt for having brought about his teacher's agony and death.

On his way to visit Chiron, Hercules was attacked by centaurs, killing several of them with arrows tipped with a poison Chiron had made. When Hercules went to find the one arrow that had missed its mark, he was horrified to find Chiron moaning in pain from the arrow that had hit him in the foot. Chiron had no antidote. The pain from his suppurating wound became so excruciating that Chiron longed for the one remedy that a god could not have. Zeus turned down Chiron's first plea for death, if only because the Thunderer was taxed by the implications of an awful precedent in allowing a god to die. In the end the king's compassion prevailed, and Chiron was placed in the sky as Sagittarius, the Archer.

Addressing the Wound

It has become fashionable in some quarters now to denigrate the image of Chiron as the "wounded healer" because such a symbol allegedly carries more victimhood than valor, and turns the would-be healer into a hopeless incurable rather than an empowered artist. This desire to shift emphasis away from Chiron's wound is understandable. But a wound, whether "real" or seen in time as illusory, is a universal part of human experience.

This scenario can be viewed in at least two ways. To people who feel deeply wounded and may play many dramas of pain, life is a story of one searing wound after another. It starts with the wound of separation from the mother at birth. Then wounds of family abuse, lost friends and lovers, and the deaths of loved ones. Wounds of loss and defeat with one's money and career, and the sadness of the body's decline in advancing age. The wounds of seeing the miseries of war and hunger, illness and loss that others bear. For some, the most acute wound is the pain of apparent abandonment by "God."

For those who see the world as energy, life may be a series of very pleasant events if one is proactive. Even birth may be a pleasure for mother and baby alike. As we'll see in Aquarian Spirituality, Jalalud-din Rumi saw the pain of separation from God as an illusion caused by the soul's blind walk through meat and mud, rain and juice, and every other heady tingle that says this splash of life is all there is. For the dervish who sees the Friend as home, all suffering goes from heavy and helpless to voluntary and skillful to right out that sandalwood door until "pain will never see me," as the Turkish poet Yunus Emre put it, and there is no more wound when we are completely whole.

Chiron's wound is a mythic model for the ways in which every soul learns compassion sooner or later from the sufferings of others. Barbara Hand Clow covers this beautifully in *Liquid Light of Sex*, so there is little need here to sketch more than the basic wound posture that each soul must play and transcend: the perpetually wounded victim who uses helplessness to manipulate others; the deliberate wounder who wins by intimidation; and the most common type, the unconscious wounder who may learn compassion from seeing the effects of what he does, or doesn't do, in the suffering of others.[105]

Chiron has an orbital period of 50 years. This means that when we reach 50, Chiron has moved around the zodiac wheel and returns to the position he was in when we were born, and thus offers a crucial opportunity to see our tendencies to wound and be wounded, and make adjustments toward relationships based in love and kindness; or miss the brass ring and suffer the unraveling that comes from seeing that our own wounds are harder to treat, and the wounds we give others are harder to forgive. The Chiron return is the last and most important of the three great rites of passage that a person meets in a normal lifetime.[106] It is no stretch to suppose that the way one handles or boots the Chiron return is the psychic second wind that drives new successes and love links, or a missed chance that invites the reverses of favor and fortune that many people meet in their early fifties.

When the Chiron return is perfectly played, the soul overcomes all perceptions of its own woundedness, and all habits of wounding others, and comes to realize its true nature by dissolving all illusions of separation. In this sense it may be best to see Chiron as one who accepted physical death as the door to the freest expression of his own power to act in service to others. Sagittarius the Archer aims his arrow at Antares, the heart of Scorpio. Is the Archer shooting to kill? Or—is he aiming a medicine arrow to mitigate the Scorpion's passion for wild experience and orgiastic death, and to keep it alive?

CHAPTER 7

AQUARIAN FAMILIES

Not "The Aquarian Family." Several of them. One of the real differences between the Piscean and Aquarian Ages is that we're moving from a "standard" family of one man and one woman who are, ideally, adults, plus a son and a daughter, to a whole cafeteria of family styles. Count 'em. One-parent families. Families with a working mother and a house husband. Two-adult households supported by the birth parent and his or her partner of the same sex. Families with three or more adults who care for their own and their adopted children in a kind of mini-community that works out the delicate balances of responsibility and leadership among the free, conscious beings in their home.

Family models are recombining in ways that make RNA genetics look elementary. The surest sign of sweeping change is in increasingly pitiless battles over "family values." The struggle is most publicly underway in the "developed" countries, where media turn the "reality" of family lives into lurid domestic dramas that are half soap opera, half cautionary tale, and all profit. But the eternal battles—between youth and authority, parents and children, individual dreams and societal rules, private consciences and religious laws, freedom and conformity—are being played out everywhere now, as old family structures crumble, and new ways appear.

It's not easy. Defenders of the traditional family are not just circling the wagons around their own territory, and the yards of their neighbors. They're fighting to make sure the kind of family they want will be what everyone else has too. Will it work? No. After much pointless trouble and pain, human beings in the Aquarian Age will rediscover many of the things that the ancient ones knew, and some indigenous peoples still know, about how to make and raise children who live in devotion to Earth, serve their communities, and practice the heart values that must be present if family values are to work at all.

It starts before birth, with the awareness that, as Tom Robbins' Kitsune the Fox puts it, "To bring a child into the world without preparing in advance for its security and happiness is a criminal act."[107] Conscious parenting views conception as a spiritual act that affirms the place of parents and child in the circle of life. Thousands of years ago, we understood what is often forgotten or ridiculed now: the simple notion that what the parents intend and feel at the moment of making a new life determines what kind of child they will bring into the world. Conceive a child in joy and love, and get a joyous, loving child. Conceive a child in craft or carelessness, and get something else.

It remains to be seen how well some of today's couples, conceiving their children in spiritual practices, even in meditative and tantric rites, will imprint their children with spiritual traits. We shall know sooner, though, what results today's parents are getting from their choices to birth their children with the help of midwives, doulas, and even dolphins; and to make sure that the first sensation that greets their new babies is the comfort of home and the sensuous languor of warm water.

WATER BIRTH

"Here," reads the epitaph of the poet John Keats, "lies one whose life was writ in water." The line clearly applies to many things on Earth now, and not only because all our lives are writ in water now as we begin the Age of Aquarius the Water Bearer. In the years to come some of our children, and many other things besides, will be born in water, with all that that implies about conscious parenting, the creative power of the sacred feminine, and birth as a simple, natural process that can be a painless, even joyous experience for mother and child. And about creating children who know from the moment they emerge from the womb that Earth is a beautiful, blessed place where people live in peace.

We know how hospital birth was for most of us, and how it still is. The emergency begins when the water breaks and the contractions come, and the mother prays that she gets to the hospital in time as her husband drives the family car like an ambulance. Excruciating pain ensues as the baby is pushed from its dark, cozy home into freezing air, the glare of fluorescent light, a chaos of blurred color, chemical stenches and noise. The terrified new arrival gets hoisted by its heels like a chicken. A monster in a white coat with coffee breath and creepy glass eyes gives the baby its first experience of touch by whacking its rear end to make it scream. Welcome to the Earth, kid! And the ordeal has only begun.

The umbilical cord is cut, and the baby takes its first searing breath of air that smells like alcohol. Then the poor new arrival, not already traumatized enough, gets whisked away from its mother—who may or may not have been allowed to touch and hold him—and gets put in a nursery next to a machine with blinking colored lights, a purring electric voice, and no sudden moves. The machine is the first thing that hasn't given the baby any pain or fear, and the child trusts it. Is it any wonder that in developed countries boys grow up to love their gadgets and cars more than their women, and girls learn that men come and go, but diamonds are a girl's best friend?

This is already changing now, as once again what we do in the Aquarian Age is nothing new, but something done well long ago, then long forgotten, and now slowly remembered and renewed. Consider, for example, Varga Dinicu's account of a birth dance ritual she witnessed in Marrakesh in 1967.

In the center of a large tent was a small hollow in the ground, lined with soft sheepskins. The pregnant woman was surrounded by three circles of women dancing a slow clockwise round, singing softly and moving their abdomens in undulating ripples and sudden, sharp contractions. The new mother would alternate between dancing in place, then squatting over the hollow and bearing down. After about an hour, she gasped, lifted her skirt to reveal the boy baby who'd just arrived, then signaled with her hand that she was not done. Another boy was born, with no pain or screams, some fifteen minutes later. The only sign of any discomfort for the mother was the sweat on her face and hair. For hours after the twins were born, and long past sunset, as though to welcome them with the joys of melody and rhythm, the women kept singing and moving, celebrating new life.[108] Before ancient Mediterranean dance became "belly dance," it was the dance of birth, done by and for women only as a sacrament of music and sisterhood that made birth painless and joyous for mother and child.

This ancient custom is well known to Russian water birth researcher Igor Charkovsky and other pioneers who are reviving the art of water birthing, sometimes with the aid of dolphins.[109] There are legends that Moses, like the other children of high priests in ancient Egypt, was born in the water of the Nile, caressed from the first moment by the living body of the lady Isis. He felt little difference between the water in the womb and the warm water of the river, and the first sight to greet him was the smile of his mother, who rubbed him with lotus and amber. She placed his ear on her breast, reconnecting him with her heartbeat, then rocked him and chanted softly to him, vibrating him with her voice until he easily blew out the fluid in his nose and began to breathe. He lay on her heart for an hour as voices, harps, and flutes gave thanks for this newest gift of beauty. When the mother was ready, she rose as light as a gazelle and danced with her son.

Which type of birth is more likely to bring us loving, happy children? It is only a matter of time before works like Barbara Harper's *Gentle Birth Choices* become better known, and more parents embrace the premise that a child raised in a peaceful, loving manner is likely to grow into a peaceful, loving adult.[110] As air is the element of intellect and water is the element of feeling, it is evident enough that when we understand the difference between being born scared in the air or loved in the water, happy new babies will not be the only things that are born in water in the years to come.

AQUARIAN EDUCATION

In *Education in the New Age* (1954), Alice A. Bailey refrained from trying to sketch in detail what education would be like in the Age of Aquarius. She envisioned education some 200 years from now, when human beings will have completed the Aquarian transition, and will have brought about changes that we can't imagine yet.[111] Her choice made sense. She was writing, after all, when technicolor was a hot new motion picture technology; small black and white TVs were in many homes but few classrooms, even in rich countries, though some schools had high-tech equipment like LP record players; computers were the size of a truck, and experts scoffed at the idea that smaller versions of these machines would be in millions of homes in a few years' time.

Education was so much easier in 1954, when I was one of millions of kids who had no idea yet why Elvis Presley's curling lips and burning hips were so dangerous. But we did know how to drop under our desks, cover our heads, and curl up into balls when our teacher set off the flashing light that was supposed to be a Russian H-Bomb. Sister Josephine got under her desk too; to show us how, when the bomb went off and blew in all the windows, we'd better be *under* all that glass that would be flying across the room. We never questioned this. Very few Americans did. It didn't occur to us to wonder if Khrushchev and his air marshals, in their red war room deep in the Kremlin, were really convincing each other that the Motherland would never be safe until Danny Furst and the rest of Overland Park, Kansas were utterly destroyed.

Nobody questioned anything. Everybody seemed to want the same things, and think everybody should have a house and two cars, a kitchen full of gleaming appliances, a TV, record player, bags full of sports gear, and a yard big enough to need a power mower and hold frisbees, dogs, and the 4th of July. We'd have been amazed to learn that in public schools, where Protestant kids didn't pray anyway, it would soon be *against the law* to pray, and people would claim that having to say the pledge of allegiance to the flag was against their child's constitutional rights, but it was okay to burn the flag, provided that when that happened, nobody took all their clothes off.

It was so idyllically simple in 1954. School was for work that was boring but easy, and home was where parents and children could relax and play away from the pressures of work and school. Sure, you still had to do homework. But it wasn't much, and teachers who tried to load you with too much of it, even pull unbelievable stunts like telling you to read a book during your summer vacation, were brought into line, and told that school is where we have to do something, and home is where we eat, sleep, play records, and watch TV. No wonder nobody thought of school as a place that could be exciting, and some parents came to think of it as kind of multiservice babysitting program. "Homeschooling" was a weird idea that made people wonder if parents who did it were too poor to afford school, or had something to hide. Nobody imagined that home and school might be the same thing, that parents would do what teachers were supposed to do.

The catch to all this was that sooner or later, maybe in college, the party would be over and you'd actually have to get to work and start to "make something of yourself . . . buckle down . . . put your nose to the grindstone" and make money in that "dog-eat-dog jungle out there," where only the fittest survived. Fortunately, one way they prepared you was by having you take tests that helped your parents and teachers, even you, understand where you'd probably wind up as you got stamped, punched, sorted, and dealt, like a buff-colored McBee card, into the slot you'd occupy for the next 44 years in the economy. If you were smart, you didn't wait for the big group tests. You figured out that while life might not be dog-eat-dog yet, it was sure getting to be puppy-nip-puppy, and the point of all those report cards, grades, and honor rolls was to help you beat the competition. You might as well have gotten going, because if you didn't you could be headed for the life of a loser.

That's how it was. Aquarian principles are now making education very different from what it was only a few decades ago. New technologies are only part of the change. While 22nd-century classrooms may be equipped with audio-visual marvels that we can only imagine, we'll use them less than some authorities do now to keep children passive and narcotized. If anything, one irony of the Aquarian classroom is that technology is much better but we don't use it nearly as much, because one of our aims is to protect our children from getting addicted to it. Our aim, as it turns out, is to develop in children such keen powers of memory and observation that using a recorder to capture and remember a lesson will seem as dishonest as using a pony to fake a Latin or French assignment.

The Aquarian elementary school classroom may look Puritan or even Spartan at first. While the walls of course have some of the children's new art works and other creations, nothing stays up long, and image turnover is high. The space is so open and simple it almost looks Japanese. It's kept clear because clutter leaves little room for imagination, but emptiness can always be filled with something, The Aquarian classroom is actually part laboratory and part meditation space, because learning how to think creatively, and preparing the mind to do it, is in fact the most basic objective in the Aquarian school.

For Alice A. Bailey, the pillars of education in the New Age were the science of mind (*Antahkarana*), meditation, and service.[112] The Aquarian classroom may have less talk and more silence, as children learn to clear and recharge the mind, and how to use images and intentions to attract and manifest their goals. We can imagine the typical school day as a structured but unpredictable set of new information and review exercises, guided and silent meditations, and teamwork sessions in which each child gets to practice group skills with teams that are often rotated, so each child gets to know all the others, and learns how to identify the strengths of each one, and complement them.

The "mystical perception" that Bailey saw as the goal of Aquarian learning goes far beyond the memorized "facts" and social rituals that pass for education in the conformist societies of the late Piscean era. The core skills are spiritual: unitary insight into the interdependence of the soul and the cosmos; love and compassion; intuition, creativity, and a respect for subjective value and meaning; a sense that the unknown is a challenge that human beings are meant to encounter and explore; and the thirst for truth, beauty, and goodness as aims that we don't just pursue, but create together every day. Will it play in Peoria? We'll see. Not far north, in Chicago, Committees for Stress-Free Schools are testing the impact of Transcendental Meditation on students' lives in and out of school.

An article published in the *American Journal of Hypertension* in 2004 reported that regular practice of Transcendental Meditation reduced high blood pressure among African-American high school students observed by the Medical College of Georgia in Augusta, Georgia.[113] Using TM in schools is not new; it's been 30 years since Robert Keith Wallace wrote about the "positive psychological effects" of TM, and studies at UCLA, Stanford, and Harvard reported that TM can "ease stress and enhance both physical and mental health and behavior." TM produces, according to Prof. Gary Kaplan, of the New York Committee for Stress-Free Schools, "a state of restful alertness that provides the body with deep, rejuvenating rest and allows the mind to reach higher levels of creativity, clarity and intelligence."

New Jersey parents got TM banned as a religious practice when their public schools first began experimenting with it in the 1970s—but times are changing. George Rutherford, the principal who adopted TM ten years ago at the Fletcher-Johnson School in Washington, DC, notes that TM seems to have cut down on school violence, and to have increased attendance and test scores. At Detroit's Nataki Talibah Schoolhouse, where students and teachers have practiced TM together for ten years, students "were happier, handled stress better, had higher self-esteem and got along better with their peers" than students at another school who did not meditate, according to the Center for Complementary and Alternative Medicine at the University of Michigan.

The genie is out of the bottle. We can't yet tell how soon we will discard the notion that the child's mind is a *tabula rasa*, a blank tablet that must be carefully filled with what authorities want it to hold, and we move instead closer to Plato's idea that the mind already holds all knowledge, and the point of education is to *educe*, or lead out, what is already there. The mind may even be seen before long as a *fons mirabilis*, a miraculous fountain whose depth and freshness we have not begun to see.

CONSCIOUS PARENTING

This is one of those terms which, in true Aquarian fashion, seems to arise simultaneously in so many places that no one is sure—and soon, no one will care—who first hatched it. One who's written about it is Dr. Bruce Lipton, whose work has led to startling new evidence about the respective impacts of nature and nurture in shaping the mind. If Lipton is right, we may soon say goodbye to the idea that we are the product of our genes, and can only grow and act the way "nature" has programmed us. New research suggests that *nurture* experiences may imprint "learned perceptions" on our subconscious minds, which in turn shape our conscious thought and actions. These learned perceptions may be even more important than our genetic makeup in influencing who we become and what we do. And the child may be affected by these experiences even before birth.[114]

Thus some parents realize that their rule about making sure not to argue in front of the children goes into effect when the child is still *in utero*, to lessen the possibility that the child will be born carrying the energy of disagreement and conflict, and will be primed to argue even before she knows how to talk. When do "learned perceptions" begin? Could they start before the first brain cells appear? Could they begin even at conception, and with the feelings that parents bring to the act of creating a child? This brings us to a question that is crucial, but no one ever seems to ask: *Why are you having a child?*

Most parents "know" the answer. There's a biological imperative. It's what everybody does. We have to replace ourselves. You have to have a kid before you die. But, while the urge to reproduce really needs no explanation, it's worth asking whether people are conscious of their motives and intentions, and what they will raise their children to be. We could even rank them with stars, like hotels or restaurants:

Table 2: Parental Consciousness Chart

RATING	PRINCIPLE	MOTIVES
☆☆☆☆☆	Love	Conceive children in spiritual intent; birth them in water or other natural, loving method; raise them to act as peaceful, loving, compassionate beings who live in high awareness and creativity. These parents adopt children. They create the next generation of conscious, awakening parents.
☆☆☆☆	Honor	Conceive children lovingly; birth them by Lamaze or other gentle method; raise them to act as solid, responsible, law-abiding citizens living in service to family, church, and country. Creating the next generation of parents who preserve traditional values.
☆☆☆	Duty	Conceive children with serious purpose and birth them to know life's pain from the top. Raise them to act as God-fearing, prudent caretakers of the family's name, wealth, and genes. Creating the next generation of controlling parents who mix and match their families' lives.
☆☆	Habit	Conceive children because we're supposed to, and our folks are really pressuring us for grandchildren; birth them the way everybody else does; raise them to stay out of trouble and do what they're told. Creating the next generation of obedient workers, lawn care experts, and consumers.
☆	Fear	Conceive children because we're not getting any younger and the biological clock is ticking; birth them in a way that is germ-free; raise them to know that their main mission in life is to care for their parents. Creating the next generation of late bloomers, depressives, and wage and tax slaves.
✗	Lust	Conceive children because condoms are no fun, and other birth control is sinful or expensive; birth them as cheaply as we can; raise them if we're awake, sober, and out of jail, and they're still around here somewhere. Creating the next generation of teenaged parents, street hustlers, and victims.

Table 2: Parental Consciousness Chart (continued)

RATING	PRINCIPLE	MOTIVES
✗ ✗ ✗	N/A	Conceive children as the annoying downside of hot sex. Abort them when this option is affordable, birth and abandon them when it's not; raise hell, Cain, the roof, and everything but children. Creating the next generation of voluptuaries, criminals, and other predators.

Clearly, different kinds of parental principles and intentions will yield different kinds of "learned perceptions" among the children who've been produced by these different sets of beliefs. And this is only the beginning, before children learn to talk and demand, claim and fight, and manipulate parents who are amazed to see how they've just been outfoxed again by little people who can't even spell "bamboozle" yet, but can already do it.

TOUGH LOVE: SAVING GRACE, OR DESPERATE MEASURE?

The phrase looks at first like a contradiction in terms. Everybody knows "love" is tender, yielding, forgiving, and gentle, anything but hard, least of all *tough*. The mere fact that a whole system of parenting was built on this curious term is an unmistakable clue that all these conditions could be in effect: (1) once-fashionable "permissive" methods don't work; (2) parents have tried everything to get their children to comply with traditional values and rules—but to no avail; (3) the social and emotional environment has shifted in ways that children perceive but their parents do not yet see; (4) children refuse to accept values that they perceive as false and corrupt; (5) consumer cultures built on convenience and instant gratification have all but dissolved the mental and spiritual fiber that enables us to set great goals and sacrifice to achieve them; (6) parents have never been so busy and stressed, nor so manipulated by corporate advertising and media to prove they love their kids by buying them every gotta-have luxury that pops up on the web and TV; and (7) little Ferris Buellers have never been so adept at working the game.

It has never been so hard for parents—and it's been decades since Kurt Vonnegut wrote about making anything come out well in a society riddled with "addictive poisons and corrupting entertainments." We need not run the litany here. It's evident enough that children have never lived in such a fun house of temptations, and have never been under such peer pressure to buy what all the other kids have—as the Age of Aquarius is the electronics floor of history's toy store—and do what all the other kids do, to be sexy and cool enough to fit in. Home and your parents cannot begin to compete.

No wonder some parents are desperate. The least creative among them, unable to come up with positive alternatives as enticing as the iPod, a PlayStation®, and MTV, may bail into harder rules and sterner punishments. Bill Cosby raised the hackles of the parents he berated for buying their kids $500 sneakers instead of books, but he's right. In theory, tough love makes sense. Children should learn that their actions have consequences—that they're not victims, but responsible agents, and that parents really do have a duty to guide and protect, even when children are as independent as the young Mark Twain. "When I was seventeen," Twain wrote, "I thought my father was a fool. When I was twenty-one, I was amazed how much the old man had learned in only four years." The learned perceptions that young Sam Clemens picked up from his parents and others in his community must have had some steel in them. Before he got to steam down the river, he worked in a print shop where he learned how to make sacrifices and pay his dues. He earned his freedom by mastering his craft—of which writing was only part.

Tough love and its anti-predecessor—a "permissive" style that many parents misapplied to the point of giving away the store—could only have been created late in the Age of Pisces, when values seem relative, even ridiculous, and threatened authorities look to shore up their walls. How to steer between the two poles? The dilemma is ancient, and is at the root of new approaches to parenting that are being tried today. Some, predictably, are as authoritarian as we would expect in cultures that turn ever more paranoid about holding on to what they think they have. One recent book on parenting urges parents to enforce "catastrophic consequences" for children who break the rules. It includes chapter headings such as "Appoint Yourself Benevolent Dictator" and "The Law of Winning the War."[115] Perhaps such an approach will actually work—if all of the family members are still alive, ambulatory, and in the house when all the conflict ends, if it does.

FLEXIBILITY

Fluidity and flexibility, the ability to adapt to changing conditions and even create them to one's advantage, are among the essential features that make an Aquarian personality and lifestyle delightful to those who love it, painful for those who don't. Flexibility is a crucial element in the parenting system that has exalted the popular Dr. Phil McGraw from a brilliant child psychologist into a TV megacelebrity who has won the trust of tens of millions of American parents, and whose books get translated into a dozen languages.

The parenting principles in Dr. Phil's *Family First* are quietly revolutionary in their departure from rigidly authoritarian parenthood. His emphasis is on negotiating and partnership, validation and nurturing, respect and communication, all within the context of a "family system" of rhythms, traditions, rituals, and other structures that are predictable enough to make life comfortable, yet have within them enough breathing room for the goals, needs, "authenticity," and creativity of each family member.[116]

Much of the genius of the *Family First* system is in its guidance on how to use and mix three basic parenting styles—authoritarian, equalitarian, and permissive—in relating to the respective personalities of rebellious, cooperative, and passive children. A passive child and an authoritarian parent, for example, will usually get along easily. The parent's main challenge will be to stimulate creativity and initiative in a child who's comfortable as a follower and listener. But when an authoritarian parent and a rebellious child march into contested territory, then the question is not if the explosion will come, but how soon.

Interestingly for those who notice the distinctive Aquarian features in this very flexible design, we can see that the three parenting styles Dr. Phil defines are a very close match with the last two Great Ages in our planet's history, and the Great Age we're entering now. The *authoritarian* parent is decisive, committed to achieving goals, controlling, and rule-bound, sometimes to the point of being rigid and dogmatic, and tends to push and dominate the other people in his or her relationships. In other words, the authoritarian parent is what we'd expect in an Aries personality. The *permissive* parent's style is more Piscean: accepting and assuring, reacting to conditions rather than planning or controlling them, and getting what it wants by pulling subtly from the shadows. The *equalitarian* parent is the most Aquarian of the three, seeking cooperation and teamwork, shared responsibility, and high creativity. This is not to say, though, that the egalitarian, "Aquarian" style is somehow better than the others. It has its pitfalls too, as we'll see.

Perhaps the most exciting and spiritually provocative point in Dr. Phil's approach is his insistence that family comes first. It must have "project status level" priority, demanding committed attention, resourcefulness, and passion, if it's to turn out well. Not only that, but parents must accept that their children are not the only ones who have to go through changes. To build the foundation on which their children will base their lives, parents will have to accept "self-examination" as an ongoing process that is happily and willingly done, so that it becomes habit. Parents will achieve the harmonious, loving results they seek only if they "clean house in yourself first," modeling in themselves the authenticity and integrity they want in their children. This is conscious parenting at its most dynamic, rooted in the evolutionary principle that the awakened soul can bring about change in its circumstances and relationships only if it first creates positive changes in itself.

ACCEPTING DIVERSITY

As everyone knows, the hot-button issue in today's family field of fire is no mere style choice about bare bellies, cerise hair, or pieces of metal worn in one's nipple or nose. There is more fury and grief in parents' responses to the sexual preferences of their children, and of other adults who want to raise children, than there is in any other area of family life. The passion is understandable. Most parents want their children to give them grandchildren. Even those who accept and love their gay and lesbian children want to protect them from bullying, and the ordeal of being who they are in a society that fears them. And millions of devout parents in dozens of countries live in stark terror that unless their "degenerate" children "go straight" and live according to "God's law," they risk an eternity of flaming agony in hell. The last thing such fathers and mothers want to hear is that now that we're in the Age of Aquarius, we're going to see a lot more cross-dressing entertainers, and—look on the bright side!—your child could be a star.

The consequences of these social stigmas and religious dogmas are already excruciating enough, in the suffering of couples who have lived together lovingly for decades but are denied the dignity, legal status, and spiritual blessing of marriage because they are of the same sex. And the pain is even greater in the fear and sorrow of children who are utterly alone, cursed by their parents, and driven out of their homes to a feral, sometimes short life in the streets. More and more kids who used to just be rebels are now refugees. One who is likely to have an easier time of it than most is Maya Marcel-Keyes, daughter of Alan Keyes, the anti-abortion activist who was a Republican presidential aspirant in 2000. Expelled from her home at 19 for her lesbian "hedonism" by parents who saw her as "supporting the enemy" after she came out of the closet at an Equality Maryland rally, Keyes was offered a scholarship to Brown University by The Point Foundation, which assists gay and lesbian youth with scholarships and other assistance.[117]

"I had spoken [in the rally] about queer kids who are homeless and the homeless youth problem," she said in a telephone interview in February, 2005. "Did you know 40 percent of street kids are GLBT [gay, lesbian, bisexual, transgender]? It's a problem that doesn't get much attention . . . I've seen a lot of friends who were queer who've been kicked out because they're gay." There is quibbling about the numbers, of course. How does one get a research sample from street kids? But 40 percent, or whatever, isn't the point. Something will have to give here, and it isn't the GLBT children. They are living their truth, and can't be expected to lie just to accommodate someone else's opinions.

One need only listen to a gay or lesbian person to understand. He did not make the choice to desire people of his own sex, and does not have the option to switch, no matter how others may recommend cold showers, sports, and religion. Nobody can "turn gay." The lesbian person gradually realizes that she is spontaneously attracted to her own sex—and then she decides whether she is going to live the truth of who she is, or conceal it. When she gathers the courage to reveal herself, she does not do this to gain attention, rebel, hurt her parents, or defy her church, though her heroic moment may be tinged with these lesser motives. She finds her true voice, and commits to authenticity because if she does not, her soul will suffocate. All that matters is that she is free, living her truth, and that she loves. In a more enlightened time, she will be loved in turn.

"I'D GIVE ANYTHING TO HAVE YOUR AQUARIUS PARENTS."

One of the cues about how parenting styles will change in the Aquarian Age is in the way Aquarians approach parenthood. We'll look now at how Aquarian Principles may suggest advantages that Aquarian parents have and other parents can borrow—and the parenting points that Aquarians can learn from others.

Aquarians love novelty, and are among the planet's easiest, liveliest communicators. They can talk to their children about anything. They tend to resist structures and rules, and can be so unconventional in their views and habits that teenagers can be hard put to rebel against them, and may even be tempted to act more conformist than they feel, just to differentiate themselves from their parents. An Aquarian household can fizz with the excitement of new activities, friends, ideas, and surprises. Life will be anything but dull. Aquarian parents are comfortable with electronic technologies, and not only know how to work the computer and the DVD deck, but are hip to the new toys. They treat their children as teammates, even equals, more readily than most parents can. Their egalitarian spirit helps them be fair, playing no favorites and hearing all points of view. They can respect the privacy of others, and recognize their children's right to set boundaries too.

What's the downside? Several things. Aquarian parents may be so enamored of what's new and fascinating that they have a hard time being consistent and setting up and keeping to the structures and rituals that glue the family's life together. They can get so focused on changing the world that they don't notice what needs repair at home, and Family First may be a second language for them at times when it needs to be primary. They may resonate effortlessly with cooperative children, less brilliantly with passive children, whom they may overstimulate; and with rebellious children, whom they may accommodate too much, only to find that the rules, when it's time to apply them, are much harder to sell. In their unwillingness either to enforce what they want or wait for it to happen organically, they can get manipulative, or damage trust that they will then have to renegotiate. As they want so much to be and have friends, they can make the mistake of asking their children to do and be the things that their adult friends are for; when an Aquarian parent is insecure, shaky collaboration can turn into co-dependent trouble.

Like any parents, Aquarians may need to fortify their weak suits, in this case by getting some fire from authoritarian parents and water from permissive ones, to make sure their family's life is not always up in the air, but sometimes, at least, on solid ground. In their love of change, their love of friendship in an era of community and their love of freedom in an age that is made for it, though, Aquarian parents are readier than most for the world we're about to live in, and so, with some love and luck, will their children be.

SPIRITUAL PARENTING

Above all, the conscious parenting of the Aquarian Age will be spiritual at its core. This is not to say that the social, political, cultural, and religious values that have traditionally defined the standards of successful parenting and sound family relationships will become irrelevant. Not at all, though old authority structures will weaken, and some will disappear. What will happen is that the values that define a person's actions as "good" or "right" will be communal and spiritual standards spoken in the heart. Spiritual values will be the touchstones for determining which other standards ought to be kept, or swept out.

The trend is already underway, and can be seen more clearly now that books and courses in spiritual parenting are crossing from the relatively narrow band of New Age media into mainstream publishing and journalism, even TV. The spiritual principles of parenting are now the compelling buzzwords that "tough love" were a few years ago. Guides on how to raise a child in spiritual terms are proliferating. Only a couple of examples here will show where the trend is heading from now to 2012, and beyond.

David Spangler, co-founder of the Findhorn Community in Scotland and a pioneer of the New Age, published his *Parent as Mystic, Mystic as Parent* in 2000. The title says it all about how parenting envisions both parent and child within the interdependent web of natural life, and the unifying divine consciousness that breathes and moves in Heaven and on Earth. Far from teaching a child to live inside the control of ever-widening sets of rules, parenting is "an opportunity to participate in the deeper mystery: the incarnation and emergence of our children's spirits and personalities."[118] Radical stuff, this. Who would have thought that the point of parenting is to support the child's soul expression?

A similar theme runs through Marilyn C. Barrick's *A Spiritual Approach to Parenting* (2004), a book largely devoted to the unusual children who have been born on Earth in recent decades, and are arriving now, "to help us calibrate our consciousness so that we function in a more attuned way and recognize our inner oneness with God."[119] We'll look more closely at these indigo and crystal children whom parents and teachers have begun to understand better only in the last few years—fittingly enough, as these children can be appreciated only in spiritual terms. This can all seem very new. But it isn't. Consider these words about the changes in family life that the New Age is about to bring:

"While the tendency is for all mankind to be one family in sympathy, more and more it will be recognized that each man requires privacy for his best development. The tyranny of the family will give place to freedom *in* the family. Strip family life of its tyranny and it may be very charming.

"The sensitive and highly charged beings of the new age would explode if they should be obliged to sit every evening round the family 'centre-table,' listening to the maunderings of the least progressive among them, who by reason of greater age assumed the right to lay down the law. This does not mean that children will not honor their parents; but under the new dispensation parents will honor their children's need for the individual life, and will give it to them—thereby securing their own freedom."[120]

The quaint style here is a tipoff that these words were written long before anyone ever heard of tough love. How long? David Patterson Hatch wrote them in 1912.

INDIGO AND CRYSTAL CHILDREN

The term "indigo child" was introduced by Lee Carroll, channel for an entity who calls itself "Kryon of Magnetic Service." Indigo refers to the deep blue color that is prominent in the auric field of the gifted and challenging human beings who have been arriving on the planet since about 1977.[121] Indigo children have also become better known through the work of musician James Twyman, who has helped them gain a sympathetic outlet for their poems, songs, and stories, and the spiritual messages they have come to impart.

This last word is precise, as the most assertive indigo children make it clear that they're here to teach, not to follow mindless rules or put up with anything that leaves no room for their creativity. They are impatient with structure unless it makes sense, and have so little shyness about declaring how things *should* be done that they can quickly become feared as troublemakers. What makes them triply infuriating is that they are usually right. They can quickly become bored in the company of less intelligent kids, and will either go within themselves, where they're much better entertained, chafe against home and school rituals that are much too rigid, or jump with nervous energy that has no way to express itself. So they have often been misdiagnosed with Attention Deficit with Hyperactivity Disorder (ADHD) or Attention Deficit Disorder (ADD) by physicians who haven't noticed that they're not dealing with a mental phenomenon, but a spiritual one.

Indigo is the color of the *ajna*, the third eye chakra that is the center of spiritual vision. Deep blue is also associated with deities of truth and learning, so it is no mystery that indigo children are beings of high mentality who can be disappointed that others cannot see what is so clear to them. Can this make indigo children insufferable? Very likely yes, to unimaginative authorities who are their natural adversaries. Even their parents, who love them dearly and remember always hearing that you don't just teach your child, your child also teaches you, can wonder at times if the lessons really have to be this severe.

Why should we believe any of this, when some of the main sources of the information are discarnate beings? Because we have the numbers. In *Children of the New Millennium*, P. M. H. Atwater reports that IQ scores among the "millennial" generation of American children—born between 1982 and 2003—have jumped so spectacularly that almost all the children tested in the area of "genius" are in the range of 150–160, and some over 180, compared to top scores of 134–140 reached only a generation or two before.[122] Test results from other countries have been similar, and often resemble the American results in one extremely significant way: the spike of 24–26 points in "nonverbal intelligence"—that is, abilities that are largely intuitive rather than intellectual.

The next wave after the indigo children, the crystal children who have been arriving since 1995, may prove harder to test. While indigo children are highly, even fiercely mental, having what Doreen Virtue calls a "warrior spirit" that is here to break apart old systems, crystal children are softer and sweeter, and more sensitive to whatever does not resonate in love and kindness. Much of the writing about these children circles endlessly back to the same question: how can these children, so empathetic and soft, so easily moved to tears and upset by the suffering of any living being that they will try to reattach a cut flower to its stem, possibly survive in the world at any time, much less now? One likely answer, as we'll soon see, may look impossible at first—before it then becomes obvious.

They have been called "crystal" children because their auric field is so pure that it looks colorless. Another explanation is that their aura has a distinctive color called octarine, which is so high in frequency that few human beings can see it. This implies, clearly, that to relate well to the crystal children, the rest of us will have to expand our powers of spiritual perception so that we begin to see what they see, hear what they hear, feel what they feel, and know what they know. In other words, unlike indigo children who can represent a stern demand for more conscious parenting, the crystal children offer a gentle invitation to it in ways that may increasingly spiritualize the people around them. Crystal children are said to be uncommonly creative and artistic, often see and communicate with angels and other spirit beings, and remember past lives, sometimes answering questions about how they learned to do something by replying, "I was good at this before." Crystal children are loving, compassionate, and kind, often acting spontaneously as healers.[123]

As crystal children often want to communicate telepathically rather than in speech, they may begin speaking years later than "normal" children do. Like baby Albert Einstein, whose story we'll visit soon, crystal children may be so unresponsive to conventional stimuli that their parents may wonder if their child is mentally incomplete. They're not. A crystal child doesn't just hear a different drummer; he has no taste for marching at all.

This presents unusual parenting challenges. How does one tempt a child with a dopey meal of a hamburger and a sugar bomb when little Ricky wants vegan food? How does one get little Alison to watch TV when—unlike indigo children who condemn televised violence as toxic and stupid—she finds electronic stimulation harsh, even painful? How should little Kosuke get hooked on an iPod when the music inside his head is so much richer? How, for that matter, are parents going to integrate their crystal children into the "real" world when the world they see is more colorful, aurally variegated and complex, and full of beings and experiences that only another crystal or indigo child can perceive?

The answer is that the parents are not going to get the child to fit into the world as they *think* it is. Rather, the child is going to get the parents to fit into the world as he or she *knows* it is. As incredible as it may seem, the way the impossibly sweet crystal children will survive in this rough world is that the world will change to accommodate them. They are, after all, masters of visioning and manifesting. And they will get what they want, for the most unselfish of reasons: that a kinder, more spiritually awakened humanity is better for the happiness of all beings who share our home on Earth. Wait and see. Within the next 20 years, crystal poets and singers will vibrate the heart of all humanity in ways we cannot begin to imagine now.

AQUARIAN PROFILE: ABDULLAH

I first met Abdullah in February 2005. His mother Rada had brought him to a meditation workshop in Cairo because, I thought at first, he was a brilliant boy, more than ready to handle metaphysical material that people in the room old enough to be his grandparents were having trouble hoisting aboard. Only on getting to know Abdullah better did I glimpse what might have been Rada's main motive: to get him out of the usual school and social ordeals, and into a place where more loving and compassionate people can accept and treasure him for what he is.

I hardly noticed Abdullah the first day. The only unusual thing about him was the hearing aid in his left ear. I hardly connected with him at all until the closing "circle of love," when his mother placed him at my left, saying "He needs you, Dan." I held his hand and felt nothing at first, neither warmth nor stiffness, neither a reach toward connection nor an urge to pull away. As the guided meditation moved along, his hand relaxed when we visualized the people we love. When we got to those who've hurt us, and whom we can now forgive, Abdullah began to shake with nervous laughter, and his hand drifted up and away. I moved my hand with his, staying in contact, following wherever he wanted to go. He relaxed and let his hand settle again when the recorded music began, then his laughter got louder and wilder, and as others began to sing along with the music, I sang too in the most soothing voice I have, as others whispered "It's all right." I felt that Abdullah wasn't freaking out from the music, but was literally jumping with an urge to play it better. As the meditation ended, an image of Mozart blandly listening to Salieri's music ran through my mind, and I mentioned it to Rada. I gave Abdullah a gentle hug, feeling his heart field very carefully. He responded with a quizzical smile.

He turned away toward his sister, and I talked for a few minutes with Rada. We agreed at once that Abdullah might be a crystal child. When I asked how old he was when he spoke his first words, she said "he was delayed." I suggested this might not be so, as his native tongue might be feeling and sound, and I told Rada the famous story about Einstein, as recollected by his sister Maja. Little Albert spoke not a word until well after his second birthday, by which time his parents had tried every way to reassure themselves that their son was neither mineral nor vegetable. One day the boy suddenly spoke up, to point out that his milk was too hot. When his amazed parents asked why he had never spoken before, he replied that "until now, everything has been in order."

Abdullah says few words, though he surges with rhythms that are trying to get out. Some features of his story are predictable: endless tests from doctors who couldn't figure out his problem and wondered if he might be hearing-impaired or mentally defective; indirect hurtfulness from relatives and others in a culture where a handicap, even an unusual condition that only looks like one, can bring bitter judgment from those who feel that the bearer of the burden, and those who must care for him, are somehow disfavored by God.

As he hits puberty, Abdullah lives at the extremes of light and dark. He's had a chance to develop his musical gifts, becoming so proficient at the organ that he amazed the adult professional musicians with whom he played at the city's most prestigious concert hall, the Cairo Opera House. He's not the only gifted one who's wished many times that he could just play music and do nothing else. But he has to interact with the world sooner or later, and when he does, other children can be relentlessly cruel.

When one imagines how vicious some of the children in middle school must be toward Abdullah—the tears in Rada's eyes tell the tale—the other famous figure who comes to mind is the one who was "despised and rejected." Is it extravagant to compare Abdullah with Jesus, and to put him in the same paragraph with Mozart? Perhaps. Yet it is easy to wonder about indigo and crystal children whose stories don't make it into the books because they aren't told with wonder and joy by parents who love and cherish them. Consider the indigo and crystal children for whom fitting in seems all but impossible, and who've had to bear scorn that other children never know. Imagine the extremely tough birth choices that these children have made, and we can see what Abdullah and other children like him have: the leonine fire of their courage and the sheer heroic beauty of their hearts. Such bravery has the power to bring change. It is the only thing that does.

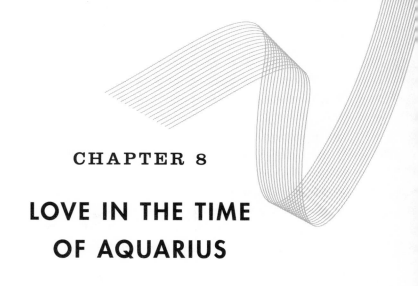

CHAPTER 8

LOVE IN THE TIME OF AQUARIUS

It's all right. Your secret is safe. No one else needs to know that you jumped right to this chapter. You even skipped the part about the money and flew like Cupid's arrow right to the most compelling question: Will I find true love? Will I keep the love I have now?

The next question flies even faster, like the light from our beloved's eyes. What is *true* love? Is love true if it endures for a long time, and weathers challenges and changes? If it is exclusive and at least generally faithful? If it holds the beloved lightly, like a bird in the hand that is free to go, and return? If it nourishes and empowers both partners, and brings out the best in each? If it is a mirror of beauty in which each one reflects the goodness that the other may not see? Is love true if it ripples out beyond itself, sending waves of kindness and forgiveness out to family and community?

Is love bound by time, or free of it? This theme is well known to readers of Gabriel Garcia Marquez's novel *Love in the Time of Cholera*, about the older couple who do not get to love one another in the usual youthful surge of passion and desire, or even in the maturity of loyalty and devotion, but in the crystalline time when most of what is left between them is the spiritual love that lives in friendship and acceptance, lightened of any sorrow over what is missing, purified by gratitude for what is still there.

Is true love a romantic notion that is impossible now? Sure, if that is what one believes. Or—are we now going to nail the question that Tom Robbins built a whole novel on: How to make love stay? No way. In the Aquarian scheme of things, quality outweighs quantity. So the value of a relationship is not in whether it lasts a lifetime, but (1) whether it hits the spiritual point it was meant to deliver; and (2) whether—however long it lasts and whenever it ends—it leaves the lovers better than they were when they first drew together. In this sense a love union, like a spiritual teacher, is not a house that we're meant to live in for life, but a bridge that gets us over the river we need to cross now.

Does this mean, at a time when many lovers aim for *serial monogamy* at best, or practice *polyamory*—that is, simultaneous liaisons in which one's two or more lovers know of, accept, and even like each other—that the traditional long marriage is on the way out, and that we'll have to bid a fond farewell to the days when happy couples raised their children, delighted in their grandchildren, and grew old together like those white-haired Japanese dolls with rake and broom that symbolize a long, happy marriage? Not at all. Marriages will still live long and prosper, enough of them to encourage couples to keep making the brave attempt, and keep finding out why Queen Christina of Sweden said, "More courage is required for marriage than for war."

Marriage will survive. Couples will find truthful, loving new ways to stay together. What will change, though, is the tissue of lies, guilt, and fear that keeps the facades of bad marriages intact as their interiors crumble away. Couples will stay married because they want to, not because they feel they must, or they dread the social pressures and religious threats that preserve appearances while smothering the soul. In "developed" societies, especially in the west, the old sexist and religious customs that once held bad marriages together are heading for landfill. Even the Middle East is in flux. Saudi Arabian judges decreed that fathers who try to force their daughters to marry men they don't love will be jailed until they come to their senses. Who knows where this may lead? If a woman can choose her husband, she may soon be free to travel out of the country without his written permission, even dress as she pleases. Aquarius is a heady and terrible time, depending on whether you are the one who gains freedom, or the one who loses control.

AQUARIAN LOVERS

The same thing applies now to love relationships, which enjoy the blessing of greater freedom, and the burden of new choices. It will even happen, though not at once—as the pain of lost love is the fuel of pop music—that women will stop singing about how a man is two-faced, and men will have to give up the refrain that a woman is a "sometime thing." In the Aquarian Age, people will be quicker to call out those who vent the usual excuses for failure. Women will tell other women, "Get over your trip about how you don't trust men. If you didn't think bad boys were so hot, you wouldn't be so unhappy." Men will tell other men, "Don't blame women. You had better choices, but you were after thrills, not love." Those who want to blame the opposite sex had best do so now, while they still can. There will be less slack for this when Aquarius is here to stay.

We're about to see how Aquarian themes and values are already having an impact on our love lives. While we'll use people born under the sign of Aquarius as our main example of how the game of love will be played for some time to come, the love skills and dynamics we'll explore do not apply only to Aquarians. Whether we're Aquarians, in relationship with an Aquarian, or doing our best to handle love in Aquarian times, the love themes and currents of the Aquarian personality will bear strongly or mildly, directly or obliquely, to everyone who has or wants a love relationship in the Age of Aquarius.

Honesty and responsibility are two of the key Aquarian love values. The Eleven Aquarian Principles are relevant too. It's not esoteric or mysterious. Just Google "Aquarius lover," and you can pick up in less than an hour most of the ways in which love relationships are changing now. You already know the main material if you're an Aquarius. If you love an Aquarius, you're already on the learning curve, though you may wish at times that it resembled one smooth hill more than a roller coaster. The main themes are these.

EQUALITY

If you're one of those men who wants the one-up spot in a hierarchic love relationship, and you even believe God wants women to submit to their husbands, please make sure you have good luggage and small bills to tip the porter. Or fortify your opinions about how women may not do what you tell them here on Earth, but they will in Heaven. If you're a woman who submits to the tyranny of a man as your "lot in life," then please accept sympathies in advance for the discomfort you're about to undergo.

Aquarians are natural egalitarians who resist authority, and even want to explode it. They chafe at rules and hate being told what to do, which is why they don't normally hook up with the most control-ling types on the zodiac wheel. In the love and family dynamics of the Aquarian Age, couples had best be ready to listen, question, and nego-tiate a lot more than our grandparents did. Even if the couple agrees that one of them will make the final decisions in their relationship, the other will have the power and the duty to "advise and consent" before the decision is made. Checks and balances will be as crucial to love as they are to constitutional law.

VARIETY SHOWS AND JOKES

Aquarians love to be entertained. And there are practical reasons why movies and other electronic stories, and comedy in general, are flour-ishing as the Age of Aquarius begins. Aquarians thrive on novelty, and are happiest in relationships that offer the curiosities and delights of something new. Does this mean that being in the bedroom with your Aquarius lover is going to be a continuous round of new toys, games, and surprises? Not really. Even for Aquarians, props are pointless without passion. But at the same time, a good Aquarian relationship does require some inventiveness. Those who invest the effort will have a longer, happier time of it. Lazy people who seek predictable routines had best choose equally log-minded lovers. One hopes that the British noblewoman whose take on sex was to "lie still, and think of England" was not married to the Earl of Aquarius.

Aquarians, being air signs, have a lively and quick temperament. They love jokes, so one no-brainer dating tip for Aquarius is the improv club or the standup act at the big hall where you and your partner will see everybody else you know. We'll see more in the next chapter about the compassionate comedy of Aquarius. For now, the rule of thumb is easy enough, though we'll have to learn by trial and error to get beyond the jokes that wound and find the ones that heal.

FRIENDSHIP AND THE LIFE OF THE MIND

As the 11th sign of Aquarius naturally relates to friendship, it's no surprise that, with some exceptions, Aquarians are among the people most likely to want both an intimate love relationship and a wide circle of friends, and they expect that the two will get along. Complaining that your Aquarius lover has more time for his or her friends than for you is probably going to get you out the door fast. More on this in a moment.

Of all the love signs on the zodiac wheel, Aquarians may be the type least likely to frolic first, ask questions later. An Aquarian love relationship tends to begin as a search for like-minded friendships before it gets intimate. Just as the one who first said "The way to a man's heart is through his stomach" might have been talking about a Taurus, the way to an Aquarian's heart—if, as we'll see, you can actually get there—is through the mind. The beautiful Roxanne in *Cyrano de Bergerac*, who prizes eloquence even above beauty, is one of the classic Aquarian lover types. She has to be won with words.

Love with an Aquarius may not require a certain hipness of mind—though that does help—but it does demand a willingness to talk about enough different and new topics to keep the conversations fresh. Aquarians love to talk about a wide range of things, and bond most strongly with others who are as curious as they are. They are loyal and devoted not only to friends, but to their convictions, which they will defend bravely, though they are open-minded and will change their views when the evidence and charm of the other are convincing. Can you bring an Aquarius around to seeing things your way? Yes, provided you do it kindly in a spirit of good humor.

As befits the revolutionaries of the zodiac, Aquarian lovers are apt to be devoted to social and political causes, and may expect you to share their passionate commitment to change for the better. What kinds of movements? Figure that Aquarians like Lord Byron and Corazon Aquino tried or achieved political upheavals. Thomas Edison was to electrical engineering what Abraham Lincoln was to slavery, Rabelais was to French literature, James Joyce was to the novel, Oprah Winfrey is to the empowerment of women, and Babe Ruth and Jackie Robinson were to baseball. All these Aquarians had liberating, transformative impacts on their fields. Is it possible that an Aquarian lover will want to have an equally transformative effect on you? Maybe not. But Aquarian relationships are dynamic, not static. Something has to change, and that something may be you.

Your Aquarian mate may at times seem more interested in changing the world than in relating to you. Does this mean you're not important? No, it means that to an Aquarius, the welfare of the many is weightier than the wishes of the one. If you want to be the center of attention—one reason why an Aquarius-Leo match can be challenging—then you may need some practice in sharing focus.

In the Aquarian Age, we'll be amazed to see how resourceful our children, and ourselves, have become when we remember that curiosity doesn't kill the cat. It frees him. We will know and explore more, not less. Our mainstream myths will shift from *Top Gun* stories about maverick stars who fit into a team to *Seabiscuit* stories about unlikely contenders who break out of their limits and through to their power, find the bravery to transcend their wounds, and take the risk of love, thereby empowering others to dare the same leap into the heart. Can we expect love in the time of Aquarius to require more courage than we've always needed for love and marriage? Yes. Is this another way in which Aquarian love relationships, and Aquarian life in general, will ask more of an effort than many of us are accustomed to making? Yes. It can't be helped. As the pace of change accelerates, the more adept we shall have to become in riding the wave—and the more women and men will adjust their protocols for trying to slow or bring change in their relationships.

FLEXIBILITY AND FREEDOM

Those of us who've been through love relationships, perhaps a marriage, know the basic drill the two sexes have about change. Though the different takes women and men have on change in their relationships may look completely opposite at first, they are in fact two sides of the same coin. Everybody "knows" that to a man, a woman is a work of art; to a woman, a man is a work in progress. A man cherishes the one he loves as perfect the way she is, a finished product that can only change for the worse, so he does whatever he can to convey, as the Billy Joel song put it, that "I love you just the way you are." He hopes that she will never change, and be always "just the way you look tonight." Is this man's wish sexist, assuming that a woman will never grow into anything more than a beautiful object? Possibly. Is it idealistic? Probably. Certain to fail? Yes. She will change, if only physically. Her hapless lover, robbed of his art treasure, will dream of a younger woman who resembles his mate as she looked decades ago.

A woman's approach is the opposite: her mate is a kind of furniture restoration project. First she wants to renovate his wardrobe. If he's an Aquarius, this can be a good thing, as an Aquarius male is apt to choose a jacket which, in Tom Wolfe's phrase, has not been introduced to his pants. Then the serious structural work begins. The man finds that his beloved is out to make radical changes in his diet, his hygiene, his home décor, such as it is, his body clock, his TV viewing habits, even his friendships. He can go one of two ways with all of this. He can resist, actively or passively, so the home becomes an arena for pointless squabbles about things that seem crucial to one spouse and trivial to the other, and he escapes whenever he can either for beer and laughs with his friends, or for some long-absent tenderness with another woman who just wants him as he is right now.

The other option is rarer. Most men sense, even if they've never seen it happen directly, that the more a man accepts everything in his mate's renovation program, and makes all the changes she wants, the sooner he will mutate into something that hardly resembles the man she first fell in love with. If he is compliant to the point of being too easy, offering her no challenge at all, the only question that remains is whether she'll lose all respect for him before he loses all respect for himself. This is why men, who fear the appearance of being weak more than they fear death, will fight every change a woman wants to make, even if they have to look defiantly boorish. It is a small wonder that Sam Shepard, before he got happy with Jessica Lange, once said that relationships between men and women, like most of those in his plays, are "terrible and impossible."

The controlling behaviors of men and women will have to be adjusted during the Age of Aquarius, as both are enemies of freedom. When a man denies a woman her freedom to change, and a woman tries to compel arbitrary changes that are mere matters of taste, both are running control games that seem opposite but are very much the same, both rooted in a desire for "love on my terms," as the hero of Citizen Kane put it. The effects of this inflexibility have been getting steadily more trying since the spring of 2005. We now see relationships splintering and cracking all around us as couples try in vain to swim against the tide of change, instead of yielding to it and letting themselves be carried safely to beaches they can't always choose or control. There is much to be said for what kayakers in Hawaii recommend: when the wave is carrying you, lie down and let go.

In Aquarian relationships, the principles of *surrender, forgiveness,* and *acceptance* that have been part of our metaphysical vocabulary for decades now are fast becoming tips for couples who intend to stay together. So is the idea of *working on oneself* to improve our relationships. One difference between the recent past and the years leading to and beyond 2012 is that New Age talk is cheap, and it's time for walking the Language of Love. In the journeys we take together now, all we really need is the love of Earth and each other, and a readiness to help increase happiness and relieve suffering. All the rest of it—images of beauty we keep as mementoes, the moot little changes we want to make in others—are excess weight that Aquarian Airlines will charge us more to carry.

SELF-RELIANCE AND BOUNDARIES

Imagine we're at a party, looking around at the people the way an astrologer might. Over in the corner, the Capricorn is fascinated with the Scorpio and is wondering if he'll survive a fling with her. Near the bar, the Sagittarius is regaling a knot of listeners with his travel stories. On the sofa, the Libra male is hitting on the Aquarius, who is cold to temptation so far, and is experiencing yet again the axiom that the curse of beauty is to have one's privacy continually invaded by passionate strangers. The Libra hasn't yet figured out the mysterious double identity of Aquarius, which can be reserved and revolutionary, flamboyant and aloof, and is liable to switch as soon as one thinks he has it figured out.

In this way Aquarians are like Hexagram 16 of the *I Ching*, Enthusiasm. Aquarians have the electrical attraction and arousing energy of thunder over the colder, receptive quality of Earth. It's appropriate that Aquarius month (Jan. 19–Feb. 18) comes when it does, with the deep ground still frozen as the surface starts to thaw. This combination of lightning above and ice below is a good symbol of the enigmatic Aquarian personality, which is so light, vivacious, bubbly, and charming that it's irresistibly attractive, yet so cool and emotionally detached that more than one person has wondered if the artist who first crafted a snow sculpture was trying to capture the heart qualities of an Aquarius.

Should you fall in love with an Aquarius? Only if your self-esteem is strong, but not if you're a high-maintenance, emotionally needy type who craves reassurance. Aquarians can be wonderfully voluble and exciting, and can communicate about anything. They can easily open their minds to us—while not letting us get within a mile of their hearts. This emotional detachment is hardest for those who like a lot of strokes and always want to know what the other is thinking. Aquarians have to have privacy to replenish energies that they can spend even to exhaustion. Winston Churchill remarked that meeting the Aquarian Franklin D. Roosevelt was like opening a bottle of champagne, yet FDR loved quiet time with his stamp collection, and dreamed at the end of his life of retiring to his farm in Hyde Park. No one was more sociable than Mozart, who found recharge and rhythms in playing billiards alone. And Virginia Woolf, maybe the classic vivid but unknowable Aquarius, wrote, "Each has his past shut in him like the leaves of a book known to him by his heart, and his friends can only read the title."[124]

As you can guess by now, Aquarian lovers are not the most tactile, demonstrative people on the zodiac wheel. Aquarians do not like love scenes that are wet and clingy, and they can be intensely annoyed by those who want to give and get affection in public. It can get very weirdly spooky to one who loves an Aquarius that the same person who was the life of the party only a couple of hours ago, when our friends were laughing and singing over our piano, can be so distant now that I'd like some intimate fireside time for just the two of us. Why is this? It's partly that Aquarius is made of air, and is more comfortable with the head than with the heart; while Aquarius can easily express what it thinks, it is, like Scorpio, a sign that has trouble expressing what it feels. Aquarius is also more strongly drawn to collective, communal situations that arouse an altruistic love of humanity than to close, romantic situations that come down to personal, passionate love for only one heart that is ready to give all, and wants to get a lot back.

When these moments of emotional truth come between an Aquarius and a lover who is more emotionally committed and engaged, they can be painful, and are doubly hard when the Aquarius is one of those who has forgotten or has not yet heard the poet Milarepa's warning that the one who always tells the truth often wounds another's heart. What looks open and vulnerable to a Piscean character can look needy to an Aquarius, who may mistake a heart that needs and deserves compassion for an emotional vampire. We've arrived at the tradeoff that makes love in the Aquarian Age a tricky prospect. We're accustomed to much more feeling in relationships than Aquarians normally want.

Can we expect in the years to come that romantic love as we've known it will die a lingering, operatic death under moonlight and clouds, oboes and strings? Is the giddy, dizzy rush of falling in love about to be history for us all?

No, thank Venus, who is still here. If anything, she gains strength now as we come to understand her forces of attraction and manifestation, the power of drawing what we seek toward ourselves—as long as it serves the highest good of all—rather than taking it in the manner of Mars, who sees only what he wants for himself. Love will still be with us. It is the strongest uniting, exalting force in the universe, and will not be overcome by fear, or sorrow, or any other dividing force.

What will pass away, though, is needy illusions that "you're nobody 'til somebody loves you" and that another person's love can validate the one who does not love himself. The Aquarian Age will have little patience with clingy lovers who fall hopelessly for people they can't have, thereby proving to themselves that they really do feel deeply, even if what they feel is mostly pain. Romantic operas about lovers who sing on their way to the guillotine, delighted that they get to ride in the same tumbrel together, will appear idiotic to the Aquarian mind, which focuses instead on how to demolish the guillotine and the punitive system that uses it. The Who could get away in the Piscean Age with a line like "I know I'm worth nothing without you." The Aquarian lover may respond to this by asking "If you're worth nothing without me, then how much can you be worth *with* me?" Needy "love" as a way to shore up self-esteem, or lose oneself in another, will get little respect, though it will still be a kind of acne phase that souls go through.

What will remain strong in the Aquarian age is the love principle that has been there all along, underneath all the dreams, beams, and desires: the power of love to purify and ennoble the soul, to catalyze the highest frequencies of kindness, compassion and mercy. As the most influential of the feminine cultures in our history—such as the French culture of the high middle ages—have shown, true love is a spiritual force that can refine and redirect even the molten mass of sexual desire into a flame that brings as much light as heat, and in the end can form a soul union much stronger than the surge of passion.

THE GODDESS RETURNS

The author confesses his bias. I'm a priest of the Moon, and this book was written largely because I do what she tells me, and I do my best to keep the appointment book straight. But isn't an allegiance to the Goddess, rather than impartiality to either sex, somehow un-Aquarian? Yes it is—but fortunately, our freedom will not be insulted in the years to come by an Un-Aquarian Activities Committee. We already know that among the core principles of Aquarius are equality and balance, including a balance of power and respect between the sexes. How, then, can anyone propose that we enter the Aquarian Age by honoring and re-empowering the feminine, and this is why the Goddess claims her place again in the center of our consciousness?

Easily, that's how, since the way to make scales balance is to place more weight in the pan that has less. To steer a ship onto a different course, we first turn the wheel hard to the new heading we want, then correct our course. It will work the same way now, as we will have to turn in the direction of the feminine in order to gain the balance we seek. The turn is already in progress, and the effects of it are visible enough. Threatened men pump themselves into taut balloons of rage—steroids and SUVs are only the physical signs—or work doubly hard to bar women from the corner office, the classroom, and the polling booth. Frightened women who are not ready to step into their power take refuge in traditional roles. Braver women glower out of faces that only a sculptor could love, and some ambitious women are already as easily corrupted by their new clout as any man has ever been, causing some people of both sexes to wonder what can possibly be the point of replacing the old domination of one sex with the new tyranny of the other. There is no way around this. We shall have to navigate it, and find the center, as smoothly as we can.

How can we be sure the turn is underway? By noting how hard those who are determined to block change are pushing against it. The two biggest new battlegrounds, at least in size and numbers, are the traditional societies of China and India, both of which have long had their ways of affirming the greater value of boy babies by doing away with the girls. China finesses this custom for the present by having enforced for years now a policy of limiting families to only one child. India, on the other hand, now enjoying an economic boom that turns this most spiritual of countries into one of the most avaricious, faces an ethical and moral issue that is thorny at the moment, and will get increasingly painful.

Officially, Indian law allows gynecologists to inform a pregnant woman about everything that her ultrasound test reveals about her baby's health, except for one thing. The doctor may not disclose whether the child is a boy or a girl, as the Indian government wishes to stop girls from being aborted by mothers whose value systems have become a lethal mix of the old and the new. India has long been a precarious place for women, averse to girls because dowries and wedding bills are high—so the new bride, while a welcome asset to her husband's family, is a rupee drain on her own. And the now-abandoned rite of suttee, in which a widow would be immolated on her husband's pyre, likewise made "economic sense," sparing her husband's family the burden of supporting one who was no longer an asset, but now only a mouth to feed.

As India gets richer, those who are under pressure to keep up with the Kumars would rather spend their money on a Mercedes with some trade-in value than on a little Indira who can only depreciate. The result is that abortion rates on girls are soaring in India's richest regions, despite the best efforts of the government, and the best ethics of doctors who inform their patients that revealing the sex of their baby is a punishable act. There are always ways around the law, even in a country less luxuriantly corrupt than India, and it's easy to find a doctor who will whisper a cryptic remark about how pink or blue booties will match the mother's sari.

A study by the Centre for Social Research shows that in South Delhi in 2004, the sex ratio at birth had dropped to 762 girls per 1,000 boys. Ratios in other areas, while not as low as this, are comparable.[125] Apart from the other relevant questions about changing outdated and cruel customs, and about abortion itself—the issue would not exist at all if human beings revered life, and practiced responsible birth control—no one seems to be asking what life in India will be like 20 years from now, when one of every four young men in South Delhi will not be able to find a mate, and will probably be about as patient and forbearing about this as frustrated young men usually are.

Another traditional society where women suffer much is Hawaii, a military base in an orchid forest, with all that this implies in bottled emotion under a surface of astonishing beauty. The islands are an uneasy mix of male supremacist elements: a male warrior ethos layered over an older, feminine aloha culture; traditional sex roles in the Chinese, Japanese, and other Asian subcultures; the sexist practices of Christian missionaries and fundamentalists; and an expanding military population. Not surprisingly, Hawaii has the highest reported rate of domestic violence in the U.S., and anyone who's lived there can see in the bruised faces and furtive eyes of women that the statistics tell only part of the story. Hawaii is, and will continue to be, a bellwether of social and spiritual ferment in areas related to the empowerment of women and the re-emergence of the Goddess. Two productions of *The Vagina Monologues* were staged there within a single year, yet Hawaii is full of men who refer to Stanley Kowalski-style halter undershirts as "wife beaters."

At the same time that old and new ways of oppressing women are negative evidence that the empowerment of women can't be stopped for long, the positive signs are rampant in the public spheres of business and popular "culture," and the question now is how long it will take to bring the inevitable changes into the private sphere of the home and the intimate space of love relationships. One thing that is clear enough is that most men view the return of the Goddess not as a sharing of power, but as a loss of it. Few of them will go along happily with the Aquarian trend toward free and equal relationships, much less help to create it. Women will have to do this. Some already are.

HUNTING WITH ARTEMIS AND SOME AMAZONS

One sign of women's new independence is the growth of organizations like *Co-Abode.org*, a website that matches single mothers in home-sharing arrangements that allow them to cut housing costs, live in safer neighborhoods with better schools, and work as a team in caring for their children and managing their house. Co-Abode founder Carmel Sullivan believes that women's need for a proactive choice, "a solution they can take in hand and not wait for social service or government," is one reason why her site has grown rapidly into a nonprofit organization with about 17,000 registered members.[126]

Co-Abode's key element is a blind email service that thousands of members have used for successful housemate searches. While not all matchups work out, most do. It helps that Co-Abode and its related networks are as expert and tenacious as they are in finding and spreading word about support groups and community health and education resources. Is this Aquarian teamwork at its most practical and effective? Yes. That's why it grows and morphs into other forms, like Golden Girl Homes, Inc., which serves single older women who don't need child-related help and news, but do want the expertise of financial planners and mortgage and realty experts who share their knowledge in classes and workshops that help members get smarter and more self-reliant with their money.

How do the men fit in to these scenarios? Sweetly and graciously, that's how. Divorced women brought together by Co-Abode and other networks work out their protocols for child visits by former spouses, who enter with permission and respect a home in which one woman is no longer struggling by herself, but two women now hold the cards and the chips. Housemates negotiate the rules and roles for male guests who stay overnight. And they find that their new teamwork makes them more flexible and inventive when the traditional man's job of authority and discipline is needed. One mother reports that she and her housemate "take turns playing the dad's role. 'If one person loses control of a situation,' she says, 'the other steps in so the other mom has a chance to collect herself.'"

Admirably enough, those who run these generally happy homes are too busy taking care of business to talk much about how empowering their life choice has been for themselves and their children. But both the negative evidence of furious last-ditch sexism, and newly confident sisterhood, are enough to show that for the old heavy hierarchy of unequal sex roles, the handwriting is now not just on the wall, as they say, but all over it. Men will have to adjust and accept relationships of balance and equality. Those who won't can still be lord and master if they want—as long as they don't mind ruling a kingdom of one.

American women, braced by decades of liberating action, can be polite but firm about all this. But African women, long pressed by the crueler agonies of tribal law and taboo, even the abomination of female genital mutilation, are taking less delicate measures. In the area of northern Kenya where the Samburu tribe lives, women who had been raped by British soldiers from a nearby training ground, and threatened with punishment by their husbands—who seek revenge not on the rapist, but on his victim—started the village of Umoja ("Unity" in Swahili) twenty years ago as a refuge for women seeking to live in safety from male violence and tribal injustice. The three dozen women who live in Umoja support themselves by making traditional bead necklaces and selling them to tourists. They've created more prosperous lives than they had before, earning enough to buy new clothes for themselves and send their children to school.

"We've seen so many changes in these women," reported Chief Rebecca Lolosoli. "They're healthier and happier. They dress well. They used to have to beg. Now, they're the ones giving out food to others."[127] So much for the idea that men are the only ones who can run an economy and gain what they want by force. An indignant husband who has roared into Umoja now and then, demanding that his wife come "home," has been sent away with a firm assertion that she doesn't need him anymore, and is better off now. "The women here are not saying they don't need men at all," says a schoolteacher who lives in Umoja. "The women are human beings and have needs. But the men who come just stay for a short time and then they go. They are boyfriends. That's all."

All that is missing in this scenario, apparently, is the bows and arrows the Amazons of Greek legend used to defend themselves from the greater size and strength of men. Will Umoja adopt the Amazons' custom of allowing men into their community only for the time needed to sire new children? In the short term, perhaps, though the longer-term Aquarian solution is likelier to be an egalitarian community of both sexes, rather than an enclave that excludes one sex in order to empower the other. Whichever way it goes in the decades to come, Umoja is clearly an example of the way Aquarian-minded people are gaining new confidence and freedom by throwing away old communal values that do not serve them, and creating new communal values that do.

SPIRITUAL LOVE

Aquarian love, in its emotional reserve and its aim of friendship and the common good, is not necessarily "higher" or "better" than the other dimensions of love we experience. It does not, and cannot, bring us to discard the passion, pleasure, intimacy, and joy we have known and treasured for so long. What Aquarian love will do is *complete* the treasure chest by adding to it the spiritual and communal love that will enhance all our other expressions of love. The richer love becomes in the soul, in other words, the richer it will also become in the body, the mind, and the heart. One way to look at this is in the four "fixed" signs of the zodiac. The symbols of the Bull, the Lion, the Eagle, and the Man or Angel, while familiar to Westerners as the four beasts seen by the prophet Ezekiel, and the four Christian gospel writers, are universal signs for the dimensions of the love experience.

Taurus the Bull is the Earth sign that rules the lusty month of May. It is sensuous, delighting in warm skin and wet thrills that get even juicier when they're served with candlelight, food and wine, heady aromas, and lush music. Taurus loves the possession of the beloved. When the song is "you're beautiful and you're mine," the Bull is singing.

Leo the Lion is the flame of love at its most joyous, in the full ripening of summer. The Lion embodies love on the plane of feeling. When the singer smiles about how "you make me feel," we're hearing Leo's voice.

The water sign of **Scorpio** is a whole system of symbols—scorpion, serpent, phoenix, and eagle—that represent different stages of the soul's alchemy. Scorpio is transformation and renewal in the chill of death after the harvest, naturally linked with the intense desire and passion of Eros, the crucible of love as purifying experience. When the song is about how love hurts and even kills, we're in the subsoil of Scorpio. When the song is about how love regenerates us, we're hearing the Eagle.

Aquarius month in mid-winter completes the cycle by affirming love as the energy of freedom, finding its highest expression in trust, acceptance of the beloved, and the release of all illusions and claims of control. When the singer says that "Love ain't for keeping," another line from The Who, then the Aquarian melody is on.

The Aquarius symbol has been called a Man, an Angel, and an Androgyne who combines the qualities of both sexes in harmonious balance. Whatever symbol applies, the bottom line is that Aquarius is by no means sexless, though his or her experience of love may be more airy than that of the other three fixed signs. Aquarius is most turned on by people who are stimulating, and share a commitment to freedom and empowerment. Those who are in the chase only for the having and holding, the joy and the juice and the risks, are apt to find Aquarius cool, even icy, when the Aquarius lives in realms of experience that are not yet seen and felt by those for whom love happens only from the neck down.

Ideal Aquarian love is less fixated on the beloved than on the friendship, altruism, liberty, and acceptance that he or she shares with the Universal Soul. In this sense the Aquarian may seem aloof when he or she is really detached, in that state of serenity, completeness, and freedom in which one does not need to possess or be validated by anyone. Like the hero Arjuna in *The Mahabharata*, who gains victory when he gives up all attachment to the outcome of the battle, the Aquarian soul realizes love most perfectly by letting go and giving the other unlimited space. Will human beings line up around the block for this? Not yet. For those who want to hold the Earth, drown in the water, and burn in the fire, the air is thin and cool way up there in the crystal sphere of total responsibility and freedom. The good news, though, is that we will not have to live there all the time in the Aquarian Age. And those who have never gone there may find their first visit bracing, even liberating. They may actually come to like the view, the easy mobility of traveling light, and the rare experience of moving at will between Heaven and Earth.

Alice A. Bailey, whose views on Aquarian education we read about in the last chapter, noted that one very attractive feature of the Aquarian Age is that we shall move beyond the heavy old tension between body and spirit, and the perception that spiritual action is an "enforced task [of] sacrifice and planetary service," founded on the Puritan premise that to free the soul, we must mortify the body. Some discipline, some process of initiation, is only to be expected as we transcend the illusions of ego and personality that come from our living in only one body at a time. Once the mind opens and the soul gains its full sweep of vision, then the awakened human being will live in service "from free choice and as a soul, conscious of intent and purpose *upon the physical plane.*"[128]

AQUARIAN PROFILE: ARUNDHATI ROY

At first glance, it's easy to wonder how this dizzyingly prolific writer and relentlessly passionate advocate of social and economic justice can possibly find the time and energy for lunch with a friend, much less for a marriage that she has sustained since 1984 to filmmaker Pradip Krishen. Yet her story is and will be one of the inspirational examples that show how the most committed Aquarian lives will get bigger and faster, spreading their force and focus from immediate families and livelihoods out to wider spheres of community, to activism on a national and global scale, and to the kinds of risks that can be taken only when one is in resonance with, and speaking eloquently for, the currents of change that are now sweeping through our planet.

Susanna Arundhati Roy was born on November 24, 1961, the daughter of a tea planter father. She started school at ten as the first "guinea pig" in a village school started by her Syrian Christian mother, the activist Mary Roy. She grew up in Kerala, studied architecture in New Delhi, and worked at an assortment of jobs until 1984, when Pradip Krishen cast her in his award-winning film *Massey Sahib*, and she began to concentrate on screenwriting. During her Saturn return year in 1991, she finished the script of her new husband's film *Electric Moon*, in which she also acted, and started work on her debut novel *The God of Small Things*, which showed how sudden and spectacular success can be when the Aquarian Age is about to begin.[129] The book was published in May 1996, was on sale in 18 countries a month later, and won the 1997 Booker Prize for Fiction.

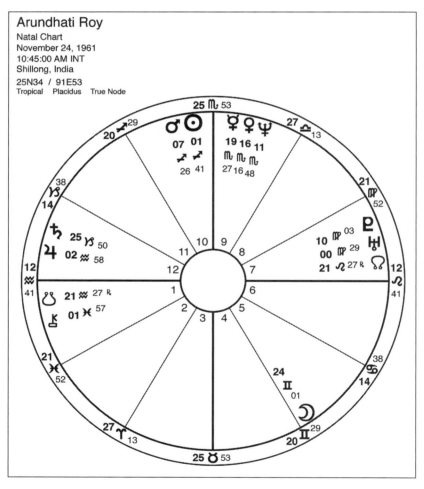

Estimated Birth Chart of Arundhati Roy

She could easily have launched a life of increasing wealth and success, and the ease and comfort that come with them. But as her astrology chart shows, she's not one to remain at a desk for long. Her birth time is unknown, and is usually reckoned at 12:00 PM, but the chart proposed for her here shows a birth time of 10:45 AM because it fits her gifts, accomplishments, and challenges, the arc of her life history, and the places on Earth where she is likeliest to live, speak, strive, and fight in the combative stance of one who speaks truth fearlessly to power.

Her astrocartograph for 10:45 AM shows planetary lines that conform closely to her experiences in India—and the lines on both coasts of her U.S. map are accurate.[130] Her Mars and Pluto lines cross near Washington, DC, showing an adversarial relationship with the American government, just as her Jupiter line through the California coast, especially San Francisco, fits an area where she is likely to gain recognition and support as an admired speaker and activist.

A look at her birth chart shows the nature of her heart and soul terrain, and the roughness of traversing it. Sun and Mars at near-conjunction in Sagittarius display a keen interest in politics and government, and a fierce courage in one's convictions. This is the chart of a brave being, having not one, but *two* T-crosses—that is, planets or major chart points across the wheel at an angle of 180°, with a third point at a 90° angle to both. Her Mars in Sagittarius squares both her Pluto in Virgo and Chiron in Pisces, indicating that much of her life will be a rumble against power (Pluto) for the sake of defending and healing the wounded (Chiron) who need a fierce, articulate voice. Her Mercury and Venus in Scorpio are in another T-cross, at 90° to her Moon's Nodes on the axis of Leo and Aquarius, so it is likely that her tenacity in pursuing her goals will attract fervent admirers (North Node) and detractors of the predictable kind (South Node), who invariably confuse opposition to governmental policies with hatred of the country itself.

As if all this were not stressful enough, the power planet Pluto also links in a powerful Y-shaped *yod* alignment with Saturn in Capricorn and the Moon in Gemini, thereby almost assuring that a highly communicative personality will work tirelessly in the combat zone where rigid, conservative forces that refuse to yield (Saturn) are in the fight of their lives with transformative forces (Pluto) that are here to sweep them away. One T-cross in a chart marks a soul who comes here knowing that life will require effort and courage. Two T-crosses and a yod are for those who accept, as Roy does, that "You have come to a stage where you almost have to work on yourself. . . . on finding some tranquility with which to respond to these things, because I realize that the biggest risk that many of us run is beginning to get inured to the horrors."[131]

As the horrors multiply, and along with them invitations to speak in so many places that she may seem at times to be a person who lives at the airport, how does Arundhati Roy find that anchor of tranquility? One way is in a long, apparently fulfilling marriage to a like-minded man who shares her view that "the world is divided into those who have a comfortable relationship with power and those who have a naturally adversarial relationship with power."[132] Roy's Venus in Scorpio signifies a person who keeps matters of the heart intensely private, as they say, who prefers a loyal, devoted relationship with her mate and requires the same fidelity in turn. While she and Krishen could easily play the power couple if they chose, their marriage, almost comically, provides no grist for gossip websites that have no choice but to list this famous pair, but can link only to "no data." Where is the scandal in a writer who dedicates her novel, as Roy did *The God of Small Things*, to "Pradip Krishen, my most exacting critic, my closest friend, my love"?

Is Arundhati Roy's love life typical of what we can expect in the Age of Aquarius? No, thankfully. Most of us will be less driven, and allow ourselves at least a little more languor, comfort and joy. Yet the features of an Aquarian love relationship are clearly here in a life that extends its focus out beyond home and family to spheres of communal, national and planetary life. And in Roy's optimistic certainty that "Another world is not only possible, she is on her way. On a quiet day, I can hear her breathing."[133]

Nothing about this life is typical. But it does show one thing about the Aquarian Age. The tough news is that we shall expend more effort, not less. But the easy news is that our capacities will expand too, so that we hit a new, empowered, more joyously engaged balance of knowing that what matters is "To love. To be loved. To never forget your own insignificance. To never get used to the unspeakable violence and the vulgar disparity of life around you. To seek joy in the saddest places. To pursue beauty to its lair. To never simplify what is complicated or complicate what is simple. To respect strength, never power. Above all, to watch. To try and understand. To never look away. And never, never, to forget."[134]

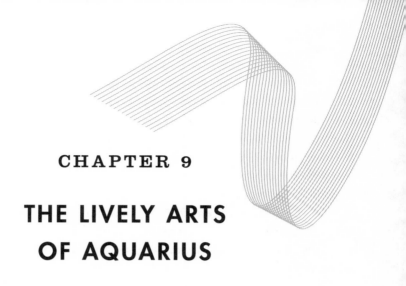

CHAPTER 9

THE LIVELY ARTS
OF AQUARIUS

Almost everybody's heard of the Seven Lively Arts, though how the phrase started is forgotten now. In 1923, amid a controversy about whether the jazz age was a dazzling new moment of bounce and joy that would liberate everyone from frock coats, black dresses, and stiff social rules—or was instead a quickstep to cultural ruin led by loose-legged entertainers who were not white in any sense of the term—Gilbert Seldes published a fearless book that took the "people's side" in yet another of the cultural struggles that have been going on, really, since the 16th century. That was when the spread of the printing press and the revolt of Luther and other Protestants broke the hold of the Roman Catholic Church over the cultural life of Europe, and opened the secular surge of the late Renaissance.

From that time, within certain limits, people were free to publish and read, paint and draw, play and sing and dance what they wanted. New, more popular art forms like the Elizabethan theatre were soon followed by newspapers and novels that reflected the lives and tastes of a rising middle class more interested in modern romance than ancient nobility. Music moved out of the church and into the home as more playable, affordable instruments made songs and sonatas accessible everywhere. People who used to endow paintings for the local church, with themselves in the corner and the saints in the center, now commissioned portraits of their families.

From the 18th century, with the church no longer a cultural censor, governmental and academic authorities have been asked to be, or have appointed themselves, the guardians of public morality. We have had a series of "culture wars" over questions of whether heroines like Emma Bovary and Hester Prynne are liberated or depraved. Whether sopranos who are not married but enjoy sex when they feel like it anyway—Violetta in *La Traviata*, Mimi in *La Boheme*, and scariest of all, Carmen, with a cigar in one pocket and a knife in the other—should be banned from the stage. It is just as well that the people in the 1880s who debated whether the waltz was obscene, and TV executives in the 1950s who ruled that the body of Elvis Presley should be shown only from the waist up, are no longer here to be knocked into apoplexy and despair by today's pop culture.

Gilbert Seldes' claim in *The Seven Lively Arts* that the new "demotic" arts of movies, jazz, and comic strips were as legitimate as theatre, orchestral music, painting, and sculpture was made possible in large measure by one fortunate meeting: between the physical genius of Charlie Chaplin, which liberated storytelling from words; and the new medium of motion pictures, which liberated even the poor from having to dress up for theatre and pay up for opera.[135] From then on stories would be fast, flashy, and funny, about characters who could be only as deep and round as two hours of running time could make them.

The term *Culture War*, both within societies and between them, is now being shouted louder and fiercer than ever before. In 2004, the government of Iran, for one, ruled that it will make an exception to its ban on all Western pop music by allowing the music of the singer formerly known as Cat Stevens to be sold in Iran. It helps, of course, that the artist converted to the Muslim faith and became Yusuf Islam only 34 years ago, in 1977. Now, rapidly changing pop culture throughout the "developed" world has placed censoring bodies in the paradoxical pinch of trying on one hand to maintain standards of cultural quality, while on the other realizing that nothing can be as useful for controlling people as mass media that are pitched to the lowest common denominator of mass intelligence. It was all problematic enough a few decades ago, when cultural watchdogs could say that when the arts are controlled by the Medici, we get Florence, and when they're controlled by commercial sponsors, we get canned laughter, crooked quiz shows, and Gomer Pyle.

Now, with hundreds of cable TV channels available in most high-tech countries, is there really any kind of cultural standard left? Is life now simply going too fast to produce culture in the way we've long understood it (and indigenous peoples still do)—as something to be grown, shaped, and refined over time? Are we in the strange position of having modern media that blasts images everywhere, yet creates little that's worth disseminating?

Not really. It only seems that way at the moment. The picture will clarify as more and more human beings awaken and realign their priorities, and especially as they develop new family structures and sources of love that fill their emotional and spiritual needs, so they'll no longer feel so terrified of silence, and so compelled to seek any stimulation, all the time, to fill the void in their hearts. The trend is already moving that way. The time is coming when the young will no longer hate their family lives so much that they'll seek any means to escape; and the old will no longer try to find in their jobs, their churches, their clubs, and everything else the acceptance and validation that people used to get in community. The more empowered we are, the less we will need to be entertained.

In the Aquarian Age, the arts will further enrich lives that are already rich, instead of only serving illusions for lives that are impoverished. What kinds of new art forms will we have in the Age of Aquarius, and what kinds of changes will we see in the arts that we already have? It's time to look at the contrast between Frank and Britney.

HOW TO SING IN PISCES,
AND LIP-SYNCH IN AQUARIUS

In 1944, when I was a day-old infant with such a thick head of black hair that the nurses at St. Vincent's Hospital in Brooklyn called me Frankie and took turns styling my hair to make me look like Frank Sinatra, professional singers had to be able to sing. Many of them looked like Frank, Tony Bennett, Bing Crosby, Nat King Cole, Ella Fitzgerald, and others who were not really hard to get used to looking at, but certainly weren't going to make it on beauty alone.

They hardly moved when they sang. They were anchored to bulky mikes on iron stands, and were lucky if the wires in this new medium of amplified sound didn't pop or boom or quit. And decades later, when they had lighter mikes that they could carry around the stage, they still hardly moved at all. Frank always said that once he got into his tux before the show, he would never sit down, even in his break between sets, until the show was over. Production values were simple: a singer in a suit or gown with an ensemble or small orchestra, and a few lighting changes, maybe none at all, during the show. Instruments were amplified only enough to back the singer, but never to compete with him, because every word of the song was important, and had to be heard. So the audiences listened.

Yes, teen audiences screamed and swooned when the singers were skinny and cute like Frankie, and later for Elvis and the Beatles. But the classic Piscean singers of the time before rock 'n' roll always preferred, when they could play them, the quieter venues, the clubs that could hold only a few hundred classy adults who sat still with their martinis, savoring every phrase of the song and the performer who seemed to be singing only to them. Each song about the memory of love's bliss and pain was so heartfelt and clear that it didn't have to last long, and usually took less than three minutes. The experience, though shared with a room full of others, was private when it really worked, and very intimate.

You can still hear singing like this in some places, though usually from rising stars, not the famous ones who can fill the big halls. The top ticket singers are now playing sports arenas and parks, to crowds so big that their video images are projected on screens next to the stage, so they can be seen by fans who can't get within a hundred yards of the stage. And what they're singing can be heard, and yes, there's a melody line, my friends here swear they heard it too, somewhere amid that cataract of amplified electronic sound. And I'm sure there were some words in there, though I couldn't tell you what they were.

Is the overwhelming sound storm and light spectacle of a rock concert a new Aquarian phenomenon? Not really. Though the technology is more sophisticated now, powerful multisensory experiences have been with us for centuries, since the first dazzling stage sets were built for baroque opera 400 years ago. Back then, court masques called for elaborate costumes and stage effects that Shakespeare never had at the Globe, where everything from Cleopatra's barge to Macbeth's dagger to the Moon were created in the audience's imagination, and no one had to see a silver crescent moving along a wire to believe that the pale, inconstant orb was really there. Now hardly anything is left to the imagination.

One of the tradeoffs we'll have to accept in Aquarius is that if we want all the brilliant spectacle and sexual thrill of beautifully toned blonde bodies bumping out a kind of vertical lap dance, we'll have to accept singers who may not even sing at all, but lip-synch the songs they recorded on equipment that enhances to the max whatever voice they do or do not have. The singer's look—at a time when wads of Britney Spears' used chewing gum sold online not long ago for as much as $14,000—is everything.[136]

Has all of the old intimacy been lost? Not entirely, because the true Aquarian musical medium is not a rock concert big enough to fill a racetrack. The new equivalent of Tony Bennett singing only to you at the Starlight Lounge is the MTV music video, now so influential that even Middle Eastern pop stars singing in Arabic are making them—they must be hugely grateful that all that belly dance practice is finally paying off.

Music videos tell us much about the coming Aquarian arts. They're longer than the old 2- to 3-minute pop songs from half a century ago, if only because no one wants to waste all the ensemble moves and big effects on a short song. The singer is shot in many costumes and sets, sometimes in a solo shot, sometimes with a dance team or crowd, or with the lover the star is inviting in or throwing out. It's all edited into a high-speed mix of images and colors, long and medium and special shots, with enough close-ups of the star's haloed face that the young person looking at it alone on the TV or computer screen can imagine, just as people did a lifetime ago, that the adored one is singing to them.

It's a tough act to compete with, and those who want to wean teenagers from electronic solitude and back into community are going to need something more potent than roller skates. This is why Aquarian communities will become both active and interactive in the way they create spiritual ceremony and entertainment. Old barriers that used to separate a worshipful audience from the idol performer will dissolve. Many who have forgotten their voices, or never found them, will discover their own resonance. Some singers will even address the heart again, not just the eye. Until we get there, though, and our people have located their voices and are ready and brave enough to use them, what kinds of new art forms can we expect, and what variations on the old ones we already have?

A WORD ABOUT THE WORD

Traditional and classical arts will continue to attract both new artists and the spectators and listeners who appreciate them, though it's inevitable that the experience of meeting the work of art will shift away from solitary encounters with a book, a painting or sculpture, or a work of recorded music that one enjoys alone, and toward communal encounters with a live performance or a recorded story seen on screen. Words will no longer be abstract units of meaning, and will become units of sound that carry vivid pictures and resonate in our hearts because of what we feel about them, not what we think they mean. James Joyce may have been correct in claiming that literature is the highest and most spiritual of the arts, but the plain fact is that we are now in a time when the sanctity of the written word has largely been lost, and it is no longer the primal tone of creation, but a marketing tool and hook of desire, a bone that anchors the muscles of a story.

Even those who still respect the word hardly have any time to read. One sign of the times has come from China, where novelist Qian Fuzhang, convinced that it is "cruel to force readers to wrestle with a 200,000-word book," has published his mini-novel *Out of the Fortress* not in print, but on the screen of a cell phone.[137] Subscribers can read a 70-word installment on their mobile phones twice a day, so in a month they'll have read the whole 4,200-word story. At this rate, reading *War and Peace* or *Ulysses* could become the labor of a lifetime, and in another century people who've read hundreds of these books could become as rare as the few Chinese sages who actually knew all 50,000 characters in the Mandarin writing system. Will literature become twitterature? We'll see.

We focus now mainly on the performing arts, and on new art media that we experience in community. The coming time will address in its own new terms the practical meaning of the poet Horace's famous phrase that poetry, and all art, should be *dulcis et utile*, sweet and useful. The sweet part is easy if the poem or story gives us pleasure, even the somber pleasure of tragedy or the intellectual pleasure of satire or philosophy. The useful part has always been much trickier. Is the work of art useful if it helps us become more morally sound and responsible? Or better parents and citizens? Or more reverent toward the gods? The common thread in all these choices is that art is useful if it brings us into conformity with religious or civil values. This was the standard of state-sponsored tragic theatre in Athens, which other codes of "redeeming social value" try to uphold today.

The Aquarian emphasis, however, will be radically different, The point of art in the coming time will be to free and heal the individual, and help bring him and her into the self-realization that awakens the potential of each one, and thereby makes the one most useful to the whole. Unlike earlier Ages, in which you didn't have to find yourself on Earth as long as you found a place in Heaven, the Aquarian Age expects you to find your gift and your power with the help of your friends, and thereby have much more to give to your community and your planet. How will you and your friends help and stoke another? With the Play of Light and Medicine Theatre.

THE PLAY OF LIGHT

Since June of 2004, we've been in the eight-year phase between two *Venus passages*—the rare event that comes once in a century, always in pairs, when Venus can be seen to move across the face of the Sun. The second and climactic Venus passage in the set we see now will come in June of 2012. These eight years, like the four Venus passages since the early 1500s, are bringing transformative new discoveries in technologies of light, and whole new ways of perceiving it.[138]

So far the Venus passages of 2004–2012 are playing true to form. We are already seeing a technological flowering extraordinary even by the standards of the last 30 years, and it is evident enough that we are at the most important transition in light entertainment and communications in more than a century. The holy grail of our present light technology, the 3D motion picture, is about to replace the old 2D movies we have had until now. This theatre of light will be the essential transformative technology of the Aquarian Age. To understand how it works, and what its implications are, it's worth our while to understand the difference between effects that are literally smoke and mirrors, and 3D video images that we'll soon be able to combine into whole 3D motion pictures.

The 3D movies of the Aquarian Age are not *holograms*, which use mirrors to shoot still photographs of an object from two different directions, then combine the 2D images to create a 3D image that can only be displayed under carefully controlled conditions. The limitations of a hologram are that it's static, monochromatic, and it can't be displayed in open space, but only on an interference medium, like stage smoke.

The 3D film and video images that are developing now look like holograms, but are made in a different way. It works like this: I dress you in a costume and put you in front of a contrasting solid-color background. I shoot video footage of you as you speak your lines and do your moves. Then we pull off the amazing effect. We project your image through a fish-eye lens onto a concave surface, so that instead of staying flat on a screen, as a 2D image does, your image pops out several feet away from the surface, and we see you in full color, talking and moving naturally in thin air.

This technique is already being used in high-tech trade shows and training seminars to create moving, full-color 3D video images about the size of your head. As the technology improves, it's only a matter of time before life-size images of humans, animals, angels, and deities can be created for theatre, appearing in surprising ways among live actors, and vanishing or moving up and out. Dolphins and whales swimming through the space. Ghosts and memories. We can't say whether Shakespeare would have used 3D video to make Macbeth's dagger appear. But he would have been tempted to use it for ghosts, or the famously unstageable scene in which phantom images of the future kings of Scotland all stream from the Weird Sisters' cauldron.

And the Madonna—the original one, the Virgin Mary—could be projected in any place where the concave projection surface is kept clear of traffic. It is easy to imagine how those who want to move devout, impressionable believers to fervid, unflinching action could make 3D images of Jesus and the saints, the dove of the Holy Spirit, Shiva, the Buddha, or Saladin appear suddenly to multitudes of people. What would preachers of the crusades not have given for a way to make St. Michael the Warrior himself appear in the cathedral and sing the call to holy war? What would *mujahedeen* in Baghdad and death merchants in Washington not give to make the Mahdi, Patton, John Wayne, or whoever else fires up the rough and the righteous, seem to materialize before their troops?

Like any new technology, 3D video will quickly be adapted to both the applications that matter most in the "developed" world: war and entertainment. The military possibilities—cloaking armies, or making ghost warriors appear, like the Angels of Mons who inspired the British in the First World War—are obvious. So are home movies, exciting enough to get couch potatoes up off their feet to fight and dance with 3D characters appearing all around them, in stories so "real" that you don't need goggles or a helmet for virtual reality anymore, and you can turn your own living room into any place in the world. This too is on the way sooner than we think. Right now a 16-year-old girl in artfully torn jeans is sending an application to the MIT Media Lab, and all she needs to get Holozone Home Fantasy off the drawing board and into the money is access to better equipment than she has at home.

REMEMBERING HOW TO REMEMBER

Those who are worried about their children turning into electronic zombies had best get used to the challenge. This danger will not go away, and tough love will not stand a chance against entertainment technologies that grow more seductive by the year, if not by the month. Decades ago, in the 1990s, the Japanese used the term *famikon adi-kuto*—family computer addict—to describe boys who'd become so attached to computers that they lost all interest in their families and friends, in school and sports, even in girls. When the computer gets so compelling that it replaces the opposite sex as the thing a boy wants, then something, and it may be more momentous than young Hiroshi, is about to shift.

Much has already been written about the deadening effects of not just the dumb-down entertainments, but also of the ways our communication technologies can stunt our ability to observe and remember, even to see what is right there in front of us. We needn't dwell on the danger to children who learn to use, as soon as they know their alphabet and some numbers, recording devices that liberate them from any need to remember anything. We can imagine with wonder how acute our memories must have been before there was any photography, even any electricity—when an experience had to be observed attentively, for there would be no replay, no chance to rewind. We marvel that people living centuries ago could hear a poem or a play once, and remember whole passages perfectly. We are charmed by stories of fathers who awakened their children in the dead of night, took them to the railroad tracks, and told them to remember what they were about to see as they waited for the train that carried the body of Abraham Lincoln from

Washington, DC back to Illinois. And the children did remember, every detail.

To some, memory itself will seem to be a casualty of the Age of Aquarius; as electronic technologies turn our communications and entertainment into rapid streams of picture and sound, so not much is likely to stay with us for long. We'll remember what we've just seen about as well as we remember a fireworks display. We'll recall the evening and the place and our companions, and the booming sounds and bursts of color. But the streaks and petals of light in the air will be impossible to describe as anything more than brief, brilliant impressions. The images of Aquarius are designed to dazzle, not to last.

Are we going to regain our powers of memory, or improve anyone else's by throwing away our home entertainment centers and limiting the time our kids get to spend with their technotoys? No, unless we want adolescent rebellion to heat into full-scale revolt. The fascination with toys is something that the soul must pass through, even if this takes more than one lifetime. To regain memory, then to purge what we don't need and keep what we do, we'll have to do what communities have always done, relying on the whole circle to help us remember what we can't recall alone. Much of what our ancient communities did, and what we now learn to do again, is memory tricks. Symbols in the village by day and the sky at night, taught from old to young. Chants of planting and reaping, blessing and mourning and welcoming. Stories of love and honor and sacrifice.

And quilts. The women who sewed them were community historians, telling each other the story of every patch and piece that went into the whole, so that a completed quilt was a work of history and memory, carrying the stories of those who were most honored and beloved. This is why the Memorial Quilt is far more than a huge work of folk art and a remembrance of loved ones who have died of AIDS. Like all true tribal mnemonics, it is an act of love—and a reminder that love and memory are inseparable. When one is strong, so will the other be. How to strengthen both? One way is by telling new mythic stories and old stories in ways that speak to us in fresh and unexpected ways, and at such depth that they heal and renew us. By creating Medicine Theatre.

MEDICINE THEATRE

Everyone who investigates how plays work and how they touch us emotionally knows the famous description of tragedy by Aristotle, who wrote that a tragic play achieves catharsis by arousing and purging the emotions of pity and fear. This is why, even though we may not feel bubbly with talk when the play is over, we feel cleansed and lightened by the experience, as though the hero's suffering has pulled out and lifted away what was heavy in us. It's easy to imagine, then, that if the "negative" emotions of pity and fear could be stimulated and boiled away, then perhaps all the lower emotional frequencies, all grief, envy, anger, shame, and everything else that is not love, could be triggered and chased, leaving us in a state of serenity and bliss.

Has anyone thought of doing this before? Yes. Many times, for many centuries. This purifying of the emotional field is the essence of the alchemical work done by those who knew, and communicated through symbols, that what we hope to find in the crucible is not just metal. What remains in the heart after the lead of grief, the iron of wrath, the tin of pride and the other lesser metals are all burned away is the gold of love.

THE ANCIENT EGYPTIAN RITUAL PLAY

Who were the first people to experiment with this? The ancient Egyptians. They were, after all, the teachers of the Greeks who invented tragedy and comedy, and the masters of so much else that Herodotus wrote of Egypt as a land of uncountable, unfathomable mysteries and wonders. As we learn more about the Egyptian festival cycle and ritual play, we now meet the tantalizing question again: Were the annual re-enactments of the great mythic stories, especially the legend cycle of Isis, Osiris, and Horus, really "plays" as we understand them, staged long before the Greek storyteller Thespis is said to have invented theatre? What evidence do we have that a director-priest in Dendera might have yelled "Louder! And faster!" long before anyone in Athens did? And if the Greeks sought to purge pity and fear in their tragic plays, what did the Egyptians aim to do with theirs?

The evidence, as deciphered and understood so far, is skimpy. We know the Egyptians celebrated the events of the Isis story each year in places all along the Nile where Isis found and buried parts of Osiris' dismembered body. We know the Egyptians celebrated in gorgeous color and music, procession and ceremony, the festivals of Ra, Hathor, Thoth, Sekhmet and other *Neters*. We have evidence in stone and papyrus for a ritual play of the battle for kingship between Horus and Set, and a duet sung by Isis and her sister Nephthys. We know that plays were enacted on stages floating in the sacred lake of Hathor's temple in Dendera. And scholars, notably Maged Samuel Ibrahim, have reconstructed actual music from the time of the pharaohs, some of it clearly meant to be sung by people in motion, perhaps as Greek choruses sang the *parodos*, or parade, as they entered the stage.

What does all of this background from some 4,000 years ago have to do with us now, at the dawning of the Age of Aquarius? Only that so much of what looks new in Aquarius is really lost wisdom so old that we've forgotten it. But we're remembering now. One of the keys to Aquarian Medicine Theatre is ancient ritual theatre as the Egyptians may have practiced it: a highly interactive, omnisensory healing art in which the participants were led through precisely calibrated frequencies of color, sound, aroma, taste, and movement, all designed to clear the cellular memories of all the people united in the sacred story.

The texture of the play is intricate, as it's designed to open all the body's chakras, or energy centers, which were as well understood by the ancient Egyptians as by their fellow adepts in ancient India. But its design is a simple sequence of eight steps. We can imagine how the priest and priestess/performers might have begun the play by leading the celebrants—all too actively engaged to be a passive "audience"—into the root chakra at the base of the spine. The red of the root chakra was the main color of costumes, curtains, and ritual objects. Songs and vigorous rhythms were accompanied by drums and sistra, as the root chakra is percussive. Incense, aromatic oils, herb teas and ritual foods would be used to help activate the root center completely. From the story of the Moon and the Serpent, respective planet and symbol of the root chakra, the play went next to the orange zone of the navel, or birth chakra, and to bowed strings played with the caressing motion of Venus. To new dances, aromas, and flavors. Then to yellow, and so on up the energy column of the body until every chakra was open and activated, and everyone in the play was cleansed, energized, and tuned. After two hours of this, all the celebrants may have come out of the temple buzzing from toe to crown, and likely would have been quite happy to come back and do it again. Is it any wonder that the Egyptian civilization lasted longer than any other, with a run of almost 4,000 years?

TRANSFORMANCE SPACES

If, as it appears, the point of the Egyptian spirit play was not just to amuse the people, and not even to honor and praise the Neters, but to bring about a spiritual cleansing of the celebrants, then the theatre space, the way it was used, and the relationship between performers and audience must have been different from what we generally experience in theatre. Aquarian Theatre, like its ancient Egyptian counterpart, will not be as passive as theatre has usually been in the Piscean Age.

It is likely that the more communal theatre we are now beginning to create will involve all celebrants in singing and even moving, as active religious rituals do, but that most of the play will consist, as plays do now, of scenes played by the main cast and watched by everyone else. Thus the new Aquarian spirit play will alternate between big interactive scenes and vignettes and musical pieces that actors will play to advance the story. This kind of design can't be played in a conventional fixed-seat auditorium. It requires an open room that can be used flexibly, like a Transformance Space.

Imagine a black box theatre, and then increase it in size into a room large enough to hold hundreds of people. Allow them all to move together, or to clear large open areas for scenes played by the main cast. There is no fixed seating, though there are mobile seats and cushions. There are movable platforms and large set pieces such as boats and temple pylons, but there is almost no solid furniture.

Scenes and objects are created by video projections, cloth curtains, and paintings. Live and recorded music will permeate the Space through wall speakers and transducers in the floor, so that vibrations of sound can enter the bodies of performers and audience through the soles of their feet, and through other parts of their bodies that touch the floor. There are also diffusers and exhaust fans for inserting and clearing aromas, and facilities for preparing and serving herbal teas and other food and drink. The most distinctive feature of the Transformance Space is its state-of-the-art technology of light. The Space will be lit with color healing filters as well as conventional gels. Some of the actors' costumes will be made of iridescent fabrics that reflect light and color. Lasers will create sacred geometric shapes, and video cameras will bounce 3D images off concave wall surfaces to create multi-colored, moving 3D light images in the air above the main playing areas.[139]

CELLULAR MEDICINE THEATRE

The point of production design is not only to make the show spectacular. The Play of Light is designed above all to realize the underlying premise of transformational theatre in the Aquarian Age: that the more light human beings can absorb into the cells of our bodies, the nearer we approach our potential as energy beings who are composed not of physical matter, but of light. In this way Medicine Theatre aims to assist, by building the light bodies of the celebrants, what the Egyptians called the Will to the Light.

The Medicine Theatre and Play of Light in the Age of Aquarius are arts of empowerment because they aim to create experiences that combine ancient and modern technologies of art and science to get the play all the way into the cells of the body, flush out the ancient fear, guilt, and pain, and lift the bodies and souls of performers and celebrants into a new freedom and a direct recognition of the Universal Soul that unites all human and spiritual beings. This knowledge is being seeded simultaneously into thousands of human beings all over the planet, with so many now working on art-and-healing experiments, and mixes of performance and holistic medicine, that no one knows "whose project" it is. The main question is how we're going to link up and play it all for everyone's benefit. Since there's only one art form that's always played fast, it's time for a look at Aquarian Comedy.

WHAT'S SO FUNNY ABOUT AQUARIUS?

As Aquarius is the 11th zodiac sign, it naturally corresponds in the astrology chart to the eleventh house of Friends, whose relationships are likely to be social, talkative, inclusive, festive, intuitive, and spontaneous, full of jokes and stories and the give and take of a game among equals rather than the wait-and-worry of life, work, and death in a hierarchy. Now if that doesn't describe the way people are in a comedy troupe, what does?

While it would be simplistic to claim that the fading Age of Pisces is tragic and Aquarius is going to be comic—our words for both tragedy and comedy came from the Greeks in the Age of Aries, and the Piscean Age gave us Shakespeare, Moliere, Gogol, Cervantes, and countless other funny people, many of whom were artists of the highest quality, goofy by design—it remains true that the arts of Pisces have been subtle, secret, silent, and profound as the sea, while the arts of Aquarius are airy: bright, quick, light, and fun.

Aquarius, as we enter it now, is an Age of the Trickster, and there's comedy tonight! The farce—a technical term for comedy of increasing confusion leading to chaos—is already underway, as the Figaro and Scaramouche scenes between the Keystone Kops on top and the Stealth Clowns in the streets seem to multiply daily. We see played out hourly the difference between tragedy and comedy:

In the tragic universe, human beings suffer because we are wicked and corrupt—and this is why stories of Saviors who come to rescue us from our own sin and E-word are hardy perennial myths, popular and marketable for millennia on end. The tragic universe is a vale of tears for believers who expect hardship on earth and fear hell after death, and "know" it will never get better because human nature is sinful and will never change.

In the comic universe, though, human beings do not suffer because we are vicious and utterly unworthy of "God." No. We get walloped in the rear end again because we are, at least for the moment, as Harry Truman once kindly put it, mentally incomplete. This is why so many comic stories are about otherwise sensible people who have been deranged by the madness of love or the glare of gold, or who are not quite shrewd enough to see the fine line between a get-rich-quick scheme and a stupid crook story.

The exception to all the folly, though, is the true mother lode of Aquarian comedy: wit and stratagem, in which the clever servant or student outwits the slow-minded boss. This scenario is, naturally, as old as the hijinks of the hoi polloi cooking up a funny thing on the way to the Acropolis. And servants in Shakespeare and Moliere pulling a fast one on Malvolio and Tartuffe. Such comedies abound when the rumble of rebellion is in the air. This is why Figaro and Scaramouche ruled the boards in Paris in the years just before the French Revolution. And Charlie Chaplin ruled the screen all over the western world when labor unrest seethed from the Great War to the 1930s. "Give me a cop, a park bench and a pretty girl, and I can make a comedy anywhere," Chaplin said, re-creating the classic formula in which Wit and Beauty team up to outwit Force.

Comedy, by its very nature, is revolutionary. This is why Tricksters grow more numerous and daring with every decade since the 1960s, in countries where authoritarian control is strongest. Apart from all the fun, though, the element that makes comedy one of the noble and compassionate art forms is its aim to bind up the wounds after the attack, heal the pain, and live together happily again. Of all the differences between tragedy and comedy, this one may be the most practical and urgent for us. In a tragedy, conflict *intensifies* into a struggle so implacable that the results are mortal; order, if it can be restored at all, can never be quite the same. In comedy, conflict *complicates* through one mistake after another, but order is restored in the end, and separation resolves into union and festivity.

The main emotional force of comedy in its purest form is the unity of all beings, as expressed in stories of people who work and fight and plot against each other until they see the misunderstanding that had set them against each other in the first place—and find some way to forgive everybody, even the one who dissed them really deep and bad. The actual ideas of Jesus are the principles of comedy, as articulated beautifully in Joseph Meeker's *The Comedy of Survival*: that everyone is included, every role is important, and in the end all is forgiven and we have feasting, marriages, and new life. When comedy works at its very best, it is medicinal and spiritual. It accepts and forgives all things.

THEN WHAT'S SO FUNNY ABOUT SEX?

Love accepts and forgives all things too. And there are other links between comedy and sexuality besides the one we've already noted, in the way love has of making mortals the fools Puck knows them to be. Comedy is always life-affirming, and usually ends in matches and marriages, and the not-so-subtle hint that the attractive young people you've seen running around in the woods for the last two hours are about to make new babies, and help the wheel of life keep turning.

Confusion in sex roles and identities is one of the richest veins in the mine of comedy, and has been long before *Twelfth Night*, when Olivia falls in love with Viola, who's pretending to be a man, then marries Viola's twin, who *is* a man, while Viola loves Orsino, who's in discomfort over his feelings for one he thinks is a boy, and so on. We can expect much more of this in the Aquarian Age, as the unique androgynous identity of Aquarius is already impacting our love lives and the ways we define our sexuality—and whatever uncertainty and confusion we experience in life, we'll meet in double measure in the comic realm, where every quirk we've got is magnified.

So stories like *The Rocky Horror Show, Victor Victoria, Tootsie, La Cage aux Folles, Shakespeare in Love*, and *Elizabeth*—in which the queen makes the tragic choice of sacrificing sex for power, and turning herself into a whitened virgin—are only the beginning. So are entertainers like David Bowie and Boy George, Alice Cooper and Elton John,

Marilyn Manson and Mick Jagger, Madonna tongue-kissing Britney Spears, and a host of Unidentified Flaming Objects.

Is much of this gender looping done just for shock's sake, and because weird sex sells? Yes, of course. But much of it is not, and reflects instead what an artist is supposed to do in exploring realms of uncharted experience, and coming back to tell the story. Some of the Aquarian stories that we shall see acted again and again are of the man who explores his female side, and prefers to make it his new home; the woman who finds her male side so empowering that she doesn't want to let it go; the couple who change places and stay together, and the couple who part when one wants to switch and the other won't budge. In ways that we're only beginning to envision, sexual identity will be one of the Aquarian frontiers where heroes dare to fly and flat men fear to peek.

More than any era in our history, the Age of Aquarius will be a time when some of us will change sex roles as comfortably as we change clothes, and even turn the round of self-reinvention into an art form in itself, a kind of ongoing detective story in which there are no bodies and no need to find a murderer, but the game becomes instead one of following a trail of shifting clues so contradictory and unpredictable that the artist's life becomes a magic show in itself, a display of Uranian trickery so dazzling that no one minds if in the end it is all flash and no finish, perhaps even a mirror ball with nothing inside. This is how it went with the one who was, in all his glory, strangeness and mystery— perhaps the first truly great Aquarian artist.

AQUARIAN PROFILE: MICHAEL JACKSON

We won't try to reinvent the wheel here by adding new facts to what may be the most tirelessly researched and gossiped life of our time. Rather we'll look briefly at this artist as both a mythic figure in himself, and as a screen on which billions projected their love and envy, fury and need, obsession, devotion, vice, and vanity. If Marilyn Monroe was right in saying, "They don't see me. They only see their own lewd desires," then what did they see when they looked at Michael Jackson?

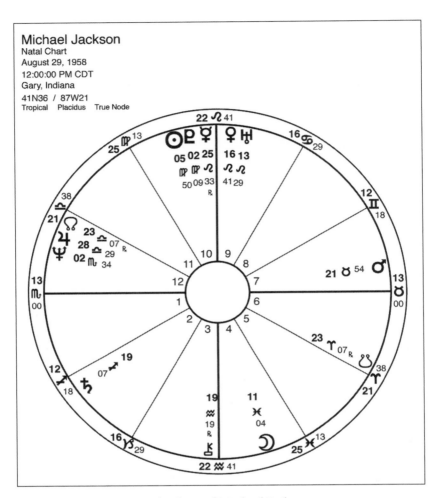

Birth Chart of Michael Jackson

The material of heroic myth is clearly there: incandescent talent and energy burned so flamboyantly that Icarus comes to mind; the trailblazing feats of breaking the color barrier on MTV and revolutionizing music video as an art form; the astonishing *Thriller* album, which sold 50 million copies and set a standard of success so impossible to equal that for the next twenty years, Jackson's other works that sold "only" 10 million or more seemed failures. The comparisons with

Mozart have often been made: in a domineering father who steered the boy away from childhood and into stardom at four; in love of clothing, games and toys; and in boyish innocence extending far into adulthood, and a yearning in both music and life to recapture the joy and freedom of getting to be a child.

Jackson's astrology chart is far more revealing than the man himself. Pluto conjunct Sun in Virgo is a combination that may indicate a drive to success so ambitious that it brings power, or at least a fierce hunger for it. Venus conjunct Uranus and Mercury near the Mid-Heaven in Leo shows an aspiration to stardom through performance, and the sizzling charisma to achieve it. His Ascendant in Scorpio is likely to manifest as a personality that is sexually magnetic, strongly emotional, yet likely to keep emotions hidden under a cloak of privacy and disguise. His Dragon's Head is in the twelfth house of mystery and secrets, so he tended to have a small circle of associates, and keep them well hidden—or have short associations, as with the groups of children whom he hosted at Neverland.

Fascinatingly, Jackson's Chiron position in Aquarius is opposite the midpoint between his Venus and his MidHeaven—and both are at a 90° "square" to his Mars in Taurus—suggesting that his relentless energy and his deep wounds may have been the price of the fame that creating beauty brings. And his Moon in Pisces is opposite to his Sun in Virgo, as he was born at a Full Moon.

This kind of Full Moon personality does have its contradictions, most easily seen in the way that the male and female features of one's being can seem not only to pull in opposite directions, but never to have been introduced to each other at all. How else can one explain a void in self-esteem so deep that the adoration of a billion fans can't fill it, and the artist feels compelled to proclaim himself the King of Pop? How else can we imagine why a man who sincerely loves children would dangle his own infant son off a hotel balcony to the horror of fans and reporters standing below? Why would a person who seems to have done no wrong in his relationships with children pay $20 million to settle a lawsuit brought by the father of a boy who testified to Jackson's innocence? And even if we accept that he had to take skin-lightening treatments in response to the pigment-destroying disease vitiligo, how is it possible that a man blessed with so much beauty would wish to destroy it with needless structural surgery on a once-angelic face?

Why would one who enjoyed a happy collaboration with Paul McCartney then proceed to alienate his friend by buying control of the entire Beatles catalog? Why, for that matter, would one who gave himself so generously to charity work, gave so much of his own money to people in need, and achieved his own extremely successful body of work, want to own the entire musical output of Elvis Presley too? This last question, as Dick Gregory explained in a radio interview in the spring of 2003, is at the core of the legal proceedings that were aimed at Jackson for decades. As the combined Beatles and Presley catalogs are worth billions and appreciate in value every year, how likely is it that the powers that be would have left such prizes in the keeping of a man who was still African American, and was far more committed to the children of Africa and the entire planet than he was to the people and institutions of any one country?

The doubts will continue, and diversify. "We're targets, you know," Errol Flynn used to say of the perils of being a movie star. And even when the famous one is not actually under attack, he will still be under incessant pressure everywhere he goes. The impulse to go to ground must become irresistible, until one decides to go one of two ways: either hide for self-preservation, or ride the public fascination like a wave, inventing whatever tricks and masks and outrages are needed to stay atop the crest.

For many people, not just megacelebrities, the Aquarian Age is the first one in which our identities have become so mobile that we are free to reinvent ourselves again and again, at least to inhabit a series of characters that others believe. In the Piscean Age, it was always understood that the public face one presents may conceal mysteries. The theme of the reality behind the appearance has been with us for millennia, ever since Plato wrote that Socrates was rough and ugly on the outside but inexpressibly beautiful within. If the Piscean image may be as deep as the sea, the Aquarian image may be only as deep as the screen on which it is projected, whether the screen has physical substance or is made only of the viewer's fantasies of who he wishes he could be. Time may never tell whether Michael Jackson was the bewildered child he appeared to be, or a master trickster whose festival of illusion captured and rode the energy of millions.

As he was born in 1958, Michael Jackson came to his Chiron return in late 2008, only months before his death.[140] Did he integrate and transcend his wounds, and thereby help to heal the countless lives that pivoted on him and tracked his light? Time may tell.

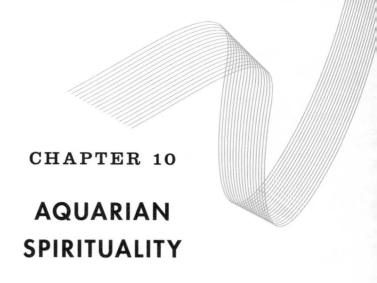

CHAPTER 10

AQUARIAN SPIRITUALITY

Will there be a new Aquarian religion? No—though there will be communities of believers who build their lives around new sacred writings and teachings, and new beliefs and principles. Such new religions always appear. But they won't be Aquarian because the Aquarian Age favors spirituality rather than religion, if only because spirituality entails union and friendship, even celebration, while religion is often a kind of organized unworthiness that sets itself the impossible task of healing a separation that does not exist. And religious scenarios can be inherently conflictive when those who imagine "God" to be a fortress will see themselves as against others, not just different from them.

In the Aquarian Age we'll be empowered together to create the new Earth, and this is why our most disempowering religions are losing their hair shirts—and have to sell their buildings, which, in a sign of the times, get turned into community centers. This power issue, as understood by Dr. David Hawkins in *Power vs. Force*, is at the core of today's spiritual shift. "The makers of the Declaration of

Independence," he wrote, "were astute in drawing a very clear distinction between that which is *spiritual* and that which is *religious*. And they must have intuitively, if not rationally, known the marked difference between the power of the two. Religion is often associated with force, sometimes disastrously so, historically and today; whereas spiritual concepts such as loyalty, freedom and peace don't create strife or conflict, much less war. Spirituality is always associated with nonviolence."[141]

Amen. Our aim here is to look at new spiritual ideas and movements that gain subtle, irresistible strength because they're rooted in the power of love, not the rush of hate. Aquarius is a time of spiritual *practice*. As the Age that now begins is for doing rather than refraining from doing, for embracing and not for avoiding, and for affirming that love is true when it moves belief into compassionate action, we gather in Aquarius to celebrate the divinity in us all.

ANGELS OF AQUARIUS

As we've already seen, especially in political events such as the American independence movement and the French Revolution, the coming Age announces itself well before it becomes "official." The same is true of new spiritual forces. Vedic hymns from the late Age of Taurus have a spiritual fire more like the monotheism of Abraham and Akhnaten than the earthy bull veneration of Crete and Mesopotamia. Late in the Age of Aries, Lao Tzu and Chuang Tzu in China taught Taoist ideas of the cosmos as a harmonious flowing of light and dark, yin and yang forces into one another. This duality, so beautiful and balanced—and the grimmer conflict of good and E-word in the religion of Zoroaster—are more Piscean than Arian in their belief that the world is not one, but two, and that life is therefore a fight at worst, a graceful juggling act at best.

It's the same with the transition from Pisces to Aquarius. We will look here at a few late Piscean religious movements, all embodying principles of Aquarius, all influential among spiritual activists who seek to draw human beings together in peace and understanding.

BAHA'I: THE PATH OF GLORY

The 19th century, in its optimistic belief in human progress and our ability to meet all our needs and solve all our problems, was the ideal breeding ground for new religions that would appear as offshoots of established faiths—and inevitably be persecuted by them—and would share a common interest in respect for all religions.

This toleration can be dangerous, as young Siyyid 'Ali-Muhammad Shirází found when he revealed to the people of Shiraz in May, 1844 that he was the *Bab* ("Gate") who shared with his disciples, called the "Letters of the Living," a mission to prepare the way for "One greater than himself" who would come to fulfill the prophecies of the world's great religions. Thus began the religion known as Baha'i, from one of the sacred names of Allah, meaning "glory." Initial results were predictable. Some 20,000 Babis were martyred, and the Bab himself was executed in 1850 at the instigation of Muslim clerics.

The promised one was already known. Before his passing the Bab privately named Mirza Husayn-'Ali-i-Nuri as the awaited Baha'u'llah, the "Glory of God." The Baha'u'llah proclaimed himself in 1863 while in Turkey, after having spent some years writing in the relative safety of Iraq. He was to spend the last 40 years of his life in prison and exile, finally passing away in Acre, then a prison city in what is now Israel, where the Baha'i World Faith headquarters are still located today.

The beliefs of the Baha'i may not seem Earth-shaking now. But they were radical when they first appeared, especially for an offshoot of Shiite Islam. Baha'is accept the unity of all religions, and their origin from the same source. What made the early Baha'i faith especially potent and magnetic was its blend of spiritual power and progressive social principles, including equality of both genders and all races, and a world government empowered to maintain freedoms of expression and assembly, and world peace. In their activism in pursuing these beliefs, the Baha'is were truly a century ahead of their time.

"The Bahá'í teachings," says Canada's Baha'i website, "promote the elimination of all forms of prejudice and uphold equal dignity and respect for all peoples, regardless of their racial, ethnic, religious, or national background. Equality of men and women, the elimination of extremes of poverty and wealth and economic justice for all peoples, universal education, and the dignity of the individual are central Bahá'í principles."[142]

This is politically explosive, if we read between the lines and see that what's implied is a world without the dividing stresses of separatist religions or countries. "The earth is but one country," said the Baha'u'llah, "and mankind its citizens." The Baha'i organization has yet to walk the talk of full gender equality—its House of Universal Justice remains an all-male ruling council—but the goal of unity remains central. The Baha'u'llah envisioned even full gender equality at some future date. He spoke like an Angel of Aquarius. "The well-being of mankind," he believed, "its peace and security, are unattainable unless and until its unity is firmly established."[143]

GREAT SOURCE: OOMOTO

By an intriguing synchronicity, the Baha'u'llah passed away in the year that the most notable of Japan's "new religions" appeared. In 1892 Nao Deguchi, a woman whose main qualification for spiritual inspiration up to that time seems to have been a life so difficult that it either breaks one's heart or opens it to God, began to receive messages from a deity who called itself Ushitora-no-Konjin. Over the years until she died in 1918, her semi-conscious "automatic writing" would fill some 10,000 small booklets, and would come to be known as the *Ofudesaki* ("From the Tip of the Ink Brush"): one of the sacred scriptures of the religion that soon became known as Oomoto, "Great Source."

Nao's writing also contained a prophecy that a great soul would soon come, who would spread the teachings of Oomoto throughout Japan and the world. He arrived in the person of a spiritual and creative genius who became the husband of Nao's daughter Sumiko, and took the name Onisaburo Deguchi. Designated along with Nao as one of the co-founders of Oomoto, Onisaburo attracted a number of devoted followers who were drawn not only by Oomoto's message of equality and brotherhood, but also by Onisaburo's magnetic personality, tireless energy, and torrential creativity as a poet, playwright, actor, painter, sculptor, potter, calligrapher, and architect whose life seemed to be one continuous creative act. "Art is the mother of religion," he said, and if his enormous output of scintillating beauty was anything to go by, something of great spiritual power had been born in Ayabe, north of Kyoto. In 1925 Onisaburo founded Oomoto's secular arm, the *Jinrui Aizenkai* (Universal Love and Brotherhood Association).

All of this would have gotten little notice from the stiff tunics who were arming Japan in the 1920s if Onisaburo's teachings had been only air and fog. But they were compelling. Given a choice between the official line that the Japanese are a divine master race and Shinto is their state religion, and Onisaburo's insistence that all human beings are equal and "all religions spring from the same root,"[144] millions of Japanese joined Oomoto. In his *Reikai Monogatari (Stories from the Spirit World)* and Oomoto's newspapers, Onisaburo was relentless in attacking Japan's imperialist and racist policies, warning of the consequences that would come if his people continued to ignore, even work and plan against, the divine laws of balance, harmony, and all-embracing love of humanity.

Onisaburo even prophesied that if the Japanese did not correct their ways, their cities would be destroyed by fire dropped from the sky. The official response was customary, and swift. Oomoto's leaders and many followers were jailed, and some were tried for *lese majeste*. Oomoto books were banned, and its newspapers closed. The faith's headquarters in Ayabe were obliterated with dynamite. The army's particular target was the main ceremonial hall, which Onisaburo had built in the shape of a cross so that visitors from throughout the world could pray facing whatever direction was central to their faith.

Onisaburo and other Oomoto leaders were released from jail after the Pacific War's end in 1945, and Onisaburo was acquitted. Like the rest of Japan, Oomoto rose from the ashes in the 1960s and emerged in the 1970s when Onisaburo and Sumiko's daughter Naohi, Oomoto's third spiritual leader, adopted a new policy of links with other religions and cultural exchanges and joint worship services in Japan and abroad. Her unofficial foreign minister was and still is her son Kyotaro, who now heads the Oomoto Foundation.

In the 1970s Oomoto launched two initiatives that placed it firmly on the world map: an exhibition of Onisaburo's works that toured to high acclaim in Paris and New York; and the School of Traditional Japanese Arts, a deep immersion in Japanese spirituality and culture, including daily practice of *Noh* dance, tea ceremony, calligraphy, and *kendo*, the way of the sword. In the early 1990s an Oomoto group even made the *Hajj* to Mecca at the invitation of the Grand Mufti of Syria, who felt that Oomoto's commitment to the principles of Islam makes Oomoto people Muslim in spirit, with the same right to travel to Islam's holiest shrine.

Oomoto's recovery was complete in 1992, when the magnificent *Choseiden* (Longevity Hall) was consecrated on the centennial of Oomoto's birth, on the site where the original great hall once stood. The Choseiden is built of wood rather than stone, to bend rather than shatter when the Earth shakes, as bamboo does and stone can't.

Oomoto has never defined itself as an Aquarian religion. It times its life in harmony with the ever-renewing cycles of nature, and its main festivals are the same midseason feasts celebrated by the Celtic/Druid and Wiccan traditions. While Oomoto works actively toward a loving and peaceful world, it does not await some transformative moment at which all of humanity achieves together a simultaneous leap into higher spiritual consciousness.

Yet the Aquarian features are clearly there: in Onisaburo's passionate, revolutionary urge to bring about a better world, in a much higher emphasis on kind, serene action than on articles of belief, in a dynamic ecumenism that began when Pope John XXIII was a boy, in an active fellowship with other faiths, and above all in universal love and brotherhood as not just a ringing iambic phrase, but as a consistent, patient habit of the heart.

GOODBYE, COLUMBUS:
THE INTERFAITH MOVEMENT

Synchronicities abound. In the year after Nao Deguchi began to receive messages from the spirit world, hundreds of delegates from Christian churches and Eastern religions gathered in Chicago at the first World's Parliament of Religions. This unprecedented synod was a highlight event of the Columbian Exposition of 1893, held to mark the 400th anniversary of Columbus's "discovery" of the New World. The parliament was imbued with the optimism that was felt in much of the Western world that now, 80 years after Napoleon, the peoples of the Earth were finally learning to overcome their differences, and link modern technologies with universalist ideas in the service of all humankind.

The delegates agreed to reject *syncretism*, or a blending together of religions in ways that would blur their distinctions of belief and liturgy; and "indifferentism," the idea that all religions are as interchangeable as spoons, and it does not matter which one—or ones—a believer chooses. There were no delegates from indigenous peoples, much less from "pagan" communities. But at least there was inter-religious dialogue, for the first time on American soil, among Christians and Jews, Hindus and Buddhists. And while the WPR did not commit itself to a program of action or to future meetings, it did affirm a desire to emphasize common principles and work toward peaceful understanding with each other.

While ignored and dismissed as naïve during the era of two World Wars and the early Cold War, the interfaith movement revived in the 1960s under the influences of a peace activism stirred by opposition to the war in Vietnam, the successes of the American civil rights movement and other forces of nonviolent social change, and a new ecumenical spirit among religions. In retrospect, it seems clear now, the strongest impetus behind the second phase of the interfaith movement may have been the birth of *ecology*, and with it an environmental activism that is naturally spiritual, based on the Gaian belief that Earth herself is a living sacred being whom people of all faiths are bound to honor and heal.

Pope John XXIII's encyclical *Nostra Aetate* (1966) was epoch-making. The title is significant, as Latin *aetas* means a human lifetime, and its use implies that a new ecumenical understanding might lead to peace and planetary health now, in *our* lifetime. Pope John's revolutionary move led the Church of Rome to create a new Pontifical

Council for Inter-Religious Dialogue. The Protestant World Council of Churches, and Jewish and Muslim religious bodies, soon took similar initiatives.

The move from word to action began in 1970 with the first World Congress on Religion and Peace in Kyoto, which now began—again through Oomoto's initiative—to emerge as a focus of international efforts toward peace, sustainable economies and environmental preservation. While existing interfaith bodies such as the International Association for Religious Freedom, the World Congress of Faiths, and the Temple of Understanding were active in furthering interfaith dialogue, the WCRP was the first to move its focus from the conference hall to the street, and propose—to the discomfort of many—that condemning the war in Vietnam was one thing on which people of faith everywhere might agree.

Different religions, even those with histories of crusade, pogrom, and jihad, now began to pray together, first on Mt. Sinai as Jews, Muslims, and Christians worshipped together in 1979 and 1984, and as Assisi hosted in 1986 the first of its annual Prayer Gatherings for World Peace. In 1993, the Year of Inter-Religious Understanding and Cooperation, a centennial World's Parliament of Religions met in Chicago. Its cast of 7,000 included thousands of women and delegates from indigenous peoples and Earth religions. Other gatherings were held, including the Kyoto Global Forum and the Conference on Ecological Responsibility, convened by the Dalai Lama in New Delhi.

And yet, in 1993 Iraqis were suffering from sanctions imposed after the Gulf War. Palestinians were still seething in agony, and new violence was certain to explode in the Middle East and elsewhere. One did not have to be an Oxford don to pose the make-or-break question discussed by two of the conferences at Oxford's International Interfaith Centre: "How effective is interfaith activity in halting and healing conflict?"[145] The blunt answer so far: Not very. This is why an ambitious new step was needed. In 1995, the Episcopal Bishop of California, William Swing, used to maximum effect his speech to commemorate the 50th anniversary of the founding of the United Nations in San Francisco. He proposed a new international body to be called the United Religions, where delegates from the world's religions could meet daily to work together on behalf of humanity and the Earth. The United Religions Initiative was founded in 2000 to "promote enduring, daily interfaith cooperation, to end religiously motivated violence and to create cultures of peace, justice, and healing for the Earth and for all living beings."[146] The URI network now includes about 200 Cooperation Circles that range in size from local groups to intercontinental organizations. A certain event of September 2001, and its divisive aftermath, has delayed for now a promising idea that seemed headed toward fruition. But in the meantime, a very old idea continues to grow again as the Earth grows, and in its rhythms of seasons and sabbats, dances and drums, keeps the momentum going.

FROM PAGANS TO EARTH RELIGIONS

While the interfaith movement may be in eclipse at the moment, one band of today's spiritual spectrum grows like fire that only looks wild. Where? One clue is in the Declaration of the 1993 World's Parliament of Religions: "We commit ourselves to this global ethic, to understanding one another, and to socially beneficial, peace-fostering, and nature-friendly ways of life."[147] The WPR's Global Ethic statement makes the new emphasis unmistakable: "We are interdependent. Each of us depends on the well-being of the whole, and so we have respect for the community of living beings, for people, animals, and plants, and for the preservation of Earth, the air, water and soil."[148]

What had redirected the WPR's thrust so dramatically? One indicator is that, as Don Frew reported, the WPR sponsors included the Fellowship of Isis, which had a local chapter in Chicago, Earth-Spirit from Boston, and the Covenant of the Goddess, "an international federation of Witches that included members of the three other groups."[149] Once these groups had made their move, the word spread rapidly among other Wiccan, women's spirituality, and "neopagan" communities. All of a sudden the witches were not only sitting and speaking in the same room with those who had burned them a few centuries back, but the witches emerged as the stars of the Parliament, attracting over 500 celebrants to an outdoor Full Moon ceremony they'd planned for fifty.

"By the end of the nine days," Frew wrote, "the academics attending the Parliament were saying 'In 1893, America was introduced to the Buddhists and Hindus; in 1993, we met the Neopagans.' As Michael Thorn said after returning from Chicago, 'This was the most important event in the history of the Craft since the publication of *Witchcraft Today* in 1954!'"[150] The Covenant of the Goddess delivered on the statement of intention it had made at its founding in 1975: to act not only as a "networking group for Witches of all traditions," but to get actively involved in interfaith work.

As is true with many new things now, spiritual language evolves as needed. "Witch" is losing its medieval fear baggage as more people come to understand—thanks, Harry Potter!—that Wicca actually means *craft*: knowledge of the properties of herbs and stones, sounds and ritual movement, and the benefits in health, work, and love of aligning oneself with the rhythms of the Moon, the womb, the Earth, and the sky. What term will be used for this kind of spirituality, whether Earth religions or Earth spirituality or Neo-Paganism, remains to be seen, now that "pagan" looks less threatening. The meaning of the word hasn't really changed. It has just gone home to its heath (source of *heathen*), the wild place where herbs grew and the Moon shone long before fearful people behind stone walls and oak doors in the town began to say the Devil lives there in the trackless woods.

Pagan simply means "field-dweller," a person who goes out into the field not just to farm it, but to live and pray there. For the ancient pagans, and the new ones who gather now amid the green leaves and waters under the stars and the Moon, the wild place is never unholy. It always was, and always will be, the root and song of life. It is small wonder, then, that the more human beings awaken now to the peril of the Earth and the sacred duty of all faiths to honor and heal her, the more the Neo-Pagan movement grows and the more exotic new orchids appear in the hothouse of Earth spirituality. And as new spiritual communities appear, they create beautiful, moving, meaningful ceremonies. Anyone who can plan a dinner party can conduct a ritual, as we'll soon see after we've visited a fire circle, and viewed a brief spirit cartoon.

For the moment, our main task is to affirm the Aquarian resonances in the interfaith movement, especially in Earth spirituality. Both see God and the Goddess as present in the Earth rather than remote from it. Both agree with the Sufis, another group who savor the juice and tingle of life, that the way of the heart is far more important than any rule or dogma. Both honor the sacred feminine. Both are inclusive, egalitarian, communal, and highly creative, and look to the time to come with everything to gain, and nothing to lose. Both understand, as some "world religions" once did and perhaps may again, that love is the remedy for fear. And both have always known that there is no point in going all the way through the Age of Pisces, the sign that rules the feet, if we have forgotten how to dance.

BURN, FIRE. BURN BRIGHT!

The *Dancin' Fool*, as Frank Zappa called him in the Disco Decade, is always with us. Today he is probably the guy who forgets to wrap his Ecstasy right, and finds that when he wants it, it has melted away in the heat and sweat of the rave. But as some of the other jumpers and shakers in the room have always known, and the authorities have always feared, there is another domain of dance where the beat of the heart meets the sound of the drum and the pulse of the Earth, where Shiva, Dionysus, and Kaminari the Thunder God run the rhythm section for rites of purification. Welcome to the fire circle, where dancers move to drums in the alchemical trance to burn grief and fear in the crucible of the heart. And where "magic" is often used to describe the experience and the results.

The ceremonies held by such groups as the Hawaii Fire Tribe typify the inclusive, active, joyous festivals that proliferate now on our planet. We focus on the fire circle because unlike the huge and famous Burning Man festival held in the Nevada desert, fire dance circles tend to keep it simple and share the hope that what gets burned is not just a spectacular effigy of a man, but the emotional iron, fluff, and mud that keep love from filling the heart.

A fire circle usually consists of a dozen or more tall poles placed around a central stone fire pit, and surmounted by torches or oil-burning lamps. The circle's entrance portal is oriented to north for the winter solstice and south for summer. The poles are connected with ropes, which may be hung with prayer flags bearing the symbols of many spiritual traditions, and prayers which the celebrants have written on pieces of cloth. Inside the circle near the entrance, there are benches for drummers, and behind them are racks and tables for gongs, crystal singing bowls, didjeridoos, and other special instruments. There is a shaker table with rattles and percussion toys that dancers play as they move around the circle. Also at the perimeter are water tables and beautifully decorated altars that hold food, tobacco bundles, and other offerings. Once the circle is prepared, the community gathers to consecrate it as sacred space.

Groups meet during the day to practice dance, drums, and chant, rehearse ritual theatre pieces, and prepare costumes and masks. Before midnight, celebrants gather at the start of the procession route. The leaders who will begin the night's festivities, dressed as the Holly King and Juno Lucina for the winter solstice, the Green Man or Pan and Luna for the summer, deliver a last few reminders. That we are about to cross from conversational space to the silence of sacred space. That everyone is encouraged, though not required, to join in chant and drumming. That anyone can leave the fire circle at any time, but should stop at the portal and be smudged with sage smoke before entering again.

The procession begins. Celebrants enter the circle, do opening rites and theatre, light the fire, and align intentions for the night. Drummers take their places and the group begins to move clockwise around the fire. As the hours go by, some dancers stand at the circle's edge and chant from there, or play drums. Some deliver poetry, song, or music, even dance ensemble pieces, in the intervals between the main drum sequences, or a group of didjeridoos plays for the dreamtime, always respecting the key principle that one must not impede those who are moving in the circle, some of whom may be entering, or already be in, the deep trance states that can come after hours of moving around the fire. This goes on through the night, and ends with an invocation to the rising Sun. The main mood each morning is not one of exhaustion—if anything, celebrants seem to get a second wind at dawn—but a mix of serenity and exhilaration.

In the Aquarian Age, as the Hawaii Fire Tribe and others like it already know, fun will be one of the keys. Communities will find for themselves where the boundaries are between reverence and awe, lightness and laughter. They will find themselves far more inventive in creating sacred play than they'd ever imagined they could be. Once our focus shifts from following rituals led by a designated holy person, we'll find our own new ways to honor and celebrate the divine in one another. Once we know that God is happy all the time and we may as well be too if we're going to be godly, we'll know what to do.

THE NEW AGE: TOY STORE OR SECOND RENAISSANCE?

Now for the selected short subject that either is a cartoon, or is often thought to be. Everyone has an opinion on the New Age. That's why many people who feel some resonance with it—if only in its sincere interest in and respect for love-based spirituality—learn quickly that the best answer to the question of whether you're a New Ager is to ask, "What do you mean by the New Age?"

If the term were any more inclusive, it would be promiscuous. It can mean a kind of Second Renaissance powered by new explorations—this time outer and virtual spaces instead of the deep seas Columbus and others braved—new technologies, challenges to established beliefs, rediscovery of ancient wisdom that was long thought to have been lost, and a humanism based on our power to realize intentions and achieve the dream of freedom. It can mean, as the Aquarian paradigm does, a time when boundaries dissolve and human beings align together as they never have before. It can mean a time when mythologists like Joseph Campbell and comparative religionists like Huston Smith show that stories of faith are the same everywhere, and we understand that all spiritual paths share the same values of love and forgiveness, kindness, compassion, and mercy.

The New Age is also a boutique and toy store for celebrities who wear symbols of ancient faith like costume jewelry. And people who decorate their homes with Tibetan thangkas, Qabbalah symbols, Buddha statues, dream catchers, a didjeridoo, and an Egyptian *ankh*, but have little time to meditate or join ceremony because they're busy getting ready to host a party for people who gush up to tell you about your sign, your aura, and your akashic record, but have not yet noticed the pesto stain on their Balinese patchwork pants.

It is easy to wonder whether those who scorn the "New Age movement" do so over differences of belief and practice, or from an aversion to sheer vacancy. So firm is the desire of some spiritual communities to distance themselves from the New Age that one Native American website has a list of "Differences between Indians and New Agers." It notes, for example, that syncretic New Age people "mix and match" beliefs, unlike Native Americans who follow only the ceremonies of their own tribe, and do not know, or want to know, the rituals of other tribes, much less other religions. And unlike New Agers who get much of their "spiritual knowledge" from books, and thereby enrich the authors, Native American people receive their religious training orally from elders who decide whether and when their students are ready, and receive no money for teaching.[151]

Some Christians see the New Age "movement" as a Satanic conspiracy that aims to wipe out "major religions" and create a new order with one government and one church. It's understandable that those who gave us the Inquisition and the witches' pyre might fear that the New Age will do unto them what they have done so often to others, and it's revealing that the only ones who refer to the New Age as a "movement" are its enemies, who attribute to it the regimentation and herd behavior of their own religions. Those who've actually lived an independent *spiritual* path, as distinct from a religious path, know that it's sometimes communal, rarely conformist, much less organized, so that "herding cats" does not begin to suggest how hard it is to get many New Agers to show up anywhere at the same time unless there's good food, music, and dancing with bare feet.

So many opinions. One wonders whether Helena Blavatsky, author of *Isis Unveiled*, who coined the term "New Age," anticipated how much venom and vanity these words would bring in the years to come. The term gained wider usage from the New Age Seminar at the Association for Research and Enlightenment, the foundation devoted to studies of Edgar Cayce. The New Age was clearly underway by the 1960s, its ideas shaped by the Findhorn community in Inverness and the Wrekin Trust, both based in the home of Celtic and Druidic spirituality. The Findhorn experiments in particular proved compelling, as they showed how the abundance of a garden is affected by the quality of one's communication with plant and animal *devas*—a Hindu word for spirits.

For those in the middle between the vacuous and the hostile, those who want information about what the New Age is, rather than mis- and dis-information about what it is not, one good place to start is B. A. Robinson's article, "New Age Spirituality." It's useful because the author is impartial, looking to clarify and define, not syncretize or condemn.[152]

AQUARIAN CEREMONIES

Besides the reading, what to *do*? We work on two things: individual soul work and self-refinement, and the communal work of building new emotional and spiritual containers to grow our lives, just as clay pots are good for plants. Communities are already anchoring these processes in their new schools, and in markets that provide healthy food, beautiful clothes and household goods, and a chance to trade with friends and neighbors. Many of these community builders are also engaged in global ceremonies and meditations like the ones in Aquarian Resources at the end of this book. Even when we are not aligning with a planet-wide meditation, but are only gathering our own people locally, the challenge is to create ceremonies that are moving, inspiring, and empowering, and also give us pleasure, so that our spiritual lives give us some juice and joy, and make us want to come back.

More and more, unless we're working within a faith that has structure but is still flexible enough to allow some creativity, we're having to wing our spiritual lives and invent our own liturgies. This can be done more easily than we think, though it does help to have in the group a few storytellers, myth minds, and actors.[153] The main challenge, in fact, is not in getting creative. It's in *staying* creative, so we don't just settle into cabin complexes of aging hippies, where new things that once were fresh start to sag into ruts and routines. To do the play of spirit in Aquarius, we will have to create it as our ancient ancestors did from the rhythms of Mother Earth and Father Sky, and the experiences that give us joy: birth and marriage, praise and acknowledgment, fulfillment and wisdom and, when we really have the hang of it, rites of smooth, swift, happy death.

DO WE NEED RELIGIONS?

This, for many, is already one of the core questions in the soulscape of today's world. Can communities practice a spiritual life without even having a religion? Is it even possible that what Abraham Lincoln said, "When I do good, I feel good. When I do bad, I feel bad. That's my religion," could be about as much religion as we really need?

The answers go deeper than the usual negatives about religions, and right into the dogma slot where the most disempowering idea has always lived: the premise that human beings will never learn to care more lovingly for each other and their planet because they are sinful and [E-word], unworthy of "God."

This question came to a head in 2003 with the release of Mel Gibson's *The Passion of the Christ*. The problem is not so much that Gibson's version of Jesus is anti-Semitic, though it is. The problem, rather, is that the film, and the gnarled grotesque of the Christian faith that it presents, is profoundly anti-human. It creates a world in which every human being who is merciful and kind is hopelessly outweighed by a hundred others who are violently hateful, stupid, cruel, drunk with lies and religious pride, and so indifferent to the agony of others that one wonders why "God" even bothers to keep humanity alive. Reviewer

Stephen Simon wrote that "the entire film seemed like the dying gasp of an old ultra-religious paradigm that is slowly fading into oblivion."[154] If he's correct, then the thing that is now dying could be the Agony Paradigm itself, the whole idea that humanity is so corrupt that "God" must die horribly for our sins and save us from hell and ourselves.

One of the real challenges of our time is expressing the Aquarian truth as gently as possible, in order not to frighten or enrage those who are married to self-loathing. The fact is that Jesus is not coming back by himself. There are no more solitary saviors on the way, as Aquarius is communal. There is no holding the truth back now. We take individual and collective responsibility for the outcomes we receive, and we all work together to awaken ourselves and each other. We work out our own sins and do not need anyone else to die for them. Not anymore. The agony scenario and the negating false paradigm it is built from must wither and blow away as the Aquarian energy of friendship spreads.

Our purpose here is not to single out any religion for criticism—most of them have their avid hell-thumpers, and people who are willing to die and to kill in the name of what they think "God" wants. Such practices do not produce individuals, much less whole societies, who will make imaginative efforts to bring about a better world for themselves or anyone else. This is why Aquarius will be a wringer for people who are stuck in religiosity.

Does this mean that religions will now fade into irrelevance in the revolutionary Aquarian Age? No, certainly not, any more than the Vedic religion of the Taurean Age passed away when the Age of Aries came, or Judaism, Buddhism, Taoism, or Zoroastrianism disappeared in the Age of Pisces. Some religions stand the test of time because they contain an enduring treasure of love and beauty. They give comfort to many people, especially those who crave a sense of belonging and of being validated by a congregation and holy scripture. They give a reassuring structure to life at a time when many are frightened by the dizzying pace of change. They offer the hope of a loving God.

What will change is our whole concept of our relationship with God. The word *religion* means "reconnection"—it's related to *ligament*—and is rooted in an idea that we are separate from "God," even that "He" is a jealous, punitive being whom human beings must obey by living in "fear of God." This premise will not survive the Aquarian Age. The less fearful and more intimate our relationship with the Universal Source, the less we will need structure and dogma, the greater our attraction will be to paths like that of the Sufis, whom we'll meet soon. Why does their practice grow more popular every year? Could it be that people who see God as the Friend and the Beloved are perfectly in tune with Aquarian currents of unity, friendship, equality, and freedom?

No way around it: stiff, stern religions have a bumpy ride ahead. Some of their adherents work valiantly to bring change. Former fundamentalist minister Michael Dowd and science writer Connie Barlow have co-created a "Gospel According to Evolution" based on their core idea that "sacred evolution" is a progressive, creative process designed by God, who for them is "the sacred name for the whole of reality, measurable and immeasurable."[155] Dowd, Barlow, and their colleague Tom Attlee have created two online Evolutionary Salons to which cocreationists everywhere are welcome to contribute philosophy and theology, sacred literature and art, ceremonies and other materials aimed at creating new evolutionary versions of Christianity and the other established religions, and also of pagan and humanist practices, politics and culture, and all other areas of human action and belief that can benefit from an evolutionary perspective.

In the end, though we may not see it in the moment, human creativity and optimism have their ways of overcoming human obstinacy and inertia, especially when traditional rites and practices of real value are under threat. At a time when, as a *U.S.A Today* survey reported in April 2010, a 72 percent majority of Generation Y "millennials" in the 18–29 age group agree that they're more spiritual than religious, it must happen, and it does, that some congregation leaders focus on the 15 percent who are still in the church.[156] Others begin to see that the flock of obedient sheep may not be any longer the best possible metaphor for the soul impulse that draws people together in a common spiritual purpose.

In the end, religious people will learn, some the easy way and some the hard way, to get with the love program. Those who give up hate and pride will see that our purpose here on the Earth plane is to master human friendship. Those who get this will live happily at this time when the shift from Pisces to Aquarius is a bloom of beauty for those who love, and a storm of struggle for those who live in fear. We will all wind up in the garden. It is our holy destiny. But first we must hold for a time the space of love and forgiveness for those who are addicted to the fight, and insist on playing their dramas out. They will be stunned to see that there is no Hell and there are no devils. They will laugh heartily when we all see Hell and all other tragedies of duality resolve into a cosmic comedy.

AQUARIAN PROFILE:JELALUDDIN RUMI

He hardly seems, at first, a likely candidate. The poet we know as Rumi lived eight centuries ago. As recently as the 1960s, all the published translations of his poetry into English were academic renderings that were more correct than compelling. Until Robert Bly suggested that Coleman Barks "free these poems from their cages," very few people outside the Middle East had any idea that Islam too had produced a great sacred poet who would be recognized one day as equal to Dante, Vyasa, and others who wrote of Heaven and Earth, bliss and suffering, the meaning of humanity and the promise of God.

Rumi is a Piscean Age poet in his all-accepting, mystical vision and his compassion. But he also fits as an Aquarian figure, and not only because he has just arrived in the world's consciousness, and has found in only a few decades more great translators than other great writers find over several centuries. Young people who are already living Aquarian love Rumi so much that in recent years he has been the poet most widely read among American college students. Rumi and other Sufi poets belong in the Aquarian shift because in their view of the world, there is no separation. All souls head toward Unity. They may inflict on themselves in their time on Earth sufferings that look like Hell. They may feel caged like birds, or lost in the dark or blind drunk, all favorite Sufi metaphors for the dullness of the soul when it drops from the blaze of Heaven into the mud of Earth.

Rumi's parents knew the theme that appears so often in his poetry: the pain of separation, and the longing to return. The family fled Kars, Afghanistan in 1201 to escape Genghis Khan, and settled in Konya, Turkey. Rumi was born in 1207, and lived as a respected scholar until the age of 37, when he got the life-changing "glance": his first meeting with the itinerant Sufi teacher Shams—the name means *Sun*—from Tabriz in Iran. The two men formed a profound spiritual friendship that changed Rumi from an intellectual who had never done much original writing into an astoundingly prolific poet. His most admired work, the *Mathnawi*, is as long as the complete works of Shakespeare.

Rumi's words were spontaneous, pouring out of him as he walked through town, usually flanked by students who wrote the lines down as Rumi spoke and people gathered to listen. His poems and stories are deliciously dramatic, and not only because of their vivid and juicy characters, their dreamlike changes of direction, and their gorgeous imagery. To those who see the strong theatrical potential in Rumi's lines, it makes sense that he spoke them in public as he walked to the school, the assembly hall, the town square, likely too "dissolved in love" to deliver "performances," much less "act" for conscious effect on an audience. Yet his conversational style, and his images that flow like jazz more than verse, often show that the poet knows others are present when he speaks. He even refers to some of them, and is aware that they may even be having fun listening to him.

Coleman Barks writes in *Rumi Illuminated*, "Rumi is the 13th-century Sufi mystic, whose ability to open the heart so dissolved the boundaries of religion that he made human friendship and the longing to merge with the Source one thing. His spontaneously-spoken poetry celebrates the sacredness of everyday life and gives voice to the soul's deepest mysteries."[157] When Rumi passed away in 1274, people from every faith walked in his funeral procession: Muslims, Jews, Christians, Zoroastrians, Hindus, and Buddhists all came to honor the one who spoke for them all, and for the truth of every sacred tradition.

While there are many Sufi orders in Turkey and other countries, the ones for whom Rumi's words are sacred are called the Mevlevi Order. They refer to the poet as Mevlana, the Master. Like other Sufi communities, they practice in their *zikr* (remembrance) meetings and in formal ceremonies a ritual that only superficially resembles "dance." Everyone has heard of the famous "whirling dervishes," but few of the dervishes try—or want to—explain what they do. Those who commit to the dervish path call themselves *semazens*, and spend years of practice in movement, song, and meditation to prepare for ceremonies called *sema* in which nine or more semazens, each holding a place in a geometric design, turn together in a communal ritual of music and turning. They always turn to the left. Why? Because the heart is to the left of the center line of the body, so by turning to the left the dervish turns on the axis of the heart. Balance is easier to keep, and the dervish can enter deep states of bliss. In turning, the dervish seeks the ecstasy of direct union with God, so that, in Rumi's words, "all qualities of doingness disappear."[158]

While Rumi expects every soul to find its way back to God sooner or later, many of his stories are about how human beings kick against the pricks until we accept divine mercy and love. The Beloved can be demanding, like any lover who wants one's best. "I am here to make your heart a shrine of love," He warns, "not a pen for holding sheep."[159]

Much of one's progress toward readiness may not be, however, so much a matter of effort as of knowing when to give up. The ecstatic Bilal says,

> In the hand of love I'm like a cat in a bag,
> lifted up and whirled around overhead.
> That's how much control I have over circumstances.[160]

For Mevlana and all who are like-hearted with him, God is the Beloved with whom our soul bond is as intimate and happy as it would be at a party. "Come in," the poet calls,

> the Beloved is here. We are all drunk.
> No one notices who enters or leaves.

Don't sit outside the door, wondering. . . .
Enter the thicket of lions unafraid of any wounds.
The shadows you fear are just a child's fantasy.
There is no wound, and nothing to be wounded;
All is mercy and love.[161]

In the end, as all the old dualities, and all the doubts, judgments, and unworthiness dissolve, we are all going home, no matter what we've done. Everyone.

Come, come, whoever you are.
This caravan knows no despair.
Even if you have broken your vow
Perhaps ten thousand times,
Come, come again.[162]

CHAPTER 11

AQUARIAN PLANET

2011 has come, and it is showtime on planet Earth at the dawning of Aquarius. As we've already seen, every one of the Great Ages in the grand cycle of the precession of the equinoxes comes at its end to a time of reversal and exhaustion, as its irresistible new energies align into structures, then in time calcify into rigid routines that become increasingly unsustainable, then collapse into a chaos that appears to many to be only ruin and disaster. But this apparent disorder is utterly necessary, for it is from the fall and recombination of old elements, and the spontaneous appearance of new ones, that the next set of rules emerges, and the new game begins.

We need not recap the political, economic, and social changes that are coming faster now than forces of manipulation, domination, and control can keep hiding the evidence. Our focus here is on how we and Lady Gaia, and all the life forms who live upon her, will be the conscious co-creators of the new Aquarian planet that we are about to plant and grow. The present emergency that compels us to act together is evident enough to us in polluted skies and seas, waters that recede from arid and fire-ravaged lands, disappearing animal and plant species, and new genetically modified death crops that proliferate even in places like Peru. Here, in what is perhaps the most brilliant farming culture and miracle of biodiversity that human beings have ever helped nature create, genetically modified Monsanto corn threatens to wipe out the native maize that Andean cultures have always held sacred. Corporatists now sell to farmers in the Sacred Valley of the Urubamba the water that has flowed down mountain *asequias* free of charge for thousands of years.[163]

It all came to a head in 2010 as an environmental news story that everyone knew about—at least insofar as they were allowed to know anything—arrived right on its Aquarian cue, precisely at the moment when the planets in our solar system formed a tremendously powerful and transformative astral alignment that didn't get on the six o'clock news at all. In the months that followed the explosion of the Deep Water Horizon oil rig in the Gulf of Mexico, as engineers worked to contain the most catastrophic environmental disaster in our planet's history, and politicians and corporatists worked to contain a public relations nightmare by shifting blame and blocking media access to the scene of the crime, almost all the "outer" planets in our sky—that is, the planets farthest from the Sun—began to form a very rare and momentous design.

Most astrologers called it the Cardinal Crosses because the planets in this dance of astral dynamics were in Aries, Cancer, Libra, and Capricorn, which are called cardinal signs—from Latin *cardo*, "hinge"—because when the Sun enters them each year, they open like a door to begin each new season. As the planets were lined up "against" each other at 90° and 180° angles that are said to be "difficult" and "stressful," and compel us to see and make changes that are overdue and now unstoppable, dire predictions spewed from doom pimp astrologers who called the "Cardinal Climax" of summer 2010 the "nastiest" and "worst" planet alignment to afflict the Earth in thousands of years.[164] Where in all of this, wondered some of the most doggedly optimistic souls among us, is there any sign that a moment of liberation and ascension into galactic, spiritual consciousness is at hand?

But it *is* there; it is all purposeful and visible. "Many of us can see the awakening happening," Daniel Pinchbeck observed, "but it seems to be coming far too slowly, in hesitant fits and starts, while the destructive force also grows in strength . . . On another level, I feel an equally uncanny presentiment that all of this is still going perfectly according to plan, that the script of our collective world movie/space odyssey has to unscroll or unfurl in just this stomach-clenching way, toward its still mysterious denouement."[165] Richard Tarnas saw the moment in similarly cosmic, even mythic terms. "Perhaps we, as a civilization and a species," he wrote, "are undergoing a rite of passage of the most epochal and profound kind, acted out on the stage of history with, as it were, the cosmos itself as the tribal matrix of the initiatory drama. Perhaps humankind has entered into the most critical stages of a death-rebirth mystery."[166]

These voices and others saw that the summer of 2010 brought something far more consequential than the technical challenge of plugging an oil well, or the police state behavior of British Petroleum and its servants in American government and media, or even the larger and philosophical and spiritual question of what ruin may come from a sacrilege of allowing the fire substance of petroleum not just to touch, but to invade and poison the water element of life itself. The Deep Water Horizon tragedy, the poisoning of the very bloodstream of Mother Earth, may in time prove to be exactly what was needed to move human beings from indifference, passivity, helpless worry, and clueless reliance on government and corporate officials whose top priority is not to heal the wound, but to control their costs and stay in office. Perhaps, finally, this was the event that caused us to hear and act upon what Gurdjieff, Peter Deunov, and others were saying a century ago about the coming time when we will no longer look for leaders and follow gurus, because we are the masters now.

The emergency is not economic, political, or even environmental. "The crisis is a crisis in consciousness," said J. N. Krishnamurti, "a crisis that cannot, anymore, accept the old norms, the old patterns, the ancient traditions."[167] This evolution in awareness, and with it the assuming of collective responsibility, is the essential Aquarian task that we now face. It will require what Richard Tarnas calls "an encounter with mortality that is no longer individual and personal but rather transpersonal, collective, planetary."[168] Like the dying and returning deity, or the shamanic traveler who is dismembered and reassembled into a being of greater strength and capacity, we as individuals, and as an entire species acting in the same resonance, will have to accept a transformative mission from which we will emerge as something no longer the same as what we were.

There is nothing immodest about envisioning both the ordeal and the opportunity in such terms. "The universe," said Henri Bergson, is a machine for making gods." He also said, ""The essence of reality is change and it cannot be known by reason." If this is true, then before we read the new operating instructions, we may have to start in the ancient depths of mythic mind, on the sixth day of our best-known, most influential Creation myth.

NATURE'S HIERARCHY: THE CHAINS THAT BIND

God said unto Adam, in the *Genesis* story from the middle of the patriarchal Age of Aries, "Be fruitful, and multiply, and replenish the earth, and subdue it: and have dominion over the fish of the sea, and over the fowl of the air, and over every living thing that moveth upon the earth." Thus humankind is instructed from the beginning to assume a dominant role in the natural world, and to do what he deems best to bring nature under his control. The Lord's next instruction hints at what's coming later in the Age of Pisces, for "out of the ground the Lord God formed every beast of the field, and every fowl of the air; and brought them unto Adam to see what he would call them: and whatsoever Adam called every living creature, that was the name thereof."[169] Thus Adam's first act of subduing nature is to name the animals and plants—and while it would take millennia before civil, military, and religious hierarchies would provide the pattern, it was only a matter of time before Christian Europe would see the world as an increasingly elaborate hierarchy in which man is outranked only by God.

Such ideas fledged into their full plumage during the age that built the great cathedrals and the edifice of scholastic philosophy, and prescribed where each man might live, what work he could do, whom he could marry, and what colors and fabrics he was allowed to wear in a system of feudal order that kept everyone rigidly in his place, and cut down swiftly anyone who dared to rise. By the late Middle Ages, monarchs who believed in the "divine right of kings" supported as well the early scientific idea of the Great Chain of Being, in which all living things "in order to their stations leap," as John Dryden put it later. Everything in nature had its proper place, ranging from the lowest bugs in the mud to fish in the sea, birds in the air and mammals of different power and degree, all the way up through the dignity of man to the throne of God.[170]

The same hierarchy ruled human societies, which remained in good order as long as no peasant tried to fight a knight or make eye contact with a king—and it was understood that breakage of order and obedience in one part of the Chain would cause other links to rupture too. The plays of Shakespeare are filled with images of shocking events in nature that come as proof and omen of high crimes in the world of men. One sign of Scotland's extreme agony in *Macbeth*, as an Old Man recounts to the thane of Ross, is that horribly, against all order in the bird kingdom, "a falcon, towering in her pride of place, was by a mousing owl hawk'd at and kill'd." And the last words of the Duke of Cornwall in *King Lear* roar his amazement that he has just been mortally wounded not by a nobleman of his own quality, but by . . . "my villein!"

Clearly, this was not a scheme of things in which anything was meant to evolve into a higher place or greater awareness. And even though the 17th century was an era of bold new movement in so many areas of life, and the generation of Shakespeare, Francis Bacon, Descartes, and the young Galileo would be the one to initiate the modern era by launching "natural philosophy" in a new direction away from religious faith and toward what would become empirical science, the Great Chain paradigm, with all that it implies about life forms staying what they are, and where they are in a hierarchy, would have the legs to walk ahead another three centuries. The famous system of classifying flora and fauna that Carolus Linnaeus devised in the 18th century remains fundamental to biology today, yet it's identical in principle to Adam's action of naming all the life forms in the Garden of Eden, and thereby bringing them all into his comprehension, and under his control. The only really significant difference between the Great Chain of Being and Ernst Haeckel's Evolutionary Tree of Life (1910) is that man is now at the top of the tree, and God is nowhere to be seen.[171]

For all of the differences in belief and method that would create an ever-widening gap between Christian religion and Western science in the years from Francis Bacon's time to our own, these two paradigms would continue to agree on one ancient and unchanging idea: that man is the ruler of nature, and his role is to understand it in order to subdue it. "Nature, to be commanded, must be obeyed," Bacon said, articulating the core idea that "The mission of modern science . . . is to dominate and control nature."[172] His premise, and the ideas of Descartes and Newton about human bodies and other life forms as machines operating by mechanical rules and rhythms rather than divine order, have been the philosophical and scientific underpinning of humankind's relationship with the natural world ever since.

From the Industrial Revolution of the 18th century through the industrial expansion of the 19th century to today's age of cybernetics, robotics, genetic engineering, and all the other technologies of industrialized globalization, this conception of nature-as-machine has driven our efforts to explore and exploit the natural world. As competition has grown terminally intense among enterprises that no longer perceive natural species as living beings, but only as "resources" to be harvested, it is to be expected that we have what has manifested now in the last gasp and grasp of the global corporatist agenda, as companies fight ruthlessly against Earth and one another to mine every metal, drill every well, and extract every atom of advantage from what is, after all, only an arrangement of machines.

Nor is it surprising, under such conditions, that authorities claim a right to spray poison and fire on plants, even the sacred herbs of ancient indigenous cultures, in an effort to eradicate species whose psychedelic properties are unacceptable within the controllers' agendas for what their people may not be allowed to perceive and dream. One bizarre result of this idea, that human beings have a right not only to control nature, but to kill whatever does not serve their aims of corporate and religious control, is the annual Cocaine Burning staged in the Plaza de Armas in Lima. It differs from the book burnings of the 1930s in one respect. The Nazis torched actual books full of ideas they deplored, while everybody in Lima—except perhaps a newly arrived U.S. embassy staffer just out of college and off the plane—knows that the hundreds of pounds of white stuff now going up in smoke is not cocaine. The police have fenced that to the CIA. The burning powder smells like baking bread because most of it is flour.

Not only has the determination of some humans to control nature brought us to a point now where more and more of us ask, as James M. Glover has, "Can we stop trying to control nature?"[173] It has also shown more and more of us that we are still stuck in a 400-year-old paradigm that robs us of all possibility of evolving into anything that is more aware, free, and dynamic. A machine cannot—at least not yet—evolve of its own will into a better model, much less into a different kind of machine, or even some other life form altogether. And presumably, if human beings are machines as well, we have as much chance of evolving into a more conscious, compassionate species as a toaster has of transmuting itself into a MacBook.

Clearly, if we're going to find some way out of the suicidal blind alley in which we now find ourselves, if we and our planet are going to survive at all, it's essential that we see in the simplest terms what is simply not working, and what new guiding ideas will help us direct our efforts toward the transformation we have come here to achieve. One essential text and starting point for understanding our possibilities now, and our responsibility for making the attempt, is a heady new mix of visionary science and daring comedy by Bruce Lipton and Steve Bhaerman, aka Swami Beyondananda.

Their 2009 book *Spontaneous Evolution* charts the ways in which the mechanistic and Darwinian views of philosophers and scientists from Descartes to Richard Dawkins have now locked us into a set of four "myth-perceptions" that have the status of "scientific law" in some quarters, even though they in fact have nothing to do with the truth or even the reality of anything. They have become widely accepted and even entrenched because they have fit perfectly the nexus of belief where a materialist "pure science" has long met the commercial interests of European colonialists, and the globalists of today, who see themselves competing, in ways that can only escalate into all-out economic warfare, for resources that are seen not as abundant and renewable, but as finite and running out fast. The myth-perceptions, as the authors see them, are these:

1. Only Matter Matters: that we live in a purely physical world, with no possibility of a metaphysical dimension in which spiritual energies are present.

2. Survival of the Fittest: in a natural world of relentless conflict and competition, with no possibility of cooperation toward shared goals.

3. It's in Your Genes: that is, our genes determine what we are and can be, thus limiting us to genetically determined routes of growth and behavior.

4. Evolution Is Random: if evolution can occur at all, it happens in ways that we cannot consciously predict or determine, so there is no possibility of conscious evolution through our collective intention of human thought and will.

We will look later in this chapter at the new ideas that Lipton and Bhaerman propose. Some are rooted in the research of Lipton and other biologists in the behavior of living cells, and their ability to adapt to environmental change, even to align with one another to alter conditions and behavior in ways that suggest a premise that has been startling until now: If new collective decisions can *emerge spontaneously* from the cells of living organisms, then is it possible that evolution might not in fact be random at all, but might happen in ways that are conscious and intentional? And might it even be possible that groups and communities of human beings might align their collective will and intention to change themselves and their conditions, even change the nature of reality itself from a *ground* of material objects, having no capacity to change, to an energetic *field* whose possibilities we have only begun to understand?

We have arrived yet again at a point of seeing that the essential difference between the old era that is now passing away, and the new time that now begins, is not mainly a matter of discovering and adjusting to new "facts" that show us relating to "external conditions" in new ways. Legitimate, non-dogmatic science does and will play an indispensable role in showing how the evolution we now achieve resembles—and can build upon—the evolutionary capacities of cells and the species they comprise. But as august and brilliant as the Nobel Prize winners and other geniuses are, they will only chart the change and get us to the head of the trail. It will be the swarm intelligence of our people, aligning as skilled, conscious agents of intention, who will brave the heroic journey and get us to our goal.

Like all heroic Aquarian stories, it may begin in the visionary actions of a few inspired individuals, even only one. But it will grow and succeed, because it has become an act of *heroic community*, committed to intention that is unstoppable because it is driven by the unifying, empowering force of love. These two key Aquarian ideas, of community and intention, are already combining to create intentional communities unlike any of the communes and other collective living experiments we've attempted before.

INTENTIONAL COMMUNITY

Like conscious parenting, this is one of those terms that seems to appear simultaneously in so many places that no one is quite sure who coined the phrase, or when. The term has been in use for at least a lifetime, though, and there's an interesting social trend and pulse in the way it comes and goes, seeming to skip a generation in the United States. When times are prosperous, and bonds of family, workplace, church, and patriotism are strong, there's less talk about intentional communities. But when hard times force us to form new links with like-minded people, then intentional communities are drawn together, as they were in the Great Depression, by shared needs and goals, rather than family history or religious belief. Sunrise Ranch in Loveland, Colorado was one of the first collective living experiments to call itself an intentional community when it was formed in 1945.

During the economic boom of the Eisenhower years and the conventional, conformist lifestyle that came along with it, intentional communities faded for a while. But they soon came back in the mid-1960s, as resistance to the Vietnam war, sexual revolution, a new counterculture, and awareness about *ecology* spurred young people to leave the cities, or try to reinvent them as earthier places where diggers might find food, and flower children could grow. Thousands of intentional communities shot up like Lucy in the Sky. Few were left by the time the Reagan decade brought new riches and the acquisitive pressures that promote competition more than community. Now, not surprisingly, there is more talk and action toward intentional community than we have ever seen in our history—and this time, as it's a core Aquarian goal and theme, it may be here to stay for a while.

In the broadest terms, intentional communities can be said to have started thousands of years ago, when spiritual seekers left home and family behind to join the first Buddhist ashrams formed by the *sangha* of believers, and the Essenes too formed associations that are as close to living communities as we can get when all our members are the same sex, and our communal life—even when it gets as nearly self-sufficient and complete as it did among Benedictines and other monastic orders—has everything but families. Most of the attempts that we've made in meeting the practical goals that communities aim to achieve—self-sufficiency and security, fulfilling work, successful nurturance and education of children in a natural, healthy environment, and group decision-making within flexible structures of communal law—have been unified by common religious belief, as were the Puritans and Shakers, the Amana Colonies and the Oneida Community.[174]

Less common are efforts like Japan's Yamagishi Communities (from 1957), which are apolitical and non-religious, and are committed to developing their members' talents by applying technical skills and teamwork to large sustainable agriculture projects that support the community's health and education programs. At the other end of the scale from such large scale-efforts are communities of a more Aquarian type that show how, under today's fluid conditions, a community does not have to stay in the same place. It may, like the Burning Man festival, draw tens of thousands of inventors, builders, and celebrants together for only a few days, in a place where no one would think of living year-round.[175] Or, like the Rainbow Gathering, it may travel across national borders from one season to the next, as it did for years in South America, its plans held together only by a loosely structured Family of Living Light.[176] The members of an intentional community may only meet each other one-on-one as they travel around the world, or they may never meet each other at all.

Take CouchSurfing, which started in 2004 and has grown into a worldwide network of a million people in a hundred countries. It has members of every age, trade, and talent, most of them in their twenties, all sharing "a vision of a world where everyone can explore and create meaningful connections with the people and places they encounter."[177] Membership is free, though CouchSurfing does ask for a one-time optional $25 donation. The way it works is simple, yet ingenious. If I want to find a place to stay in your city, I open the CS directory page that profiles all the CouchSurfers in your area. Then I send an "I'd Like to Surf Your Couch" message, with my CS name, so you can see the profile I've posted about myself, and also—far more important for making sure you don't welcome into your home an ax murderer, a Fox News polemicist, or worse—comments from people who've hosted and vouched for me. And there's one more clever kicker. When I open up my profile, I see only the positive comments. But when you open it, you'll see the negative ones too.

CouchSurfing introduces one to the most unexpected teachers, like C. L. Hickerson, whose Locust Grove Farm in Greensboro, North Carolina is also a ceremonial center complete with a monument to C. L.'s parents, a standing stone circle, fire circle, and art installations in wood, ceramic, and stone, all designed as a ritual space for the intentional community of farmers, artisans, and students who work and celebrate there. My time with C. L. was full of teaching stories, like the one about how C. L. asked young Andrew Trump if he wanted to become the custodian of Locust Grove, and Andrew answered that that discussion would best begin when he knew the name of every tree on the farm. I've rarely received such lessons in original action and abundant creativity as I did from these two men, whose every word and move was an education in conscious living, moment-to-moment awareness, communal creativity, and impeccable stewardship of Earth.

Such experiences, and CouchSurfing is loaded with them, show how the Aquarian transition is happening far away from major media markets, in places where modest masters are walking the talk of the New Earth in ways that raise the essential questions: What if, in the same way that we wouldn't dream of fouling our hostess's home, harming her family, and stealing her possessions, we also see that we are here as guests of Mother Earth, grateful for the bounty of her table and the hospitality she offers it in a Grace that welcomes and forgives all, and waits patiently for us to learn how guests behave? What if Earth were the ultimate youth hostel, where we arrive in a spiritual adventure that brings us into friendship with all nations and cultures, into conversations in new languages and music in new keys as we learn one another's songs and sing them into the night?

What if we could even join with others, with thousands and even millions of them, in a Great Game that challenges us to solve our problems and save the Earth, and have fun doing it in an intentional community of hugely talented and optimistic people? The game is already underway. Called the Avant Game and Urgent Evoke as it continues to evolve, it's the brainchild of game designer Jane McGonigal, who sees an invaluable resource of creativity where no one else had thought to consider it.[178] McGonigal, who describes herself as "exuberant" rather than "rational," says her goal for the next decade is "to try to make it as easy to save the world in real life as it is to save the world in online games."[179]

In her view, the 500 million young people on our planet who've devoted so much of their childhood and adolescence to playing online and video games are by no means the nervous little bundles of unutilized, even wasted talent that they may seem to be in the eyes of those who wish their children and other people's were engaged in something "productive" or "useful" or "real." Rather, as McGonigal sees them, young gamers are an invaluable creative resource. The 10,000 hours they spend playing games during their childhood—compared to the 10,080 hours they spend in classrooms from the 5th grade through the end of high school—make them gaming "virtuosos" by the time they're 18, ready if they have a way and a chance to devote to the real world and its problems the same skills and values they've learned from more years of gaming than the rest of us have devoted to the skills we use. What are all these virtuosi getting so good at? At what could almost be, as McGonigal sees them, a list of Aquarian virtues:

1. "Urgent optimism: extreme self-motivation . . . the desire to act immediately to tackle an obstacle, combined with the belief that we have a reasonable hope of success.

2. "Skill at weaving a tight social fabric . . . we like people better after we play a game with them [because] it takes a lot of trust to play a game with someone.

3. "Trust that [we] will play by the same rules, value the same goal, [and] stay with the game until it's over. . . . And we actually build stronger social relationships as a result.

4. "Blissful productivity . . . we're actually happier working hard than we are relaxing, or hanging out . . . we are optimized, as human beings, to do hard meaningful work.

5. "Epic meaning. Gamers love to be attached to awe-inspiring missions to human planetary-scale stories . . . they aim consistently at the epic win."

None of this is a guaranteed sell, and McGonigal draws some laughs— at least at the top of what she has to say, from people who are not yet ready to believe that young World of Warcraft gamers are ready to handle pollution, poverty, ethnic and religious violence, and the rest of the heavyweight game pieces in today's cluster of planetary crises. And more than one person has wondered whether the World Bank Institute's motives in sponsoring the Urgent Evoke game are purely altruistic and progressive, or an attempt to co-opt what could become a threat to corporatist agendas of control, or at least to identify promising and temptable talent among the young gamers.

Yet Urgent Evoke now attracts a growing number of players, attracted by the challenge of the game itself, the crucial importance of the planetary stakes, and the obvious fact that when what we are doing is not working, we must reach a point where, as Franklin D. Roosevelt put it at the beginning of the New Deal, we "Do something. If it works, do more of it. If it doesn't, do something else." There's little doubt about McGonigal's brilliance, her sincerity and infectious enthusiasm in marshalling the energies of so many toward an Epic Win for planet Earth: "An outcome that is so extraordinarily positive you had no idea it was even possible until you achieved it. It was almost beyond the threshold of imagination. And when you get there you are shocked to discover what you are truly capable of."

Other examples of intentional community abound, including those, like Circle of Sound, whose members link up synchronously across the Earth to align in Global Harmonization ceremonies that anchor the frequencies of Acceptance, Love, Compassion, Unity, and Peace for the benefit of all beings. Several communities of this kind are listed in the Aquarian Resources at the end of this book. For now, the best way to culminate the subject of intentional community is to look at what may be, in Sam Shepard's phrase (from *Fool for Love*), the extra long black Mercedes Benz of intentional communities.

A LABORATORY FOR HUMANITY'S FUTURE: DAMANHUR

It has been called "The Eighth Wonder of the World," and many other things besides, since it was established in 1975 near Turin in the Piedmont region of northern Italy by spiritual teacher, author, and holistic health practitioner Oberto Airaudi and two dozen other founding members. In the years since, the Federation of Damanhur has grown into "an eco-society based on ethical and spiritual values, on social commitment, on volunteer work and solidarity [whose] citizens apply these principles in order to realize their collective dream of a more sustainable and equitable world, built upon People and Communities."[180] Damanhur was given a United Nations Global Settlement Award in 2005 as an outstanding model for a sustainable future, and has received many other honors for bringing its optimistic vision to practical realization.

The 1,000 members of the main Damanhur settlement live in a network of independent and largely self-sufficient villages that comprise together a sophisticated, highly evolved city-state with its own constitution, currency, businesses and civic services, a daily newspaper, medical and scientific research facilities, an open university, and a school system that teaches children from nursery through middle school. The name of the region that houses the center of Damanhur, in the foothills of the Alps, hardly conveys the tireless reach and effort that the community brings to everything it does. *Valchiusella* literally means "closed valley," but Damanhur is anything but isolated in space, or in its aims. It has grown to include some 20,000 members living in satellite communities in Europe, the Americas, and Japan. It has created relationships with many international organizations, including Wisdom University, with whom Damanhur is committed to the goal of supplying 100 percent of the world's electricity from renewable sources by 2018.

From its beginning, in a hundred ways, Damanhur has always fused the practical business of life on the Earth plane with a joyous mystical vision and alignment with energies in the *field* (more about this soon) that are no less potent and "real" for not yet being completely understood. Determining the location where Damanhur's "cathedral" had to be built was not only a matter of finding the right spot on the ground, but of building at the precise depth *under* the ground where "synchronic lines" flow in "rivers of energy that link the Earth to the cosmos." When the time came to sink the shafts into the mountain, everyone—teachers and elders too—got down and dirty, hauling up the rock and mud in bucket brigades, even late into the night, because Damanhurian spirituality is above all "extremely pragmatic, for proposing complex thought, which is realized through complete and responsible action."[181]

The grand result of the years of effort that followed, much of it in mudslides and bleary exhaustion, has often been compared to the great cathedrals of medieval Europe because the Temples of Humankind—the Halls of Water, the Earth, the Spheres, Metals, and the Labyrinth—are filled with astonishingly beautiful works of painting, sculpture, mosaic, and stained glass, all built underground in resonant sound spaces, some of them linked by secret stairways and doors that open when one follows the clues in the murals. But Damanhur's cathedral differs from the great works of Christian architecture in one crucial respect: the Temples of Humankind do not encode the symbols of only one religion. Rather, Damanhur's spiritual principles are eclectic and Earth-based. Ancient Egypt is a major influence, as the name Damanhur comes from *Temen-Hor*, the "town of Horus." Like an Egyptian mystery school, Damanhur uses Horus the Falcon as the "stellar/solar symbol of light, towards which the initiate guides his path of consciousness."[182]

Otherwise Damanhur can hardly be said to have a belief system, much less anything resembling dogma. The community's spiritual principles, as set forth in Oberto Airaudi's three *Books of the Initiate* and other writings, consist mainly of core ideas common to many mystery traditions: that within each human being is a divine energy or force that must be awakened through individual effort that enables us to break away from limiting habits, and discover and pursue each one's talents and dreams. While his emphasis on such personal fulfillment is high, Airaudi—who as Damanhur's guiding Horus figure uses the initiate name Falco and writes through the personae of OroChritshna and other teachers—also makes it clear that we can develop and emerge only through honoring our responsibilities to others and working with them in a spirit of fully engaged, committed living in relation to other human lives, our communities, and our planet.

This is never quick and easy, as we know. It is a process of *Dying to Learn*, as the first of Airaudi's *Books of the Initiate* is entitled, and requires at some point the making of "the esoteric choice [that] can only ask EVERYTHING of you. Choose or stop. Get off the train or endure and continue the Journey, with joy, enthusiasm, courage and a spirit of adventure."[183] What makes this challenge bearable and doable for Damahur's brave souls? It helps that the community's philosophy and style are grounded in practical activity on the Earth plane, in empowering discoveries of talents that one didn't know were there, in teamwork and relationships, and in an outlook that is consistently optimistic and joyous.

One example, in the Hall of the Earth, is in a mural that is startling at first glance because the last thing we expect to see in this serene, exquisitely beautiful place is a battle scene. A closer look shows that, curiously, the warriors wear armor and carry shields that look ancient Roman—but they have no weapons, there are no dead or wounded on the field, no blood to be seen anywhere, and everyone is laughing and grinning as though they've never had so much fun. In the background are masses of gray, faceless beings who look nearly human in form, but are not quite there. To become realized as individuals, to gain full color and expression, these yet-unformed candidates for humanity will have to join the battle that is joyous because each one who fights it full-out is winning the victory over everything within himself that is small, timid, and uncommitted to awakening that divine spark and principle of the human being in the full emergence of his light.

Damanhur has always encouraged, and done all but require, the creative expression of each of its members in whatever art medium gives him or her joy. While not one of the two dozen founding members of the community was an accomplished professional artist, the Temples of Humankind, the outdoor temples, labyrinths, parks, and buildings have been filled over the years with sculptures, murals, and other installations that show what works of beauty are waiting within each one who is willing to learn from those of more developed skill, and to challenge old assumptions about what one cannot make and do. The results appear everywhere at Damanhur in images like this one from the elder care house, which shows the community's departed ones as smaller than the flowers, plants, and insects because as human beings we are here not to dominate nature or control it, but to find our place among beings who are equal to us in dignity and beauty— and who, like us, are emerging into their possibilities as they, and we, form the interdependent connections that help us grow together in the field, and find our dynamic roles in the conscious evolution that fulfills us all.

PLAYING THE FIELD

We have now come full circle from the first chapter of this book, and its Aquarian ideas about the physical and spiritual environments that we live in and seek to transform through our conscious, concerted intentions. It's time to look at what feels like, and appears to be, the solid and "real" material dimension of our experience on Earth in relation to the mysterious, unseen *field* of energetic forces that the pioneers of quantum mechanics began to investigate a century ago, and which today's scientists have begun to imagine as not only an unlimited domain of potential from which anything can emerge spontaneously, but even as a kind of artist's palette or energetic laboratory that human actions and intentions may affect and direct toward specific goals for the sake of our conscious evolution into a species living in greater capacity, awareness, and compassion toward one another and our planet.

To Albert Einstein, the invisible energy matrix that modern scientists have called *the field* was "the sole governing agency of matter"—thus implying that the physical universe we have accepted as "real" for all these thousands of years, because we can perceive matter with our senses and imagine the atomic particles that comprise it, is not only controlled in some way by the energy forces at work and play in the field. It may even be true, as Einstein ventured, that "there is no place in this new kind of physics both for the field and matter, for the field is the only reality."[184] For Lynne McTaggart, whose seminal book *The Field: The Quest for the Secret Force of the Universe* (2002) helped galvanize today's growing surge of interest in the nature of the field and our relationship to it, the field is "an ocean of microscopic vibrations in the space between things—a state of pure potential and infinite possibility."[185]

So far, so easy to agree on. The points of contention are in whether the forces at work in the field are only random and mechanical, unaffected by the presence or consciousness of observers, or whether there is, in fact, as Werner Heisenberg ventured, such a thing as an "observer effect," whereby our very act of perceiving or measuring material things might somehow affect their behavior—and if so, whether the intention of one or more observers could in fact bring about changes in the energetics of the field, and in matter itself. The same question applies as well to the nature and behavior of genes and the cells that comprise them: are they mechanical and thereby basically immutable, so that "it's in our genes" and there's nothing we can do about it—or might there be some kind of cellular intelligence that is capable of making decisions about an environment, even changing it?

As Bruce Lipton shows in *Spontaneous Evolution*, "the new science of *epigenetic control* reveals that life is controlled by something above the genes [that] provides a gateway to understanding our proper role as co-creators of our reality."[186] Not only this—but if our cells are indeed "smarter than we are," and millions of them can act smoothly in concert to respond to conditions in their environment, then it is not only possible but *necessary* that "we live by our higher nature as cells in the body of Mother Earth and in the spirit energy of the eternal universe.[187]

A growing body of research conducted for decades now brings increasingly convincing evidence that everything in the field is indeed affected by everything else, and conditions in the field can indeed be affected by the intentions of teams of people who direct their energies in prayer, meditation, and sound toward effecting changes in the behavior of human hearts and minds. As the evidence continues to accumulate and point to some inescapable conclusions, it is only a matter of time until we act more expertly to replicate the kind of experiment reported by Gregg Braden, in which the crime rate in a given city plummeted when the number of people practicing transcendental meditation there reached the square root of one percent.[188]

The implications of Braden's experiment—that only a fraction of one percent of us are needed to create changes of consciousness and behavior in the entire human morphic field—are the basis of *The Intention Experiment*, Lynne McTaggart's book about "the World's Largest Mind-Over-Matter Experiment,"[189] and the countless scientific tests, meditations, ceremonies, and other intentional alignments that bring us together at every solstice and equinox, every lunation, every moment of environmental crisis.

The results are far from conclusive yet, as we are only beginning now to co-create the new Aquarian Planet. But our hypothesis is easy enough to articulate. More of us awaken every day, and when we do, we don't go back to sleep. We are by no means a naïve, dreamy minority. We are an intentional force that grows in numbers, strength and clarity of intention every day, every hour. Time is on our side, as we hold in mind the New Earth we've come to make together. We envisioned this role long ago in the celestial grand opera we knew we would come to play together now. Curtain Up! Light the Lights!

AQUARIAN PROFILE: WANGARI MAATHAI

Some of today's most sonorous and powerful new Aquarian vocabulary is coming from Africa, which has preserved some of its communal traditions, and may thus have an easier transition to societies that closely resemble Old Culture communities, where the young grow up living between the spirit realm of Heaven and sacred Earth, knowing that they are linked to and embraced by all the lives around them, seen and unseen, in the house and the river, the forest and the sky.

The Ndebele word *tshwane* comes from the name of a revered chief who was named for the river where his people lived in South Africa before they migrated during in the 1800s to what is now Zimbabwe. Tshwane has been in the news because it was proposed as a name to replace Pretoria. "Tshwane" would not memorialize colonial rule through apartheid. Tshwane affirms unity rather than division because it means "we are the same" or "we are one because we live together."[190] African languages are filled with such words to express that we are one and the same, that this is in fact a point of pride for us, and we are responsible for one another. This is why, as Julian Hewitt wrote, the African word *Ubuntu*, which means that "I am a person through other people . . . my humanity is tied to yours" may be "the single most important aspect of living in a highly connected planet: Our humanity is tied together. We must respect each other, and we must always keep our interconnection in mind."[191]

There is a practical mysticism in this. While the Aquarian core values of friendship and equality, freedom and flexibility and acceptance will all be important for keeping all kinds of relationships together in the Aquarian Age, the last two values of spirituality and community are the fast track of the soul. Thus community without spirituality may help us for a time to gain and spread happiness. Spirituality without community can steer us through a series of love unions and soul mates. But for the long haul, loving spiritual bonds had best be planted in the spirit of community like green growing things firmly rooted in the Earth, in the way that Wangari Maathai envisions them.

Maathai raised quite a few eyebrows in Europe and North America when she won the Nobel Peace Prize in 2004. For a century, the Nobel Committee had usually chosen laureates who brought an end to war, and so they occasionally honored even war criminals like Henry Kissinger. Or the prize went to activists who sought to ban land mines, or to end religious conflict or racial strife. But Wangari Maathai brought a whole new premise to the consciousness of the planet: that the main problem now isn't conflict among human beings, as painful as that still is. The most dangerous issue, as others are beginning to see, is an unhealthy relationship between human beings and their mother, the Earth.

Wangari Muta Maathai was born in Kenya in 1940. After earning her bachelor's degree in biology from Mt. St. Scholastica College in Atchison, Kansas and her M.S. at the University of Pittsburgh, she became the first woman from East and Central Africa to earn a Ph.D. from the University of Nairobi (1971), where she served as associate professor and chairwoman of the Department of Veterinary Anatomy. In 1976 she joined the National Council of Women of Kenya, and launched the idea for which she is best known: the Green Belt Movement, an inclusive grassroots initiative that aims to organize women, and the men who will join them, in efforts to plant trees and thereby preserve the environment. Since its beginning, the Green Belt Movement has coordinated the planting of almost 40 million trees in Kenya's farms, towns, and villages.

In 1986 the effort grew into the Pan African Green Belt Network, teaching the program to community leaders from Tanzania, Uganda, Malawi, Lesotho, Ethiopia, Zimbabwe, and other countries. Maathai's sphere of action got wider as her 60th year approached. As co-chairwoman of Jubilee 2000 Africa, she led campaigns to cancel the debt of poor African countries, and to stop ruinous exploitation of forests and other natural resources. By the 1990s her tireless leadership had brought her numerous awards and honorary degrees, culminating in a triumph that is especially close to her heart. In 2002, in the watershed election that replaced the corrupt Daniel arap Moi regime with a democratic government in Kenya, she was elected to parliament with an amazing 98 percent of the vote in her district. She still serves as Kenya's Assistant Minister for Environment, Natural Resources and Wildlife.

Maathai's main working concepts—for example, that "the symbiotic relationship between the sustainable management of natural resources and democratic governance [is] relevant globally"—are the kinds of ideas that have often been thought before, but have somehow never been so well articulated, or put into such effective practice.[192] Perhaps the people of the world, seeing clearly now that nations that are fighting over oil will soon be at war over water and food, are receptive to Maathai's warning that "Unless we properly manage resources like forests, water, land, minerals and oil, we will not win the fight against poverty. And there will not be peace. Old conflicts will rage on and new resource wars will erupt unless we change the path we are on."

Wangari Maathai's vision sees human life in all its dimensions—from the individual to the family, the community, society, and the whole planet, as a set of love links unified by devotion to the health and happiness of Mother Earth. The implied question in her world view, as it affects all our relationships, is simple: can the quality of our love for other human beings really be any better than the quality of our love for our planet? Intuitive answers are evident enough, as the societies that continue to damage the Earth most are precisely the ones in which citizens' love relationships are most unhappy and unstable. Time will tell whether one thing that now grows taller and stronger among all those tens of millions of trees in Kenya is a new culture of love based in values that are healthy, nourishing, and sustainable. It's time to learn the stories that Africa tells, and spread them everywhere like seeds that will sprout and rise to green and heal the Earth.

CHAPTER 12

AQUARIAN STORIES

We close our journey and begin the voyage toward 2012 with a few stories and scenarios that serve here as what medieval poets called an *envoi*: a word of thanks and a reminder that farewell means go happily and in peace.

THE STATION MASTER

The morning train pulls into a station in the country. A man gets off, walks up to the station master, and asks him, "What kind of town is this?" The station master replies, "What kind of town did you just come from?" The man smiles and says, "It was great. Beautiful and pleasant, and the people were friendly and kind. I can't wait to go back and visit there again." And the station master says, "Well, you'll probably like it here. That's the kind of town this is." Later the mid-day train comes, and a man gets off and asks the station master the same question. The station master asks him, "What kind of town did you just come from?" The man says, "It was horrible. Ugly and run-down, and the people were hostile and mean. I never want to go back there." And the station master tells him, "Well, then you may not like it here very much either. That's the kind of town this is."

THE SHIP IS REALLY THERE

When Magellan's expedition to sail around the world stopped off the coast of what is now Argentina to send a party ashore for provisions, the native people on the beach were astonished to see small boats suddenly appear as if from nowhere, coming toward the shore. Each boat was full of white-skinned, bearded men, and carried a leader in a shiny hat who stood up and watched as the others rowed. The natives were amazed that men in such tiny boats could have come across the big water, and ran to tell their shaman. He saw at once some large wooden houses with folded white wings that were floating offshore at about the distance of an arrow shot. They must have brought the little boats. Once the shaman described the Spanish ships, the others in his tribe could all see them too.

BE KIND TO LAWYERS

Two professions will stand in the unemployment line of history when the Age of Aquarius really takes off.

One is lawyers. They thrive on conflict and oppression, and their desire to win at all costs has often made them so loathsome that Shakespeare's Dick the Butcher invariably gets a laugh when he shouts, "The first thing we do, let's kill all the lawyers" (*Henry VI*, Part 2). Attorneys have to be well-dressed, and not just because a prosperous image is vital to their success. They pay a lot for custom-tailored clothes because freedom of movement is crucial when one has to walk a tightrope between secrets and lies, and dance gracefully through terms like plausible deniability, which only a lawyer could have invented.

No more of this in Aquarius, as each one's value will be weighed in how well he heals, teaches, and serves his community, not in what he can squeeze from one person, or all of them. His first response to an accidental injury will be to ask if anyone else is hurt. His first thought when he meets someone from one of the vanishing breeds—ego climbers, empire builders, vindictive wounders, winners by intimidation—will be to wonder what is causing the other's pain, and making him lacerate those who want to love him.

The trend is already underway as popular movies now deliver stories of a kind not seen before: of lawyers, corporate raiders and other organized crime figures, giving up their old ruthless lives of domination and trickery, and even persuading whole ballrooms of other sharks and shareholders that there are more important things in life than screwing the other guy. Before too long, textbooks about storytelling and screenwriting may add a new scenario to describe what more people are doing, and how good it makes them and everyone else feel. At first these may be called Abdication stories, as their focus is on what the hero is giving up. But later such stories will be seen as the Homecoming. The return of the son who's been prodigal with the truth. Surrender and liberation.

Once we acquire the essential Aquarian mind-linking skills, and everybody is transparent and telepathic, it will be impossible for anyone to use or practice law as they do now. How can a defendant pretend he's innocent when everybody can read his mind and see he's not? How can a jury convict a man who everybody knows is not guilty? How can attorneys get away with hiding evidence and attacking the credibility of honest witnesses? About as easily as a crooked judge can serve a political or corporate agenda when everyone can see what's really under his robe and in his soul. The good news about law is that it has sometimes served its noble purpose of protecting honest people. The tough news is that when we are living in harmony so open that we no longer need to fight and lie, lawyers will find new livelihoods as teachers and actors. We'll need those.

PLEASE HUG A SPY

Another group that will need new job training are spies, the people who make their gadgets, and all of those who earn their living my making and breaking codes, hiding secrets and cracking them, snooping on others, and hiding themselves. Who can cover anything up when everybody's telepathic, or try to earn money by selling information that everybody else already has?

For investors in spyware, Aquarius is a tragedy. It comes just as their field is ready to explode into dazzling new possibilities. You might know. The U.S. Congress and courts had already agreed that anybody from the government can enter your house at any time, provided they don't wake you up if they come at night, and thereby infringe your right to remain asleep during legal proceedings that affect you. For all anyone knew, all the constraints that used to prevent governments from spying on all their people, all the time, were about to evaporate. So spooks wouldn't have to place a concealed microphone, video camera, and heat sensor by your mattress or futon. Everything—video deck, the digital sound recorder, the sensors that show whose body temperature is going up or down, and in what room, could be mounted inside an attractive box that resembles a bird feeder, and could be bolted to the outside of your house, like the electric meter.

And now Aquarius comes. Everybody will be telepathic. You may as well unload those shares in the Cryptomate Group right now.

THE TRUTH WILL SET YOU UP

There is a wonderful story about the famously unfaithful Brooklyn Dodgers pitcher Kirby Higbe, whose wife came home one day to find her husband in their bed with another woman. Higbe jumped out of bed, ran out of the room and down the stairs, then shouted back up at his wife, "It wasn't me!"

Good luck with this in the Age of Aquarius. Relationships will be more fluid and less possessive anyway, and philanderers had best have their fun now, before women become telepathic as well as intuitive. A woman will always know when a man is lying, and vice versa. There will be zero slack for the slick:

"Do you think this dress makes me look fat?"

"No."

"Yes you do. Looking at me in this dress made you think about pork."

"I'm just getting hungry."

"You just ate. And you didn't like the food."

There is no escape. The New Honesty will, mercifully, come gradually, not all at once. The deeper consequences will appear by and by. At the moment, Aquarian transparency stories all look comic. Here's one that somebody may be working on now, given freely here in defiance of the usual Piscean paranoia about how story ideas should be kept hidden because somebody may steal them. Please steal it now. It needs to get out there.

Hal Ravitch, a devious producer and notorious cad from the Los Angeles pop music industry, picks the wrong woman to cross: Wendy de Noire, who is secretly a witch. She gets her revenge by sending Hal a thousand years into the future, where he reappears in the middle of the Age of Aquarius. It's a nightmare. His credit cards are useless, as banks no longer exist. Artists and communities work together directly, so nobody needs a producer, and show business as Hal's always known it is history.

Fortunately, he's still attractive enough to get help, but now, for the first time, women have his number from the first glance. He's so used to lying that he can't score with anyone, and this is really strange at first, until he learns that the rules have changed. Now women don't care if they have to share a man, as long as he's honest about it. Hal goes through romantic purgatory and spiritual hell as he hits the rock bottom of unworthiness as a man who can't stop lying. But when he comes through the dark night of the soul, his life changes. He finds that he's a great stage manager, and two women in his commune are more than happy to share him and love him. He feels confident and happy for the first time, and tells the Goddess, "I don't know what you did to bring me here, but thank you so much. You've saved my life." At that moment he vanishes.

Wendy, it turns out, has gone through her own changes, and regrets the ways she's punished others who've wronged her. She sends Hal back to 2011. He finds himself in the conference room of the most feared, sinister talent agency in LA, still wearing his pink and silver Aquarian jumpsuit, seated across from Roy Scrodnick, the Prince of Sharkness himself, who has just heard Hal say, "I don't know what you did to bring me here, but thank you so much. You've saved my life."

The meeting is a catastrophe. Hal has no idea what's up, and can't tell a lie. He and Wendy meet again, of course, and she tells him what happened. He wants to go back to Aquarius and invites her to go too. At first she doesn't want to go, but then she does. Are we talking sequel now? But of course. The only question is how many. *The Truth Will Set You Up* could be a blockbuster.

THE DRAGON AND THE DOLPHIN

Asians and westerners perceive dragons very differently. For eastern peoples, notably the Chinese, the dragon is a lucky omen and mighty blessing, symbol of the divine creative fire that brings light to the world, and seeks wisdom.

But in the European tradition, the dragon is the fear that manifests in possessiveness and jealousy as a kind of snake in the manger who won't let anyone near the gold, which he can't spend, or the girl, whom he can't love. The dragon gets his kick of empowerment from denying others what they want—but he creates nothing, least of all new dragons. Ever hear of mom and pop dragons having a brood of little dragaroos and dragonettes? Neither has anybody else. The Dragon is solitary because it is armored against love.

Its energy is blocked in the solar plexus domain of fear and courage, and has not accelerated into the love frequency of the heart. Since the Dragon has all these unsexy qualities, how, then, does it reproduce? It doesn't. It is created when some other being, like the giant Fafnir in the Nibelung legends, decides that the best way to hoard what he has is to turn himself from a sexual being into a gigantic asexual reptile.

Once the dragon appears, St. George or Siegfried or St. Michael usually comes to kill it with a sword or a lance. But killing the dragon won't get rid of it for good, since its blood can enter the soil like seeds and wait to become another dragon later. Killing the dragon symbolizes a problem we have always had with violence: that it never settles anything, but only guarantees that another dragon will come later. One does not have to be a myth master like Carl Jung or Joseph

Campbell to see that the dragon slayer's blade or spear is a straight line that represents the penetrating power of masculine intellect, which by itself can never free the dragon, but can only confine or kill it for now. Why do the earliest dragon fighter stories that we still tell in the West appear in the millennia before Jesus, during the Age of Aries? Because that's when the patriarchal, male-dominated cultures overcame the matriarchal goddess cultures of the Taurean Age, which sought above all to protect and empower the fertility of the womb and the soil.

After over 4,000 years of bloody background, we can go the new Aquarian route of transforming the dragon into a being of love, even one as happy as a dolphin. The dragon will not move toward such freedom willingly. It can only be freed by the force of love. We will soon be able, for the first time in Earth's history, to link the concerted intentions of awakened and loving beings in order to send love to the dragon, and liberate him. It's easy to work up interactive Free the Dragon plays. When the celebrants have entered the circle, people playing such Earth figures as Pan, the Green Man, Loki, Isis, Gaia, and Hera enter. The wise women speak about what they bring tonight. Then the dragon—played most easily by several lithe people linked with black and red cloth into a single scary being, enters roaring and tries to take over. When the others resist, the moment escalates into threats and worse. Then the Earth clowns lead the celebrants in a love chant that dissolves the dragon's fear, and turns it back into a being of love.

THE TRUTH LANDS SAFELY

The divine principle of Truth seems always to be a Goddess. The Egyptians depicted her as Ma'at, who had wings and wore a single feather in her hair. The Greeks called her Astraea, the "starry one." Like all ladies of Truth, Ma'at and Astrea seem to have lived on Earth during some Golden Age, then went to live in the Heavens when life among humankind turned coarser, and lies made the floor of the world fetid and slippery.

At least one good thing was that the goddess was always safe up there in the sky where no one could do her harm. Until now, that is. The premise of this story is that people in the late Piscean Age who have turned lying into an industry become obsessed with the fear that as long as Truth remains alive somewhere, even up in the sky where no one can see her, they'll never be completely in control of what people on Earth believe. Media-wise "developed" nations lead the hunt, and the book, movie, serial, and novelty rights to the story all ride on whether Truth can be taken alive. Her domain name, truth.com, is already a lock for some quick entrepreneur. But her living energy field is still at large. No authority will be safe until she's in the slammer, the bottle or the box. The hunt is on.

Tricksters help her, of course, in what could be, in the right hands, the most intricate philosophical buddy movie since *Don Quixote*. Truth learns to look the other way as long as outrageous scams work for the benefit of all; and Kokopeli, Maui the Trickster, clever servants from Moliere, and others amaze themselves by acting in completely disinterested service. Chaplin as the Tramp is captured when he stops to make sure that the Keystone Kop he's just whacked with a board is all right. In the end, the audience is happy to learn what they somehow knew all along but never realized: that you can't love and lie at the same time, because Truth is really the robe of Love.

EVERYBODY GOES TO HEAVEN

People all over the world are attracted now to the Sufis and their happy view that there is no Hell. Everybody goes home to God sooner or later, and the only question is how each one will fight against this before giving in. In the meantime, though, so we won't shock too terribly the ones who still believe in Hell, it may be best to visualize Heaven this way:

> *It resembles at first what we've always expected: golden sunlight, blue sky, fleecy white clouds, stairways of marble, and gates of pearl. No one*

wonders at first why it is that, like Elvis, the angels seem to hold their harps, but do not actually play them. At the gate is not St. Peter, but a quiz show host who asks each new soul, "Would you like to look down at Hell for a moment before you go into Heaven?"

Those who say, "Not really" or "No, thanks" go at once through a silver silk curtain, and those who say "Oh, boy! Yes!" are escorted onto a terrace, where they see a horde of people, bending over the balustrade at the edge, some of them yelling at the staff:

Southern Baptist: I still can't see Hell. Where is it?

Mather: You just have to keep looking. You know it's there, right?

Taliban Fighter: Of course we know it's there. Why can't we see it?

Pope Alexander VI: You just have to be patient, and keep looking. Don't give up!

Tea Party Host: Well, it feels like I've just been here forever. Where is it?

Torquemada: You sound really indignant about this.

Crusader: Well, yes. This is taking forever. Why can't we just go in?

Innocent III: You said you wanted to see Hell first. So you have to do that. You can't go in until you see Hell first.

Khomeini: Don't get mad at us just because we're staff, and the customer's always right.

Ashcroft: Ruhollah's telling it like it is. We don't get to go in until all of you do.

And so on. The staff is not allowed to say that Hell isn't there. Nor do they get to say that so many vengeful souls were really hoping that the highlight of the whole trip would be looking down into Hell and seeing those bastards we hate screaming and sizzling in the lake of fire. The most avid Hellwatchers, like Captain Ahab nailing a Spanish gold ounce to the mast of the Pequod for the first sailor to see Moby Dick, long to be the one to say,

Rev. Fred Phelps: Look! There! He breaches! It's Clinton!

Hannity: I knew it! Where?

Rev. Pat Robertson: There! Up in the burning hawthorn tree, surrounded by those devils with weed whackers!

And so on. Is it fair that the most foolish and punitive souls can eventually get off the terrace and into Heaven? Sure it is, even if they strain and squint for a glimpse of Hell for so long that they'd get balustrade burn if they had bodies. This is Heaven. It's all good.

Every now and then a soul on the terrace smiles quizzically and disappears. When other souls nearby notice this and ask what's happened, the staff say that he or she must have seen Hell, and has just rematerialized inside The Lounge. What the staff don't say, can't say, is: there is no Hell, there never was.

The most unexpected people are inside that silver curtain, in the Lounge. A smiling Mr. Cheney, Mr. Stalin, and Lucrezia Borgia invite the newcomer to be a fourth for bridge. Mr. Hitler, a much funnier guy than anyone expected, is serving champagne and shrimp toast. Catherine de Medici is singing popular favorites from every century and country. Caligula leads the dance team, and there's magic in Dracula's Big Black Box. Attila the Hun, in his striking tufted horsehair tuxedo, is the emcee. In a banquette near the Moon Window, witty and flirtatious as always, is Henry Kissinger, and nobody is surprised to see that the old war criminal is as mellow as a baked pear. Everybody is. All have played their roles to perfection, all have suffered the fires of their own self-scourging and have burned all their wounds and judgments away, and all have come home.

All are one. And always have been. And are perfect in their love and joy. Welcome. This seat is waiting for you. Some Chateau d'Amour?

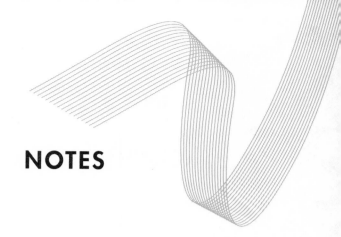

NOTES

CHAPTER ONE

1   "Aquarius/Let the Sun Shine In," from *Hair, the American Tribal Love Rock Musical*, Book and lyrics by Gerome Ragni and James Rado, Music by Galt McDermot, 1968.

2   Ken Keyes, Jr., *The Hundredth Monkey*, 1981. Keyes' story is based on an account by Lyall Watson in *Lifetide*, pp. 127–148. See also *www.testament.org/testament/100thmonkey.html*.

3   Rupert Sheldrake, *The Presence of the Past*, pp. 177–181.

4   Report of the Global Consciousness Project on observations of Sept. 11, 2001. Published on the GCP website at *www.noosphere.princeton.edu*.

5   Ibid.

6   GCP report on the Harmonic Concordance of Nov. 8, 2003, "Harmonic Concordance Nov 8/9 2003," n*oosphere.princeton.edu/harmonic.concordance.html*.

7   Ervin Laszlo, *CosMos: A Creator's Guide to the Whole World*, p. 93.

8   Richard C. Hoagland and David Wilcock, "Interplanetary 'Day after Tomorrow'?," May 14, 2004, *www.enterprisemission.com/_articles/ 05-14-2004_Interplanetary_Part_1/Interplanetary_1.htm*.

9   Thom Hartmann, *The Last Hours of Ancient Sunlight*, p. 97.

10   In this story from *Meetings with Remarkable Men*, the young Gurdjieff saw a group of boys tormenting a smaller boy from the Yezidi cult by drawing around him, in the dirt of the playground, a circle from which the boy believed he could not escape. Gurdjieff freed him by erasing a part of the circle, giving the Yezidi boy a way out. See *www.gurdjieff-legacy.org/40articles/ yezidism.htm*.

CHAPTER TWO

11   " . . . the vernal equinoctial point will cease to be in the constellation of Pisces, sign of the Christian era, towards the year 2010—in forty-four years." Louis Charpentier, *The Mysteries of Chartres Cathedral*, p. 166. See also Wynn Free with David Wilcock, *The Reincarnation of Edgar Cayce?*, p. 303.

12   Andrew Raymond, *Secrets of the Sphinx*, *www.revealer.com/ platonic.htm*.

13   Thom Hartmann, *The Last Hours of Ancient Sunlight*, pp. 14–25.

14   *Neter*, which rhymes with "knitter," is often mistranslated as "god." To the Egyptians, a neter (female netert, plural neteru) was one of the physical forms and forces in which the One manifested in the natural world. That is why neter is the source of our word *nature*.

15   From *Sono un Gran Bugiardo*, documentary film by Damian Pettigrew, 2003.

CHAPTER THREE

16 Stefan Theil, "The End of Welfare," *Newsweek*, July 26, 2004, p. 25.

17 Mohandas K. Gandhi, *Gandhi on Nonviolence*.

18 Dalai Lama, Nobel Prize lecture at Oslo University, Dec. 11, 1989, *www.dalailama.com/html/nobel.html*.

19 Edward Gibbon, *The Decline and Fall of the Roman Empire*, *www.ccel.org/g/gibbon/decline/volume1/chapter4.htm*.

20 Arthur C. Clarke, quoted in David Elkington, *In the Name of the Gods*, p. 367.

21 Joseph Meeker, *The Comedy of Survival*, pp. 24–35.

22 Kurt Vonnegut, "Cold Turkey," *In These Times*, May 10, 2004, *www.inthesetimes.com/site/main/article/cold_turkey*.

CHAPTER FOUR

23 The source of the statement attributed to Mussolini—"Fascism should rightly be called Corporatism as it is a merge of state and corporate power"—is questionable. See *quotes.liberty-tree. ca/quotes_by/benito+mussolini*. On the steadily growing power of capitalism at the expense of democracy, see Robert Reich, *Supercapitalism*. See also Youssef M. Ibrahim, "The Collapse of Capitalism as We Know It," first published in *The International Herald Tribune* on March 10, 2004, reprinted at *www.gulf-news. com/Articles/opinion.asp?ArticleD=113241*.

24 Virgil, *Eclogue 4*, tr. J. W. MacKail, 1934. See *The Eclogues of Virgil* at *www.sacred-texts.com/cla/virgil/ecl/ecl04.htm*.

25 Faisal Islam, "Bailed-Out Banks Make Huge Profits," *The Real News*, August 3, 2009, *therealnews.com/t/index.php?option=com_ content&task=view&id=31&Itemid=74&jumival=4075*.

26 Kim Zetter, "Big Business Becoming Big Brother," first published at *Wired.com*, reprinted at *truthout.org*, Aug. 9, 2004; John Perkins, *Confessions of an Economic Hit Man*; Ellen Hodgson Brown, *Web of Debt: The Shocking Truth About Our Money System and How We Can Break Free*; "The Zeitgeist Addendum" at *www.zeitgeistmovie.com*; and Daniel Estulin, *The True Story of the Bilderberg Group*, 2009.

27 Matt Taibbi, "The Great American Bubble Machine," *Rolling Stone*, July 2, 2009, *www.rollingstone.com/politics/story/28816321/the_great_american_bubble_machine*; "Blowing Bubbles," Universal Festival Calendar Mythic prelude for November, 2008, *www.hermes3.net/nov108.htm*.

28 Tom Robbins, *Fierce Invalids Home from Hot Climates*, p. 362.

29 Learn more about Nations Lite at *www.trendwatching.com/resources/images/NATIONS-LITE.html*.

30 A *derivative* is "A financial instrument whose characteristics and value depend upon the characteristics and value of an underlier, typically a commodity, bond, equity or currency. Examples of derivatives include futures and options. Advanced investors sometimes purchase or sell derivatives to manage the risk associated with the underlying security, to protect against fluctuations in value, or to profit from periods of inactivity or decline. These techniques can be quite complicated and quite risky." See *www.investorwords.com/1421/derivative.html*.

31 From the annual report of Berkshire Hathaway for 2002, *www.berkshirehathaway.com/letters/2002pdf*.

32 George Soros in interview with Judy Woodruff, "The Financial Crisis," *New York Review of Books*, May 15, 2008.

33   David Chalmers, "Notes on Emergence Theory," *consc.net/notes/emergence.html*.

34   David Bonabeau and Christopher Meyer, "Swarm Intelligence: A Whole New Way to Think about Business," *Harvard Business Review*, May 2001, p. 1634. Swarm intelligence gained greater cachet in 2006 with Barbara Shipman's work on the "quantum intelligence" of bees, and its possible applications to the human mind. See *discovermagazine.com/1997/nov/quantumhoneybees1263*.

35   James Surowiecki, *The Wisdom of Crowds*, pp. 119–135.

36   Sam Foster on chaos theory at *easyweb.easynet.co.uk/˜sfoster4*.

37   "Comfortable with Chaos," *www.hermes3.net/nov108.htm*.

38   Alan M. Webber, "Secrecy in Business: Only Fools Stifle Truth," *USA Today*, July 13, 2004, p. A15.

39   Mark Landler, "Deutsche Bank Chief Gets a Slap on the Wrist." *International Herald Tribune*, July 23, 2004, p. 5.

40   Martin La Monica, "Breaking the Rules with Open Source." *CNET News*, Aug. 2, 2004, *news.com.com/Breaking+the+rules+with+open+source/2100-7344_3-5290983.html?tag=nefd.lede*.

41   Ibid.

42   Ibid.

43   Marek Kohn, "Why an Unequal Society Is an Unhealthy Society," *homepage.ntlworld.com/marek.kohn/unequal.html*. All quotes in this and the next two paragraphs are from this source.

44   Floyd Norris, "Confidence of Founders May Harm Google IPO," *International Herald Tribune*, August 14–15, 2004, p. 6.

45   "Google Goes Public," *International Herald Tribune*, August 22, 2004, p. 8.

46   James Howard Kunstler, "Zombie Economics: Don't Bail Out the System That Gave Us SUVs and Strip Malls," November 25, 2008. *www.alternet.org/economy/108481/zombie_economics:_don't_bail_out_the_system_that_gave_us_suvs_and_strip_malls*

47   Katherine Zaleski, "Local Currencies: Communities Printing Own Money to Keep Cash Flowing," *Huffington Post*, April 6, 2009, *www.huffingtonpost.com/.../communities-print-own-cur_n_183497.htm*.

48   "Companies Issue Own Money, 'Detroit Cheers'," March 23, 2009. See Crain's Detroit Business at *www.crainsdetroit.com/article/20090323/FREE/903239995#*.

49   Jeremy Brecher, T. Costello, and B. Smith, "Lessons from Hard Times Past," Truthout Perspective, July 22, 2009, *www.truthout.org/072209R*.

50   Karen Goldberg Goff, "Barter System Reborn," *Washington Times*, April 1, 2009, *www.washingtontimes.com/news/2009/apr/01/barter-system-reborn*.

51   John Leland, "With Advocates' Help, Squatters Call Foreclosures Home," *New York Times*, April 9, 2009, *www.nytimes.com/2009/04/10/us/10squatter.html?_r=1*.

52   Michael Shuman, "Small-Mart: Ideas and Tools for Building Healthy Local Economies," *www.small-mart.org*.

53   Wendy Call, "Reclaiming Corn and Culture," *Yes! Magazine*, Summer, 2008, *www.yesmagazine.org/issues/a-just-foreign-policy/reclaiming-corn-and-culture*.

54   Benjamin Dangl, "Argentina: Turning Around: An Interview with Mark Dworkin and Melissa Young," July 22, 2009, *www.zmag.org/znet/viewArticle/22083*.

55   Ethan Miller, "Other Economies Are Possible," *Dollars & Sense*, July–August, 2006, *www.dollarsandsense.org/archives/2006/0706emiller.html*.

56   Doreen Carvajal, "Champions in Hearts of Employees," *International Herald Tribune*, August 11, 2004.

CHAPTER FIVE

57   Letter to James Madison, Jan. 30, 1787, *www.earlyamerica.com/review/summer/letter.html*.

58   The seven tentative uniformities are (1) a period of economic reversal and hardship following a time of sustained economic development and rising prosperity; (2) growing tension between social classes, and exploitative, predatory actions by the upper class against the lower classes; (3) disaffection with the existing order among intellectuals who form common cause with the lower classes; (4) inept, negligent and corrupt government; (5) failures of leadership by a ruling class unable to perceive and respond effectively to changing conditions; (6) fiscal irresponsibility and corruption, resulting in large financial losses and maldistribution of wealth; and (7) inept and inconsistent use of force in foreign military misadventures and increased domestic surveillance and police harassment of the country's own citizens. See Crane Brinton, *The Anatomy of Revolution*.

59   See James Chowing Davies, "Toward a Theory of Revolution," *American Sociological Review*, February, 1962. See also Davies' *Why Men Revolt*, ed. James C. Davies, 1997.

60   Davies, op cit., article abstract, p. 5.

61   Sara Robinson, "When Change Is Not Enough: Seven Steps to Revolution," Campaign for America's Future, February 22, 2008, *www.alternet.org/politics/77498/?page=entire*.

62   Al Jazeera video series, "Battle for the Amazon: People vs. the Government," *therealnews.com/t/index.php?option=com_content &task=view&id=31&Itemid=74&jumival=4116*.

63   David Spangler, "A Call to Action: Fear and Loathing in the World," Aug. 29, 2009, *www.nhne.org/news/NewsArticlesArchive/ tabid/400/articleType/ArticleView/articleId/6095/Default.aspx*.

64   Martin Luther King, Jr., *Strength to Love*, 1963.

65   Marjorie Cohn, "Chavez Victory: Defeat for Bush Policy," *www.truthout.org/docs04/082004.htm*. See also Oliver Stone's 2010 film, *South of the Border*.

66   Ibid.

67   Medea Benjamin, "Venezuela's Referendum and the Nation's Poor," *www.truthout.org/docs04/081604.htm*.

68   John Pilger, "Empire, Obama and America's Last Taboo," San Francisco, July 5, 2009, *coto2.wordpress.com/2009/08/20/john-pilger-empire-obama-and-america's-last-taboo/*.

69   David Ignatius, "Primer for a Revolution," *Washington Post*, July 6, 2004, *www.truthout.org/docs04/070604.htm*. All quotations from and about Saakashvili and the Rose Revolution are from this article.

70   Kwame Nkrumah, *Handbook of Revolutionary Warfare*; Tariq Ali, *The New Revolutionaries: A Handbook of the International Radical Left*.

71   Naomi Wolf, *Give Me Liberty: A Handbook for American Revolutionaries*, p. 3. See also Ron Paul, *The Revolution: A Manifesto*, 2008.

72   Nicolas Truong, "The New Insurrectional Thinking," first published as "La nouvelle pensée insurrectionnelle" in *Le Monde*, July 8, 2009, *www.truthout.org/071009G*.

See also The Invisible Committee, *L'insurrection qui vient* (The Coming Insurrection); "U.S. Support Committee for the Tarnac 9," p. 91, Aug. 2009; and "Comfortable with Chaos," November, 2008, *www.hermes3.net/nov108.htm*.

73   Daniel Terdiman, "Text Messages for Critical Masses," *Wired*, August 12, 2004, *www.truthout.org/docs04/081204.htm*.

74   Greg Mitchell, "How Obama Won: The Rise of Web 2.0," *www.alternet.org/media/123192*. See also Mitchell's *Why Obama Won: The Making of a President 2008*, 2009.

75   Alan Rosenblatt, "Progressives Gather Forces on Twitter," August 24, 2009, *www.huffingtonpost.com/alan-rosenblatt/progressives-gather-force_b_267223.html*.

76   Information about *Outfoxed* is available at *www.outfoxed.org*.

77   Jose Ortega y Gasset, *Revolt of the Masses*, p. 38.

78   David Ignatius, op. cit. See note 69 above.

79   *Baltimore Evening Sun*, July 26, 1920, *www.whale.to/a/mencken.html*.

80   From Che Guevara's farewell letter to Fidel Castro, written April 1, 1965, as Che left Cuba for South America. See *www.hey-che.com/quotes-from-che-guevara.html*.

81 Anthony Shadid, "Free of Qaddafi, Town Tries to Build New Order," *New York Times*, March 6, 2011, *www.nytimes.com/2011/03/07/world/africa/07rebels.html*.

82 Xiao Qiang, "The Great Leap Online That Is Stirring China." *International Herald Tribune*, August 6, 2004, p. 7.

83 James Borton, "A Blogger's Tale: The Stainless Steel Mouse," *Asia Times*, July 22, 2004, *www.atimes.com/atimes/China/FG22Ad04.htm*. See also Jayati Vora, "How Human Rights Groups and 'Hacktivists' Are Using Internet Technology to Buck State Censors," May 23, 2008, *www.alternet.org/rights/86248*.

CHAPTER SIX

84 Russell Mokhiber, "The Top 100 Corporate Criminals of the 1990s," *www.littlepageboothlaw.com/CM/PressCoverage/PressCoverage75.asp*.

85 Associated Press, "Bristol-Myers Squibb Agrees to Pay $150 Million to Settle SEC Charges." *International Herald Tribune*, August 5, 2004, p. 11.

86 "Schering-Plough to Sell Stock." Ibid., p. 11.

87 For more on the Pfizer and Swine Flu stories, see *www.hermes3.net/oct.109.htm*.

88 *NOW with Bill Moyers*, "Losing Medicaid in Mississippi," July 16, 2004, *www.pbs.org/now/transcript/transcript329_full.html*.

89 Pam Belluck, "Vermont Will Sue U.S. for the Right to Import Drug." *New York Times*, August 11, 2004. Reprinted at *www.truthout.org*.

90 Herbal Medicine Panel at *www.nmst.org.html*.

91   *Prevention Magazine* data on the American Holistic Health
        Association website at *www.ahha.org/statistics/preventionsurvey.htm.*

92   Hawaii Health Guide at *www.hawaiihealthguide.com.*

93   Cairo Women's Group for Health and Well-Being at
        www.theessencesofegypt.com/PresentDay.html.

94   See *www.communityacupuncturenetwork.org.*

95   Dinshah Ghadiali was born in India and emigrated to the
        United States just before the First World War. He developed
        a highly effective system of color healing that used light boxes
        to project light through color healing filters. His work was
        suppressed in the usual manner. His grandson Darius Dinshah
        coordinates the Dinshah Color Healing Society, which no
        longer makes and sells light boxes, but does make and sell color
        healing filters. Harry Hoxsey was a naturopathic physician
        and veterinarian who developed an effective herbal remedy for
        cancer. He was suppressed in the usual manner.

96   Information about the American Holistic Health Association
        health search service is available at *www.ahha.org/ahhameb.htm.*

97   See Matthias Rath, M.D.'s advertisement, "From 'Pharma-
        Fraud' to 'Pharma-Terror'," *International Herald Tribune,*
        September 2, 2004, p. 9.

98   Shirley's Wellness Café at *www.shirleys-wellness-café-com/
        overview.htm.*

99   Ibid.

100 Figures compiled from reports by the National Nutrition Institute
        of America, Centers for Disease Control and Prevention, National
        Safety Council, U.S. National Center for Health Statistics, and
        the Journal of the American Medical Association.

101 Cecilia W. Dugger, "Short of Physicians, Africa Trains Substitutes," first published in the *New York Times*. *International Herald Tribune*, November 25, 2004, p. 3.

102 Geoffrey Crowley, "Medicine Without Doctors," *Newsweek*, July 18, 2004, p. 48.

103 Kevin Trudeau, *Natural Cures "They" Don't Want You to Know About, www.naturalcures.com.*

104 Stan Brock and Remote Area Medical at *www.ramusa.org/about/stanbrock.htm.*

105 Barbara Hand Clow, *Liquid Light of Sex*, pp. 121–145.

106 The three main spiritual rites of passage as timed by planet transits are these:

The Saturn return, which almost always comes in one's thirtieth year, when Saturn has gone round the zodiac and arrives again at his natal position. This moment usually triggers decisions either to remain on one's present life course, or alter it.

The Uranus opposition, which comes between the ages of 39 and 42, when Uranus has gone halfway around the wheel and is opposite to his natal position. This transition may herald sweeping changes in one's livelihood, residence, relationships and other major life areas.

The Chiron return, at 50, which brings up for seeing and clearing each one's issues of woundedness, healing, and integration within oneself and with others.

CHAPTER SEVEN

107 Tom Robbins, *Villa Incognito*, p. 35.

108 Iris J. Stewart, *Sacred Woman, Sacred Dance*, pp. 95–96.

109 Timothy Wyllie, *Dolphins, Telepathy & Underwater Birthing*, pp. 49–66.

110 Barbara Harper, *Gentle Birth Choices*, p. 88.

111 Alice A. Bailey, *Education in the New Age*, pp. 95–97.

112 The three aspects of mind that *antahkarana* aims to integrate are the sensory or "concrete" mind, better known as common sense; the individualized mind, or soul; and the higher abstract mind, or intuition.

113 Dana Micucci, "Meditation Helps Some Students." *International Herald Tribune*, February 15, 2005, p. 21. All quotes in this paragraph are from this article.

114 Bruce Lipton, "Conscious Parenting." *www.brucelipton.com*.

115 Ruth Peters, *Laying Down the Law*, 2002.

116 Philip C. McGraw, *Family First*, pp. 44–56.

117 Matthew Cardinale, "Maya Keyes Sets the Record Gay in Interview Exclusive." *YubaNet*, February 15, 2005. All quotes in this paragraph and the next are from this article.

118 David Spangler, *Parent as Mystic, Mystic as Parent*, p. 34.

119 Marilyn C. Barrick, *A Spiritual Approach to Parenting*. This excerpt is quoted from *www.spiritualpsychology.com*.

120 David Patterson Hatch, *Last Letters from the Living Dead Man*, *www.earthlypursuits.com*.

121 Lee Carroll and Jan Tober, *The Indigo Children*. Also Doreen Virtue, *The Care and Feeding of Indigo Children*.

122 P. M. H. Atwater, "Children of the New Millennium." Published on the website of *New Dawn* magazine at *www. newdawnmagazine.com*. Atwater has republished her findings in *The New Children and Near-Death Experiences*.

123 Doreen Virtue, *The Crystal Children*, p. 4.

CHAPTER EIGHT

124 This quote has been attributed to Seneca, Danton, and, most commonly, Virginia Woolf. See *www.borntomotivate.com/ FamousQuote_VirginiaWoolf.html*.

125 Amelia Gentleman, "India Still Fighting to 'Save the Girl Child'," *International Herald Tribune*, April 22, 2005, p. 1.

126 Constance M. Green, "One House, Two Single Moms," *Washington Post*, April 5, 2005, p. C09.

127 Marc Lacey, "In One Kenyan Village, Women Run the Show and Build New Lives," first published in the *New York Times*. Reprinted in the *International Herald Tribune*, December 8, 2004, p. 7. All quotes in this paragraph are from this article.

128 Italics in original. Alice A. Bailey, *Esoteric Astrology*.

129 Saturn has an orbital period of 29½ years. The Saturn return occurs when Saturn has completed a full circuit of the zodiac and returns to his position in one's natal chart. It typically marks a moment, or at least offers an opportunity, either to commit one's life more strongly to the direction in which it is already going, or to make a radical change of course toward a new career and life purpose.

130 Astrocartography ("star mapping") is a branch of astrology that projects a person's birth data onto a world map to create sets of

planetary lines that show a person's best—or least good—places for living and working, and for relationships with employers, teachers, backers, audiences, love partners, healers, and whatever else each one seeks. See, for example, the astrocartography of Barack Obama at *www.hermes3.net/july108.htm.*

131   Interview with Amy Goodman of Democracy Now, May 20, 2004, *www.countercurrents.org/ie-roy200504.htm.*

132   Arundhati Roy and David Barsamian, *The Checkbook and the Cruise Missile*, p. 46.

133   Speech at the 2003 World Social Forum in Porto Alegre, Brazil, *www.choike.org/nuevo_eng/informes/738.html.*

134   September discussion with Howard Zinn, September 18, 2002 in Santa Fe, NM, *nmazca.com/verba/roy.htm.*

CHAPTER NINE

135   Gilbert Seldes, *The Seven Lively Arts*, 1923. See also *xroads. virginia.edu.1%ZEPHYR.SELDES.choi.htm.*

136   "People," *International Herald Tribune*, September 4–5, 2004, p. 9.

137   Howard W. French, "A Bit at a Time, Author Redefines Short Fiction." *International Herald Tribune*, September 12, 2004, p. 6.

138   "The Mirror of Venus," *www.hermes3.net/may104.htm.*

139   For more on the Transformance Space, see *www.hermes3.net/ theatre.htm.*

140   For the implications of the Chiron return, see chapter 6, note 106.

CHAPTER TEN

141 David Hawkins, *Power Vs. Force*, p. 87.

142 From "Human Rights," Bahá'í Community of Canada, *www. ca.bahai.org.*

143 B. A. Robinson, "The Beliefs and Practices of the Baha'i Faith," *www. religioustolerance.org/bahai3.htm.*

144 Kyotaro Deguchi, *The Great Onisaburo Deguchi*, p. 4. See also Oomoto's website, *www.oomoto.or.jp/English/enHist/jiken-en.html.*

145 Marcus Braybrooke, *Faith and Interfaith in a Global Age*, p. 51. See "The Interfaith Movement in the Twentieth Century," *www.nain.org/library/movement.htm.*

146 From the opening of the URI Charter. See *www.uri.org.*

147 Marcus Braybrooke and Peggy Morgan (ed.), *Testing the Global Ethic*, p. 4. See also Stephen Fuqua, "The Global Interfaith Movement" in the April, 2003 edition of *Fertile Field*, at *www. fertilefield.org/articles/archives/000009.html.*

148 Don Frew, "The Covenant of the Goddess and the Interfaith Movement," *www.witchvox.com/white/coginterfaith.htm.*

149 Ibid.

150 Ibid.

151 For information on differences between Indians and New Agers, see "Response to the 'New Age' Movement," *www. yvwiiusdinvnohii.net/articles/1995-98articles/NoraBunce9502 NewAgeMovement.htm.*

152 B. A. Robinson, "New Age Spirituality," *www.religioustolerance.org/newage.htm*.

153 See "Aquarian Ceremonies," *www.hermes3.net/aqcerem.htm*.

154 Stephen Simon at *www.edgenews.com/simon/passion_of_christ.html*.

155 See Dowd and Barlow's website at *www.TheGreatStory.org*.

156 Cathy Lynn Grossman, "72% of Millennials 'More Spiritual Than Religious,'" *U.S.A Today*, April 27, 2010, *www.usatoday.com/news/religion/2010-04-27-1Amillfaith27_ST_N.htm*.

157 Barks, Coleman, *The Illuminated Rumi*, p. 9.

158 "Rough Metaphors," from *The Essential Rumi*, p. 174.

159 "I Cried Out at Midnight," translation by Jonathan Star from *Rumi: In the Arms of the Beloved*, p. 81.

160 "Full Moon, Bilal" from *The Hand of Poetry*, p. 82.

161 "The House of Love," translation by Kabir Helminski, from *Love Is a Stranger*, 1993.

162 These lines appear in many versions and melodies, and are often sung at the Dances of Universal Peace. See *www.mevlana.net*.

CHAPTER ELEVEN

163 See "Sowing the Wind," Universal Festival Calendar prelude for September 2009, *www.hermes3.net/sep109.htm*.

164 See "The Crosses of 2010," *www.hermes3.net/2010.htm*.

165 Richard Tarnas, "Our Moment in History as an Initiation for Humanity," *www.nowopolis.com/.../779-our-moment-in-history-as-an-initiation-for-humanity.*

166 Ibid.

167 "The Zeitgeist Addendum," 2008, *www.zeitgeistmovie.com.*

168 Tarnas, op. cit.

169 *Genesis* I, 28 and II, 19.

170 See especially A. O. Lovejoy, *The Great Chain of Being*, pp. 5–19.

171 Ernst Haeckel, *The Evolution of Man*, 1910. See Sheldrake, *The Presence of the Past*, pp. 49–51.

172 Bruce Lipton and Steve Bhaerman, *Spontaneous Evolution*, p. 127.

173 James M. Glover, "Can We Stop Trying to Control Nature?," *www.wild.org/blog/can-we-stop-trying-to-control-nature.*

174 Geoph Kozeny, "Intentional Communities: Today's Social Laboratories," *www.gaia.org/mediafiles/gaia/resources/GKozeny_IC-SocialLabs.pdf.*

175 See *www.burningman.com.*

176 Rainbow Gathering; Rainbow Family of Living Light, *www.welcomehome.org.*

177 CouchSurfing, *www.couchsurfing.com.*

178 Jane McGonigal, The Avant Game, *www.avantgame.com.*

179 Jane McGonigal, "Gaming Can Make a Better World," video, March 23, 2010, *www.ted.com/talks/jane_mcgonigal_gaming_can_make_a_better_world.html.* All quotes from Jane

McGonigal in this section are from this presentation. These ideas and other results of McGonigal's game experience were published in January, 2011 in her new book, *Reality Is Broken*.

180 "Damanhur: Community, Spirituality, Research and Action," *www.damanhur.org*. All quotes about Damanhur that follow here are, except as noted, from pages on the Damanhur website.

181 Oberto Airaudi, *Dying to Learn*, Foreword by Stambecco Pesco, p. 7.

182 Ibid., p. 124.

183 Ibid., p. 101.

184 Bruce Lipton and Steve Bhaerman, op. cit., p. 101.

185 Lynne McTaggart, *The Field*, p. 22.

186 Bruce Lipton and Steve Bhaerman, op. cit., p. 28.

187 Ibid., p. 66.

188 Gregg Braden, *The Divine Matrix*, pp. 116–117.

189 Lynne McTaggart, *The Intention Experiment*, p. xxvii.

190 Michael Wines, "Marching to Pretoria? Consider Tshwane," first published in *The New York Times*. Reprinted in the *International Herald Tribune*, January 5, 2005, p. 2.

191 Julian Hewitt, "'Ubuntu' of Globalization," first published in *The Boston Globe*, reprinted in the *International Herald Tribune*, Nov. 6, 2004, p. 9.

192 Wangari Mathai, "Planting a Tree for Democracy," *International Herald Tribune*, December 12, 2004, p. 6.

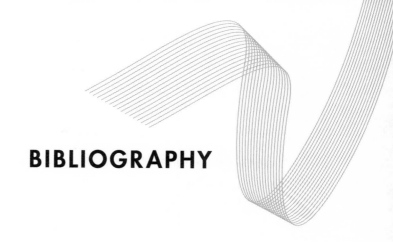

BIBLIOGRAPHY

Airaudi, Oberto. *Dying to Learn: The First Book of the Initiate.* Zagreb, Croatia: Graficki Zavod Hrvatske, 2005.

Ali, Tariq. *The New Revolutionaries: A Handbook of the International Radical Left.* London: Morrow, 1969.

Amao, Albert. *Aquarian Age and the Andean Prophecy.* Bloomington, IN: Author House, 2007.

Ardagh, Arjuna. *Awakening into Oneness: The Power of Blessing in the Evolution of Consciousness.* Boulder, CO: Sounds True, 2007.

Argüelles, Jose. *The Mayan Factor: Path Beyond Technology.* Santa Fe, NM: Bear & Company, 1987.

Atwater, P. M. H. *The New Children and Near-Death Experiences.* Annapolis, MD: New Dawn Publishing, 2004.

Bailey, Alice A. *Education in the New Age.* Chicago, IL: Lucis Publishing, 1971.

———. "Esoteric Astrology." *www.kingsgarden.org/english/ organizations/omm.gb/womenwriters/alicebailey/sevenrays/ astrology/astr1053.html.*

Barks, Coleman, and John A. Moyne. *The Essential Rumi*. New York: HarperOne, 1997.

———.*The Illuminated Rumi*. New York: Broadway Books, 1997.

Barrick, Marilyn C. *A Spiritual Approach to Parenting: Secrets of Raising the 21st Century Child*. Gardiner, MT: Summit University Press, 2004.

Bateson, Gregory. *Steps to an Ecology of Mind*. London: Paladin, 1973.

Berry, Thomas. *The Great Work: Our Way into the Future*. New York: Bell Tower, 1999.

Blavatsky, H. P. *Isis Unveiled*. 2 vols. Pasadena, CA: Theosophical University Press, 1972.

Bonabeau, David, and Christopher Meyer. "Swarm Intelligence: A Whole New Way to Think about Business." *Harvard Business Review*, vol. lxxx, no. 5 (May, 2001).

Braden, Gregg. *Awakening to Zero Point: The Collective Initiation*. Bellevue, WA: Radio Bookstore Press, 1993.

———.*The Divine Matrix: Bridging Time, Space, Miracles, and Belief*. Carlsbad, CA: Hay House, 2007.

Braden, Gregg, P. Russell, D. Pinchbeck and others. *The Mystery of 2012: Predictions, Prophecies and Possibilities*. Boulder, CO: Sounds True, 2007.

Braybrooke, Marcus. *Faith and Interfaith in a Global Age: The Interfaith Movement's Offer of Help to a World in Agony*. Henley-On-Thames, UK: Braybrooke Press, 1995.

Braybrooke, Marcus, and Peggy Morgan (ed.). *Testing the Global Ethic: Voices from the Religions on Moral Values*. Ada, MI: Conexus Press, 1998.

Brinton, Crane. *The Anatomy of Revolution*. New York: Vintage Books, 1965.

Campbell, Joseph. *The Masks of God: Creative Mythology; Primitive Mythology; and Oriental Mythology*. New York: Penguin Books, 1969.

——. *Thou Art That: Transforming Religious Metaphor*. Novato, CA: New World Library, 2001.

Capra, Fritjof. *The Tao of Physics: An Exploration of the Parallels between Modern Physics and Eastern Mysticism*. Boston, MA: Shambhala, 1975.

——. *The Turning Point: Science, Society, and the Rising Culture*. New York: Bantam Books, 1982.

Carroll, Lee, and Jan Tober. *The Indigo Children*. Carlsbad, CA: Hay House, 1999.

Carter, Mary Ellen. *Passage to the Millennium: Edgar Cayce and the Age of Aquarius*. New York: St. Martin's Press, 1998.

Chalmers, David. "Notes on Emergence Theory." *consc.net/notes/emergence.html*

Charpentier, Louis. *The Mysteries of Chartres Cathedral*. East Sussex, UK: RILKO Books, 1972.

Christian, Diana Leafe. *Creating a Life Together: Practical Tools to Grow Eco-Villages and Intentional Communities*. Gabriola Island, Canada: New Society Publishers, 2003.

Clow, Barbara Hand. *Liquid Light of Sex: Understanding your Key Life Passages*. Rochester, VT: Bear & Company, 1991.

Dalai Lama. Nobel Prize lecture, Oslo University. Dec. 11, 1989. *www.dalailama.com/html/nobel.html*.

Davies, James Chowning. "Toward a Theory of Revolution." *American Sociological Review* 27, no. 6 (February 1962): 519.

———, ed. *Why Men Revolt*. New Brunswick, NJ: Transaction Publishers, 1997.

Deguchi, Kyotaro. *The Great Onisaburo Deguchi*. Tokyo, Japan: Aiki News, 1998.

Dossey, Larry. *Healing Words: The Power of Prayer and the Practice of Medicine*. San Francisco: HarperSanFrancisco, 1993.

Duncan, Adrian Ross. *Astrology: Transformation & Empowerment*. Boston, MA: Weiser Books, 2002.

Edwards, David. *Burning All Illusions: A Guide to Personal and Political Freedom*. Boston, MA: South End Press, 1996.

Eisler, Riane. *The Real Wealth of Nations: Creating a Caring Economics*. San Francisco: Berrett-Koehler, 2007.

Elkington, David, and Paul Howard Ellson. *In the Name of the Gods: The Mystery of Resonance and the Pre-Historic Messiah*. London: Green Man Publishing Ltd., 2000.

Emoto, Masaru. *The Hidden Messages in Water*. New York: Atria, 2005.

Fellowship for Intentional Community. *A Comprehensive Guide to Intentional Communities and Cooperative Living*. Rutledge, MO: Fellowship for Intentional Community Press, 2010.

Ferguson, Marilyn. *The Aquarian Conspiracy: Personal and Social Transformation in the 1980s*. Los Angeles: Jeremy P. Tarcher, 1980.

Forrest, Steven, and Jeffrey Wolf Green. *Measuring the Night: Evolutionary Astrology and the Keys to the Soul*, Vol. 1. Borrego, CA: Seven Paws Press, 2000.

Free, Wynn, with David Wilcock. *The Reincarnation of Edgar Cayce?* Berkeley, CA: Frog, Ltd., 2004.

Foster, Sam. "Chaos Theory." *www.easyweb.easynet.co.uk/˜sfoster4*

Fuller, Buckminster. *Operating Manual for Spaceship Earth*. Reprint of 1969 Edition. Carbondale, IL: Southern Illinois University Press, 1976.

Furst, Dan. *Dance of the Moon*. Woodbury, MN: Llewellyn Worldwide, 2009.

——. "The Universal Festival Calendar." *www.hermes3.net/ufc.htm.*

Gandhi, Mohandas K. *Non-Violence in Peace and War*. In *Gandhi on Nonviolence*. Boulder, CO: Shambhala, 1996.

Gibbon, Edward. *The Decline and Fall of the Roman Empire. www.ccel.org/g/gibbon/decline/volume1/chapter4.htm.*

Goleman, D., Braden, G., and others. *Measuring the Immeasurable: The Scientific Case for Spirituality*. Boulder, CO: Sounds True, 2008.

Green, Deva. *Evolutionary Astrology: Pluto and Your Karmic Mission*. Woodbury, MN: Llewellyn Publications, 2009.

Green, Jeffrey Wolf, and Steven Forrest. *Measuring the Night: Evolutionary Astrology and the Keys to the Soul*, Vol. 2. Borrego, CA: Seven Paws Press, 2001.

Green, Liz. *The Astrology of Fate*. Newburyport, MA: Red Wheel Weiser, 1984.

Grof, Stanislav. *Human Survival and Consciousness Evolution*. New York: State University of New York Press, 1998.

Harper, Barbara. *Gentle Birth Choices*. Rochester, VT: Healing Arts Press, 2005.

Hartmann, Thom. *The Last Hours of Ancient Sunlight*. London: Hodder and Stoughton, 1999.

Howell, Alice O. *The Heavens Declare: Astrological Ages and the Evolution of Consciousness*. 2nd, revised ed. Wheaton, IL: Quest Books, 2006.

Hume, Basil. *The Intentional Life: The Making of a Spiritual Vocation*. Orleans, MA: Paraclete Press, 2004.

Ibrahim, Youssef M. "The Collapse of Capitalism as We Know It." *International Herald Tribune*. March 10, 2004. Reprinted at *www.gulf-news.com/Articles/opinion.asp?ArticleD=113241*.

Jackson, Hildur, and Karen Svensson, eds. *Ecovillage Living: Restoring the Earth and Her People*. London: Green Books, 2002.

Jenkins, John Major. *Galactic Alignment: The Transformation of Consciousness According to Mayan, Vedic and Egyptian Traditions*. Rochester, VT: Bear & Company, 2002.

———. *Maya Cosmogenesis 2012: The True Meaning of the Maya Calendar End Date*. Rochester, VT: Bear & Company, 1998.

Keyes, Ken, Jr. *The Hundredth Monkey*. Uncopyrighted book, 1981. *www.testament.org/testament/100thmonkey.html*.

Khan, Hazrat Inayat. *The Hand of Poetry*. New Port Richey, FL: Omega Publications, 1993.

King, Martin Luther, Jr. *Strength to Love*. New York: Pocket Books, 1963.

Kohn, Marek. "Why an Unequal Society Is an Unhealthy Society." *New Statesman*, July 26, 2004.

Korten, David C. *Agenda for a New Economy: From Phantom Wealth to Real Wealth*. San Francisco: Berrett-Koehler, 2009.

Kunstler, James Howard. *The Long Emergency: Surviving the End of Oil, Climate Change and Other Converging Catastrophes of the Twenty-First Century*. New York: Grove Press, 2006.

Laszlo, Ervin, and Jonas Salk. *Evolution: The Grand Synthesis*. Boston, MA: Shambhala Publications,1987.

Laszlo, Ervin, and Jude Currivan. *CosMos: A Co-Creator's Guide to the Whole World*. Carlsbad, CA: Hay House, 2008.

Law, Jacky. *Big Pharma: Exposing the Global Health Care Agenda*. New York: Carroll & Graf, 2006.

Lipton, Bruce, and Steve Bhaerman. *Spontaneous Evolution: Our Positive Future (And a Way to Get There from Here)*. Carlsbad, CA: Hay House, 2009.

Lipton, Bruce. *The Biology of Belief: Unleashing the Power of Consciousness, Matter and Miracles*. Santa Rosa, CA: Elite Books, 2005.

Lovejoy, A. O. *The Great Chain of Being*. Cambridge, MA: Harvard University Press, 1936.

Marcus, Rose. *Insights into Evolutionary Astrology: A Diverse Collection of Essays by Prominent Astrologers*. Woodbury, MN: Llewellyn Publications, 2010.

McGonigal, Jane. *Gaming Can Make a Better World*. Online video, 2009. *www.ted.com/talks/jane_mcgonigal_gaming_can_make_a_better_world.html*.

———. *Reality Is Broken: Why Games Make Us Better and How They Can Change the World*. New York: The Penguin Press HC, 2011.

———. "World Without Oil." Interactive game, 2007. *www.boingboing.net/2007/05/03/play-jane-mcgonigals.html*.

McGraw, Philip C. *Family First*. London: Simon & Schuster UK, 2005.

McKenna, Terence. *The Archaic Revival*. New York: HarperSanFrancisco, 1991.

McKenna, Terence, and Dennis McKenna. *The Invisible Landscape: Mind, Halluciongens and the I Ching*. New York, HarperSanFrancisco, 1993.

McTaggart, Lynne. *The Field: The Quest for the Secret Force of the Universe*. New York: Harper Perennial, 2002.

———. *The Intention Experiment*. New York: Free Press, 2007.

———. *What Doctors Don't Tell You: The Truth about the Dangers of Modern Medicine*. 2nd ed. New York: Thorsons, 2005.

Meeker, Joseph. *The Comedy of Survival*. 3rd ed. Tucson, AZ: University of Arizona Press, 1997.

Meltzer, Graham. *Sustainable Community: Learning from the Cohousing Model*. Bloomington, IN: Trafford Publishing, 2005.

Merchant, Carolyn. *The Death of Nature: Women, Ecology, and the Scientific Revolution*. San Francisco: Harper & Row, 1987.

Mokhiber, Russell. "The Top 100 Corporate Criminals of the 1990s." *www.littlepageboothlaw.com/CM/PressCoverage/PressCoverage75.asp*.

Moore, Thomas. *The Care of the Soul: A Guide for Cultivating Depth and Sacredness in Everyday Life*. Reprint ed. New York: HarperPerennial, 1994.

Myss, Caroline. *Anatomy of the Spirit: The Seven Stages of Power and Healing*. New York: Three Rivers Press, 1997.

———. *Defy Gravity: Healing Beyond the Bounds of Reason*. Carlsbad, CA: Hay House, 2009.

Nkrumah, Kwame. *Handbook of Revolutionary Warfare*. Atlantic Highlands, NJ: Humanities Press International, 1968.

Ortega y Gasset, Jose. *Revolt of the Masses*. New York: W. W. Norton, 1994.

Paul, Ron. *The Revolution: A Manifesto*. New York: Grand Central Publishing, 2008.

Payton, Michelle A. *Healing What's Real: Expanding Your Personal Power with Mind Over Matter Techniques*. Asheville, NC: The Left Side, 2008.

Pearce, Joseph Chilton. *The Biology of Transcendence: A Blueprint of the Human Spirit*. Rochester, VT: Park Street Press, 2002.

Perkins, John. *Confessions of an Economic Hit Man*. San Francisco: Berrett-Koehler, 2004.

Pinchbeck, Daniel. *2012: The Return of Quetzalcoatl*. New York: Jeremy P. Tarcher/Penguin, 2006.

Raymond, Andrew. "Secrets of the Sphinx." *www.revealer.com/platonic.htm*.

Reich, Robert. *Supercapitalism: The Transformation of Business, Democracy and Everyday Life*. New York: Alfred A. Knopf, 2007.

Robbins, Tom. *Fierce Invalids Home from Hot Climates*. 6th ed. New York: Bantam Books, 2001.

———. *Villa Incognito*. New York: Bantam Books, 2004.

Roy, Arundhati. *Field Notes on Democracy: Listening to Grasshoppers*. London: Haymarket Books, 2009.

Roy, Arundhati, and David Barsamian. *The Checkbook and the Cruise Missile: Conversations with Arundhati Roy*. Cambridge, MA: South End Press, 2004.

Rumi. *Love is a Stranger*. Translated by Kabir Helminski. Aptos, CA: Threshold Books, 1993.

Russell, Peter. *The Awakening Earth: The Global Brain*. London: Ark Paperbacks, 1982.

Schwaller de Lubicz, Isha. *The Opening of the Way: A Practical Guide to the Wisdom Teachings of Ancient Egypt*. Rochester, VT: Inner Traditions, 1981.

Schwaller de Lubicz , R.A. *Symbol and the Symbolic: Ancient Egypt, Science, and the Evolution of Consciousness*. Rochester, VT: Inner Traditions, 1981.

Sheldrake, Rupert. *The Presence of the Past: Morphic Resonance and the Habits of Nature*. Rochester, VT: Park Street Press, 1995.

Spangler, David. *A Pilgrim in Aquarius*. Findhorn, Scotland: Findhorn Press, 1997.

———. *Parent as Mystic, Mystic as Parent*. New York: Riverhead Books, 2000.

———. *Revelation: The Birth of the New Age*. Findhorn, Scotland: Lorian Press, 1976.

Star, Jonathan. *Rumi: In the Arms of the Beloved*. Los Angeles: Jeremy P. Tarcher, 2008.

Steiner, Rudolf. *Evolution of Consciousness: As Revealed through Initiation Knowledge*. London: Rudolf Steiner Press, 2007.

Stewart, Iris J. *Sacred Woman, Sacred Dance*. Rochester, VT: Inner Traditions, 2000.

Surowiecki, James. *The Wisdom of Crowds: Why the Many Are Smarter than the Few and How Collective Wisdom Shapes Business, Economies, Societies and Nations*. New York: Doubleday, 2004.

Talbot, Michael. *The Holographic Universe*. New York: Harper Perennial, 1992.

Targ, Russell, and Jane Katra. *Miracles of Mind: Exploring Nonlocal Consciosusness and Spiritual Healing*. Novato, CA: New World Library, 1998.

Tarnas, Richard. *Cosmos and Psyche: Intimations of a New World View*. New York: Plume/Penguin, 2007.

Tefft, J. C. *The Christ Is Not a Person: The Evolution of Consciousness and the Destiny of Man*. Bloomington, IN: iUniverse.com, 2009.

Teilhard de Chardin, Pierre. *The Phenomenon of Man*. Cork, Ireland: Collins Press, 1959.

Trudeau, Kevin. *Natural Cures "They" Don't Want You to Know About*. Homewood, AL: Alliance Publishing, 2005.

Truong, Nicolas. "The New Insurrectional Thinking," first published as "La nouvelle pensée insurrectionnelle" in *Le Monde*, July 8, 2009. *www.truthout.org/071009G*.

Tolle, Eckhart. *A New Earth*. London: Penguin Books, 2005.

Virtue, Doreen. *The Crystal Children*. Carlsbad, CA: Hay House, 2003.

Vonnegut, Kurt. "Cold Turkey." *In These Times*, May 10, 2004. *www.inthesetimes.com/site/main/article/cold_turkey.*

Wann, David. *Reinventing Community: Stories from the Walkways of Cohousing.* Golden, CO: Fulcrum Publishing, 2005.

Watson, Lyall. *Lifetide*. Sevenoaks, UK: Hodder and Stoughton, 1979.

Wilcock, David. *Convergence I-III. www.Ascension2000.com.*

Wolf, Fred Alan. *Mind into Matter: A New Alchemy of Science and Spirit.* Needham, MA: Moment Point Press, 2000.

Wolf, Naomi. *Give Me Liberty: A Handbook for American Revolutionaries.* New York: Simon & Schuster, 2008.

Wyllie, Timothy. *Dolphins, Telepathy & Underwater Birthing: Further Adventures Among Spiritual Intelligences.* Rochester, VT: Bear & Company, 1993.

AQUARIAN
RESOURCES

This brief list could be much longer, and contain hundreds of worthy websites, email newsletters, and other resources. What follows here is a set of starting points, each of which will open many new trails. All resources were accessed in May, 2011.

COLLECTIVE INTENTION PROJECTS AND EXPERIMENTS

The **Global Coherence Initiative** is a scientific experiment created by the **Institute of HeartMath** to coordinate millions of people worldwide in "heart-focused care and intention to shift global consciousness from instability and discord, to balance, cooperation and enduring peace. See *www.glcoherence.org*. The GCI uses its **Global Coherence Monitoring System** to "directly measure fluctuations in the magnetic fields generated by the earth and in the ionosphere."

See *www.glcoherence.org/monitoring-system/about-system.html*.

Common Passion is "a global social cooperative of individuals and communities who share compassion as a common passion," and aim "to create social and environmental harmony through science-based applications of collective consciousness."

See *www.commonpassion.org*.

The Intention Experiment is the subject of Lynne McTaggart's book of the same title. This "Largest Mind-Over-Matter Experiment in History" is "a series of scientifically-controlled, web-based experiments testing the power of intention to change" conditions in the world.

See *www.theintentionexperiment.com.*

The Call for Conscious Evolution combines the efforts of well-known "Evolutionary Leaders" who are united in their "aspiration to become more conscious through subjective practices including meditation, reflection, prayer, intuition, creativity, and conscious choice making that accelerate our evolution in the direction of unity consciousness and inspire us to deeply align our collective vision."

See *www.care2.com/greenliving/a-call-for-conscious-evolution.html.*

INTENTIONAL COMMUNITIES AND COMMUNAL NETWORKS

The Global Ecovillages Network (GEN) is "a global confederation of people and communities that meet and share their ideas, exchange technologies, develop cultural links" that help in the transition to a more sustainable future on Earth.

See *www. gen.ecovillage.org.*

The Ecovillage Design Education, founded under the aegis of Denmark's Gaia Trust and launched in 2005 at Findhorn by a group of educators calling themselves the GEESE (Global Ecovillage Educators for Sustainable Earth), "draws upon the experience of some of the most successful ecovillages and intentional communities in the world."

See *www.gaia.org/gaia/education.*

The WorldShift Network and its State of the World Forum were founded by Ervin Laszlo, founder of the Club of Budapest. Its six spheres of activity are "Unity of Humanity and Nature, Global Subsistence Economy, Salutogenesis, Global Wisdom Culture, Participative Civil Society, and Planetary Peace and Freedom." See *www.worldshiftnetwork.org/home/index.html.*

The **Earth Charter Initiative** is a global network of people, organizations, and institutions who participate in promoting the Earth Charter, and implementing its principles in practice. The mission of the Earth Charter is "to promote the transition to sustainable ways of living and a global society founded on a shared ethical framework that includes respect and care for the community of life, ecological integrity, universal human rights, respect for diversity, economic justice, democracy, and a culture of peace." See *www.earthcharterinaction.org.*

The **Fellowship for Intentional Community** originated in Rutledge, MO, and has published two editions, most recently in 2010, of its *Comprehensive Guide to Intentional Communities and Cooperative Living.* Its website offers an extensive, up-to-date, worldwide clearing house of community resources, directories and information. See *www.ic.org.*

The **Conscious Community Network**, active since 2003 in Reno, Nevada, organizes various resources in the city of Reno and the surrounding area in pursuit of common economic, social, and spiritual objectives. CCN's actions, and its commitment to "the universal spiritual values of Love, Integrity, Courage, Service, and Respect" have been widely influential. See *www.consciousmedianetwork.com.*

GLOBAL MEDITATIONS AND METAPHYSICAL EVENTS

The **Earth Rainbow Network** began in 2000 to link its members in synchrony across many time zones in a series of global meditations, each aimed at a specific Focus topic. It has evolved since into "a dynamic forum in which people from around the world share information, visions and feedbacks" on environmental issues, and join in efforts like the Inconvenient Truth and Perfect Storm series to respond to events that require concerted responses.

See *www.earthrainbownetwork.com.*

For information on worldwide meditations, ceremonies, and sacred other sacred events, **Global Meditations** provides excellent coverage of the current and following month, and of major events on the 3- to 4-month horizon. Barbara Wolf of Global Meditations also sends a free monthly events list to subscribers (email: *bjwolf@ rochester.infi.net*).

See *www.globalmeditations.com.*

The website of sound healing pioneer **Jonathan Goldman** is a useful resource for information about global chant and toning ceremonies such as World Sound Healing Day, held annually on February 14. To facilitate such events, Goldman has created the world's first interactive sacred sound temple, where people can project intentionalized sound 24/7 for Global Harmonization.

See *www.healingsounds.com* and *www.templeofsacredsound.org.*

The **World Peace Prayer Society** applies the premise that "thought forms create an energetic field strong enough to empower the course of planetary destiny." The Society organizes and disseminates word of events aimed at spreading the message May Peace Prevail on Earth.

See *www.worldpeace.org.*

Since 2004, **Global Love Day** has attracted increasing interest and support in over 100 countries for its synchronized events and ceremonies held annually on May 1.

See *www.thelovefoundation.com.*

Since 2001, **Circle of Sound** has coordinated Global Harmonization ceremonies on the solstices and equinoxes, uniting hundreds of circles throughout the world through the synchronized sounds of quartz crystal singing bowls, other instruments, and voices in holding the intentions of Acceptance, Harmony, Compassion, Love, Joy, and Peace.

See *www.circleofsound.org.*

The **Prophets Conference** gathers cutting-edge scientists and thinkers for progressive discussions aimed at achieving an optimistic critical mass toward the moment of planetary awakening in 2012. Its Great Mystery web pages are especially valuable.

See *www.greatmystery.org.*

Dan Furst's monthly **Universal Festival Calendar** carries extensive information and links on astral and worldwide mythic events.

See *www.hermes3.net/ufc.htm.*

ABOUT THE AUTHOR

Dan Furst has been an actor, author, astrologer, and ceremonial artist in New York, Japan, Scotland, India, Indonesia, Hawaii and Egypt. His Universal Festival Calendar, published since 1998 on his website, *www.hermes3.net/ufc*, and his book *Dance of the Moon*, have made him one of the world's most respected experts on mythology, sacred calendars, astrology, prophecy, and evolution into higher spiritual consciousness. As a Moon priest and festival clown, Dan has created ritual theatre at many Earth festivals and has played Jupiter, Neptune, Saturn, the Green Man, the Holly King, Pan, and other roles. He is also the first actor ever to play the beloved Sufi poet Jalaluddin Rumi. He lives in Pisac, in the Sacred Valley near Cusco, Peru, and is at work on his next book, *Double Harmonies*, about the sacred music and sound science of ancient Egypt.

TO OUR READERS